CHURCHILL'S
UNDERGROUND ARMY

Major General Sir Edmund Ironside, C-in-C
Allied Expeditionary Force, with his ADC,
Captain Colin Gubbins, during the Allied
intervention in North Russia in 1918.

CHURCHILL'S
UNDERGROUND ARMY

A History of the Auxiliary Units in World War II

John Warwicker, MBE

Foreword by

Lord Ironside

FRONTLINE BOOKS, LONDON

Churchill's Underground Army
Hardback edition published in 2008,
this new edition published in 2013 by Frontline Books,
an imprint of Pen and Sword Books Ltd,
47 Church Street, Barnsley, S. Yorkshire, S70 2AS

www.frontline-books.com

Copyright © John Warwicker, 2008, 2013
Foreword © Lord Ironside, 2008, 2013

ISBN: 978-1-84832-717-7

CIP data records for this title are available from the British Library
and the Library of Congress

For more information on our books, please visit
www.frontline-books.com, email info@frontline-books.com
or write to us at the above address.

Printed and bound in Great Britain by
CPI Group (UK), Croydon, CR0 4YY

Contents

Contents

Dedication

To the men and women of the WWII GHQ Auxiliary Units –
both civilian and military – who volunteered for dangerous
secret service when Great Britain most needed them – and
who were then allowed to disappear without recognition.
Almost.

Illustrations

Acknowledgements

I must first thank Members of the Museum of the British Resistance Organisation – part of the Parham Airfield Museum complex, near Woodbridge in Suffolk – for providing access to all the good things the Museum has to offer, and which provided many short cuts for research. Patrons and Friends, and many veterans, relatives and supporters on the mailing list, have been a conduit for the accumulation of unique, high quality archive information, exhibits and expertise. In particular I must thank former curators Graham Bines, Raymond Carter, Carl Raby, and weapons expert and volunteer guide Richard Ashley, for their guidance, knowledge, and dedication to authenticity.

Lord Ironside, the principal Patron of the BRO Museum, and Lady Ironside have been greatly encouraging and supportive throughout.

It is not possible to name every single helper; after all, some just arrived as visitors to the Museum, then handed over documents or exhibits as anonymous donations – and disappeared again. Having been steeled in the need for secrecy from the very start, they saw no reason not to continue. In some cases, donors opted to place into proper custody, long treasured items of debatable provenance and ownership.

Very special thanks are due to Auxiliers Robert Millard (Bathampton Patrol) and Donald Handscombe (Thunderseley, Essex), both of whom unstintingly contributed their research, and reminiscences of life within typical or untypical Auxiliary Units Operational Patrols. Similarly, Lieutenant-Colonel Norman Field, OBE, after recharging his memory, painted a unique picture of his findings in, and development of, the XII Corps Observation Unit. Photographs have been assembled from the many offered by veterans and their families but special thanks must go to Nora Trego for providing unique action images of her husband's Sandford, Dorset, Auxunits patrol during training.

Prominent among those helping were the late Yolande Alston and her family; William E. ('Bill') Bartholomew; the late Brigadier Geoffrey ('Bill') Beyts, DSO, MBE, MC; Geoff Bowery; the late Geoff Bradford; Donald Brown, author of *Somerset versus Hitler*; the late Reginald F. J. ('Rex') Chaston and his family; Ronald Chisnall; Ralph Clarke; Roy Coleman; Colin Cooke; Captain Barbara Culleton, TD; Colin Durrant; the late Lieutenant-Colonel J. W. Stuart Edmundson, TD, and his family; Ann Fielding and her late husband John; Major Peter Forbes; Gerry Fryer; the late Arthur Gabbitas; Eric Gray; C. Jack Grice; the late Major R. F. Hall, MC; Alwyn Harvey; Stephen Hogben; Kate Ingram; the late Herman Kindred; the late David Ingrams; the late Stanley Judson; Roy Lewis; Bernard Lowry; Paul McCue; Jill Monk; Ivan Mower; Daphne and Ken Nunn; Joy Oxenden; the late Peter Robins; Lieutenant Roy Russell; Alison Smith; David Steed; Chris Stennet; Doris Steward; Andrew Taylor; Phil Tomaselli; Captain Ken Ward; Dr William Ward; John Williams; and the late Miss E. ('Willie') Wilmott. WWII researchers Mick Wilks and Bernard Lowry, authors of *The Mercian Maquis*, and Tim Wray have never tired in their dedicated quest to penetrate the mysteries of the Auxiliary Units and have conscientiously passed their findings along the line and given unconditional permission for their use.

I have been given unrestricted access to the field work of Dennis Walker in the north-east of England, and the North Yorkshire and Cleveland WWII Study Group has kindly supplied technical drawings. Research carried out in the National Archives by Tony Evans has provided critically important insights into hitherto firmly prohibited territory.

The remarkable research undertaken by a dedicated team from the Vintage and Military Amateur Radio Society (VMARS), headed by Richard Hankins, has provided the first detailed description of the design of the unique radio transceiver operated by the Auxiliary Units Special Duties Section. VMARS's skills and research over a number of years have been invaluable.

Transcription from original audio archive material was kindly undertaken by the late Christine Montagu and Captain Barbara Culleton, TD.

For Frontline/Pen and Sword Books, Michael Leventhal has been a model of courtesy and a fund of wisdom and good advice; and his Senior Editor, Kate Baker, has produced a series of invaluable guidelines with the greatest patience and good humour.

Finally, special appreciation is due to Ann Mary Warwicker who encouraged the author to dedicate three of his remaining years to this project and who was blessedly on hand to unravel the complexities of the modern electronic age – on the not infrequent occasions when they were beyond normal understanding.

*

All National Archives' material is Crown Copyright and reproduced with the permission of Her Majesty's Stationery Office. Copyright commitments have been taken seriously and apologies are offered where attributions may inadvertently been less than adequate.

Foreword

In putting together this keynote account of the British Resistance organisation, John Warwicker's fascinating story of how the undercover services of the United Kingdom were put on watch in 1940 provides an authentic insight into how they grew up into an effective intelligence and irregular forces network, which eventually undermined the military might of the Axis powers and led to their defeat in 1945.

His researches have brought to light the stealth behind the pre-war Intelligence services which clouded over the military vision of the government, even though Parliament had sanctioned massive defence loans for re-armament. My father had studied the defence of the UK whilst he was the General Officer Commanding, Eastern Command, in 1936 and had represented the War Office at the manoeuvres staged by the German Army in that year, and knew from his experiences as a hands-on C-in-C in the North Russian Campaign of 1918 that he needed rapid-reaction commanders in the east of England, where the threat of German invasion was greatest. Although be could not implement his ideas until he was put in command of the Home Forces in 1940, he was able to pick Colin Gubbins with confidence to command the Auxiliers in the underground army of Auxiliary Units, whose role was to observe and hinder every action of the supposed German occupation force. In 1918, Colin Gubbins had been picked by the DCIGS at the War Office to be my father's ADC, so that he was able to learn first-hand about Gubbins's two year service as a Boer ox-wagon driver under contract to the German Army in South-West Africa in 1901, as well as see his methods of fighting the terror of Communism within the Arctic Circle.

After my father had served beyond his retirement in 1940 and had been rewarded by his field marshalship and when Colin Gubbins had given up command of the Auxiliary Units on 9 November 1940 after the threat of invasion had receded, John Warwicker goes on to describe how the stay-behind force of Auxiliers established their Operational Bases from which they could strike out at an occupation force. To cap his services in helping found the Museum of the British Resistance Organisation at Parham, he was instrumental in securing a lottery grant for constructing a replica Operational Base to show all visitors to the museum what life was like for men of the underground army.

His descriptions of the Special Duties Section, which was formed to feed forward into activities behind the enemy lines with the SOE and Long Range Desert Group, add to the list of achievements of the British Resistance organisation and his researches show that there are still a lot of secrets locked away from public view in the National Archives for no good reasons. He has shown that the role of the Auxiliers should not be written off and his vivid accounts of how they thought, worked and lived are worth reading. After the early war *Blitzkrieg* the German forces became overstretched and *Der Tag* became a past cry, but the author shows why the British Resistance organisation should not become a forgotten memory.

Lord Ironside,
2008

Preface

'. . . to explain Britain's rich diversity today, our history closer to home may be forgotten . . . But it is a timely reminder to those of us toiling in the archives that while we labour to recover the overlooked from the disparagement of history, we must also always take care not to be forgetful ourselves.'

Lisa Jardine, Radio 4, Points of View, 23 December 2007

GHQ Auxiliary Units were one of the nine British secret services of WWII. It was a deliberately nondescript title. The other eight were the Security Service (MI5); the Secret Intelligence Service (MI6); the Escape and Evasion Service (MI9); the Double Cross Service; the Radio Security Service; the London Controlling Section; Special Operations Executive; and the Political Warfare Executive. With self-defined justification that to function properly a secret service must remain secret forever, skilled techniques of deliberate deception were imposed on them all as a matter of routine. By still withholding much of the sensitive information in their vaults, and being economical with the truth about the rest, responsible government departments – by choosing to operate without the intrusive scrutiny of Parliament or the public – give support to the concept of the 'bureaucratic inertia which thrived on Whitehall's cult of secrecy' according to Professor M. R. D. Foot, the leading historian of WWII Special Forces. Auxiliary Unit personnel, civilians, and servicemen alike, were therefore subjected to severest conditions of secrecy, both during wartime and afterwards, at a stricter level than other combat units and well outside the normal constraints of the Official Secrets Acts.

Just as the authorities had calculated, this exposed quicksands for post-war researchers. While a drip-feed of inside stories did gradually pass to the public domain from individuals who, for one reason or another, felt free to publicise their secret WWII service (or who were tacitly authorised to do so on a nod-and-wink basis) the mass of information held in Whitehall archives was intended to remain under wraps for ever. This included almost everything to do with the Auxiliary Units.

When confronted with this iron curtain of security, and safe in the knowledge that no one was likely to emerge to contradict them, Auxiliary Units' researchers sometimes tended to follow the easiest route, by concentrating disclosures around the soft underbelly of the subject, that is the civilian men of the Operational Patrols. These men – hurriedly recruited, trained and equipped as saboteurs from mid-summer 1940 – were tasked to stay behind the lines after the German invasion that, following the fall of France, was expected every day. Auxiliers, as they are commonly known, were sometimes willing post-war witnesses, sometimes not. It depended less upon their individual integrity – usually of the highest order anyway – and more on their final debrief when stood down in 1944. Without a central directive, this oral advice came from the almost equally under-informed understanding of their local officer-in-charge. The inevitable results were confused guidelines for veteran Auxiliers to follow and a maze of conflicting data for researchers to try to unravel.

Historical research is anyway endemically faulted, no matter how many so-called 'authentic' sources may be quoted. Given time, rumour matures into substance, dubious material is upgraded, and official reports are sanitised. Individuals' accounts are sometimes marred by subjectivity. Each stage of this reprocessing may gain a little more apparent authority until 'facts' are firmly established for the uninquisitive. Media men are the greatest source of the conversion process.

By concentrating on the Operational Patrols, researchers missed the real essence of the Auxiliary Units – the Special Duties Section, men and women spies also trained to stay behind the lines, this time to collect and communicate intelligence about the enemy from within his ranks. These civilians were, initially at least, recruited directly by Section D of the Secret Intelligence Service, MI6. This in itself ensured that the *complete* Auxunit organisation could expect to be kept permanently secret and almost impenetrable.

While the history of the men and women of the Auxiliary Units is no exception to the rules of fallible research, every effort has been made here to check and cross-check authenticity, but it will soon become obvious that these elite bands of intended stay-behinds were a different thing to different people, in different places, at different times, and under different commanders.

Inevitably, with this shifting curtain of official secrecy goes a commensurately cast-iron guarantee of continuing public interest in a small but innovative part of Britain's fight for survival through the critical months of WWII – no doubt to the enduring displeasure of the very government departments which have tried with such dedication to keep the whole story to themselves.

While not written with the intention of bringing discredit to any individual or agency, this book could, perhaps, help to ensure that healthy public interest remains alive and well.

Introduction

This England,
July 1940

The following extract from an editorial in the *New York Times* sums up the situation:

> It is twelve o'clock in London. Hitler has spoken and Lord Halifax has replied. There is no more to be said. Or is there? Is the tongue of Chaucer, of Shakespeare, of Milton, of the King James translation of the Scriptures, of Keats, of Shelley, to be hereafter, in the British Isles, the dialect of an enslaved race?
>
> Let us try to see clearly. We have to look back a good many centuries to find the beginnings of English liberty. We see it as a rough and obstinate growth, heaving the rich soil under the oaks of lordly estates, breaking out in Wat Tyler's time, and in Cromwell's and in the day of the second James, forcing through the Reform Act, never perfected, never giving up. We see the spread of democracy and of empire, side by side, confused and turbulent. But we see democracy ever marching on.
>
> It is twelve o'clock in London. Not twelve o'clock for empire – there is no empire any more. Not twelve o'clock for the old 'dominion over palm and pine'. Twelve o'clock for the common people of England, out of whom England's greatest souls have always come. Twelve o'clock for all that they are and have been, for all those things which make life worth living for free men.
>
> Twelve o'clock – and the wisest prophet in Christendom cannot say what is to come. The folk, old towns of Britain, the hills and cliffs and shores and meadows, rich with history, the homes and lives of forty-five million people, the great British traditions of

human worth and dignity, the folk sayings, the deep wisdom and the long-suffering hopes of a race – these, not being pleasing to Hitler, are condemned.

We know little, and for a time shall know little of this unparalleled spectacle of the nation rising as by a single impulse to the defence of –

This blessèd plot, this earth, this realm, this England.

From our own shores we cannot see the shadow over ancient gardens, over houses hoary with age, over the graves of poets and philosophers, and the tombs of the martyrs. We know only that one of the green and lovely oases of civilization in the wilderness of man's time on earth, is foully threatened and that the whole world for evermore will be the poorer if it falls.

Words falter. There are no phrases for the obscene ambition that attacks, for the magnificent mobilization of a people that defends, unshaken and unafraid. We can only pray that soon the time will come when the vultures no longer defile British skies, and the cry goes out from John o' Groats to Land's End –

'Twelve o'clock and all's well!'

*

Suffolk farmer Herman Kindred well remembered the day in July 1940 when, at twelve o'clock, he was called to do his bit for the blessed plot. 'I was simply amazed. The whole place was surrounded by soldiers on armed guard. No one else was allowed anywhere near.' Herman Kindred, normally leading an uneventful life, had unexpectedly been plucked from routine duties with the local Home Guard and ordered to Little Glemham village hall, near Saxmundham. Never a particularly military man, he was paraded before a couple of officers.

> The one who was in command – I found later that he was a fellow called Croft – asked me if I would consider joining something special. He seemed to know a lot about me already and warned me the job might be dangerous and had to be kept absolutely secret.

Kindred decided that anything was better than 'standing around on everlasting guard duty, bored stiff and without a firearm to fight with', and he cautiously replied 'Well. Perhaps I wouldn't mind.'

Captain Croft's reply was equally understated:

> You may be the man we are looking for. We have already started work along the south coast and are now in a hurry to sort out East Anglia. You will be checked out. Could you get another five or six men you can absolutely trust? They have got to be patriotic and determined and, above all, must know the land like the back of their hands. You see, the Germans are coming and they are a ruthless lot. We have to make special preparations *because they could invade at any moment.*

With the cover title of 'Intelligence Officer', although he was not associated with the Intelligence Corps, Croft and other carefully selected officers were now working day and night to enlist civilian men for a stay-behind task in those parts of Britain most vulnerable to invasion by Nazi Germany. Little Glemham was not his first stop in East Anglia but was, for the moment, the last – for the northern boundary of his area stopped at a line stretching inland from the East Coast holiday town of Aldeburgh.

Also in July 1940, Lieutenant J. W. Stuart Edmundson, Royal Engineers, and Captain Donald Hamilton-Hill, Seaforth Highlanders, were unexpectedly ordered to an office in Whitehall, and briefed as 'Intelligence Officers' for south-west England and Lincolnshire respectively. A month later Cyril Hall and Geoff Bowery, soldiers in the Suffolk Regiment, were *told* to volunteer for 'something special'. Yolande Bromley, serving with the ATS in Yorkshire, was soon more courteously *invited* to do so. Later still, Jill Holman was enrolled in Norfolk and Roy Coleman in Port Talbot. Both were aged sixteen and below the age of military service. Captain Peter Fleming, of the Grenadier Guards, was ahead of them all, commanding the first 'Auxiliary Unit', known originally as XII Corps Observation Unit, from his headquarters at Bilting, near Wye in Kent. These and many more men and, for a different stay-behind task, women too, were being individually recruited in great secrecy for post-invasion roles – to commit mayhem or collect intelligence behind German lines.

It was intended that these men and women, and hundreds more, were to be put in at the sharp end in a serious way, either as spies or saboteurs. They were now being called upon to volunteer for unconventional tasks which would leave them liable to immediate execution if captured by the Nazis. Although they were sometimes told that the job was a dangerous one, few, if any, realised just how vulnerable they might become. To be fair to the powers-that-were, neither did anyone else.

They were the spearhead of a very special partisan army indeed called – although very few were allowed into the secret – the GHQ Auxiliary Units. Secrecy would be paramount for their operational safety. Above all, however, it was necessary to prevent anyone knowing that Britain was responding to Nazi ruthlessness with a cauldron of dirty tricks of its own, developing innovative forms of irregular warfare, and doing so in full awareness at high level that the plans were contrary to the conventions of warfare and, therefore, almost entirely illegal. Officers in charge called it 'Scallywagging'.

Although Parliament was never informed or consulted, so frequently were the Auxiliary Units intended to penetrate the boundaries of internationally accepted legality, their very creation had demanded the authority of the inner War Cabinet chaired by the prime minister, Winston Churchill himself.

Chapter One

Appeasement

'War is to be avoided at all costs . . . '

Neville Chamberlain and the Chiefs of Staff in the late 1930s

In 1918 the German Kaiser's great army was retreating to the motherland from France and Belgium and, after years of stalemate, many of its men were in a hurry to get home. However, it was far from a beaten force.

The Treaty of Versailles into which Germany entered after the armistice of 11 November 1918 was, it has been argued, a political and economic humiliation disproportionate to Germany's military position. Germany was stripped of its colonies and subjected to punitive terms of reparation to the Allies, notably to France – allegedly without the German Army having been comprehensively beaten in battle.

It may have been difficult for German staff officers to understand the political imperative for an armistice at all, isolated as they were in their secure headquarters. There had been no fighting or destruction on home territory. Germany was still intact. Admittedly, the British were advancing with determination, at last on the ascendant following years of costly stalemate, and General Pershing's still growing American army was now making a real difference to Allied military superiority.

Distanced from the civilian population, senior German Army officers were perhaps unaware of hardship on the home front, following the Royal Navy's sea blockade of essential supplies and foodstuffs. The result amounted to near famine and, although reports differ, up to a million were said to have died from starvation. In contrast, the Army, for all the horrendous loss of life on the Western Front, was more or less intact and still comparatively well-equipped, well-fed and formidable.

It was, in any event, domestic rather than military pressures that finally persuaded the German government to seek an armistice.

And so it was not surprising that – during the years of Allied occupation and severe economic hardship at every level – the German nation, and the military in particular, came to resent bitterly the punitive conditions imposed by the Treaty of Versailles. Latent militarism was not difficult to discern. Revenge must have seemed an attractive option too. Winston Churchill wrote:

> Adolf Hitler was the child of the rage and grief of a mighty Empire and race which had suffered overwhelming defeat in war. He it was who exorcised the spirit of despair from the German mind by substituting the not less baleful but far less morbid spirit of revenge.

It was into this near-revolutionary ferment of overheating political, economic and social discontent and national humiliation that Adolf Hitler and his confident new Nazi Party emerged in the late 1920s with promises to rebuild the nation and then, crudely and undemocratically, seized political power in the early 1930s. It is not difficult to imagine how welcome they were, even to many of their countrymen who disapproved of all the brash triumphalism, the bombast and glitter, the provocative speeches and violence, and the hatefully racist political agenda of the Nazi Party.

Even the most sceptical Germans began to count the value of the Reichsmark in negotiable tens and hundreds rather than the worthless millions to which they had been unhappily accustomed for a time in the 1920s. It could not have been all that difficult to ignore deteriorating moral values and – as individuals prospered and the nation declared its renewed strength on the international scene in blatant defiance of embargos on rearmament and treaty obligations – simply to look the other way.

Although the reacquisition of former German colonies was not apparently given immediate priority, a certain attraction to the electorate was Hitler's disclosed intention of reuniting those German-speakers who had been separated from the nation state by the Treaty of Versailles, such as the majority population in the Czechoslovakian Sudetenland and a substantial minority, at least, in western Poland. He also made little secret of his intent to absorb Austria – Germanic enough by any standards.

As he made his longer-term plans, Hitler tested the resistance and determination of the World War I victors, notably France and Britain, by marching to remilitarise the Rhineland in 1936. This provocative move was completed without opposition other than the passage of diplomatic notes, demands for ambassadors' explanations, and bold declarations at the League of Nations. Significantly for the Nazis, there was no serious sabre-rattling from the Allies.

While still isolated in a political backwater, and out of favour with the Conservative Party, Winston Churchill found that Britain was as yet too preoccupied with its own economic depression and associated unemployment to respond positively to German provocation with a programme of rearmament. Of the three British armed services, the Royal Navy had suffered the least financial constraint, but the Royal Air Force and the Army had slipped badly behind the Luftwaffe and the German Army in terms of manpower, weaponry, training and new equipment, through sheer lack of investment and political direction.

*

Britain's political and diplomatic response was, instead, an official policy of appeasement. Appeasement is defined as '. . . soothing threatening enemies by satisfying their demands – to calm, to assuage, to allay, to make peace'. It is a technique not unknown to all of us when confronted with a bully and imminent danger to health and welfare. Although on occasion an intensely sensible option, it does, unfortunately, smack of cowardice. Nevertheless, this policy was accepted in pre-war Britain, if not with enthusiasm, without notable resistance, except by a relatively few people of influence. Notable among them was Winston Churchill. His group was never to show favour for Chamberlain's shuttle diplomacy from Croydon Airport to Munich for conciliatory talks with Herr Hitler. Sympathetic Whitehall insiders coined the ditty: 'If at first you can't concede, / Fly, fly, fly again.'

When the Prime Minister, looking by today's criteria intensely old-fashioned and out of touch with reality, returned from Germany on 30 September 1938, waving a paper agreement in which he had effectively conceded Czechoslovakian Sudetenland to the Nazis, declaring 'Peace with honour – Peace in our time' a collective sigh of relief was the reaction from the majority of Britons. They could now get back to work, where there was any, and look forward to next year's holiday at Clacton-on-Sea.

Support for appeasement came from influential circles, such as Parliament, writers and broadcasters, and many of the land-owning upper classes, as well as a population still reeling from the casualty lists of World War I and the widespread unemployment and economic slump which followed. Most, if not all, preferred to resist a renewal of hostilities at almost

any cost. They hoped instead, to live in peace, if not unqualified content-
ment. For the moment at least, anti-Fascism was not in political ascendancy.

The Right Honourable Neville Chamberlain, leader of the Conservative
Party and Britain's coalition prime minister from 1937 until May 1940, died
a few months after his resignation, largely unaware that he was the target
of a conspiracy – including political friends as well as enemies, the press,
parliamentarians and later, historical researchers and apologists too. Any
blame for Britain's lack of preparation in advance of World War II was laid
firmly and permanently on him.

It is clear enough now that he hardly deserved such a coalition of
condemnation, much as the notion suited some writers and commentators,
who found him an easy scapegoat, a laughable, brolly-bearing, wing-collared
caricature, a spokesman for a minority of British wimps who kowtowed to
the German Führer as he advanced inevitably into confrontation, ruthlessly
pursuing one objective above all others – European military and economic
domination. Comparisons with that great British bulldog, his successor
Winston Churchill, left 'lapdog' Chamberlain ridiculed as the principal
figurehead for his government's unfortunate policy of appeasement.

In spite of all the recrimination heaped upon him, it is doubtful whether
Chamberlain himself ever believed his own fine words about peace in our
time. Out of touch he might look at first sight, but he was an experienced
politician with access to a variety of the best available military and
diplomatic threat assessments, as well as secret service intelligence. No doubt
much of the advice was conflicting but still with enough substance to give
a full brief on just how many beans made five with Adolf Hitler. Moreover,
Neville Chamberlain was certainly no coward.

*

After Britain declared war on 3 September 1939, the event was followed at
first by a flurry of self-righteous recrimination, focusing largely on the
country's lack of military preparation. Once there was more time to think
about it, some of Chamberlain's detractors slowly became influenced by
second thoughts. Later still, some objective writers developed a new
understanding, profiting both from a growing library of WWII
autobiography and the release of records from Whitehall's sacred vaults.
Previously unexplored opportunities for book sales and media fees became
evident, and Winston Churchill's perceived infallibility was placed under

renewed scrutiny – sometimes unfairly. Neville Chamberlain's reputation was looked at again, this time in a more favourably impartial light.

Discussion started to refocus upon Chamberlain's role in more detail. A good example is to be seen in W. J. M. Mackenzie's historically authoritative *The Secret History of SOE*. Soon after the end of WWII, the author, whose informed objectivity is not in question, was commissioned by the Cabinet Office to compile the best possible account from surviving SOE records. He discusses (page 753) Chamberlain's part in the pre-war government's policy of peace at all costs. He considers the possibility that his 'disgrace' was merely one of the efforts of crypto-fascists to conceal their own pro-Nazi tendencies. Mackenzie goes on to discuss the possibility that Churchill himself, sensing a golden opportunity, may have gone along with this in order to contrast the apparent timidity of Chamberlain with his own pro-Empire and pro-Royal Navy image.

Although it is impossible to imagine this line of thinking being supported or encouraged by dedicated pro-Churchill supporters, the arguments would have been invaluable to a public debate had they appeared in print earlier. However, for reasons unexplained, having commissioned the book and permitted circulation to just a very few privileged outlets in the inner circle of Whitehall, the Cabinet Office banned publication for *fifty years*, *The Secret History of SOE* did not appear on bookshelves until the very end of the twentieth century.

It now seems possible that appeasement may not have been so dishonourable, so unpatriotic, or so unwise after all. Instead, if it did gain useful time for Britain's industry and the armed forces to make belated progress toward a blueprint for rearmament, this apparently feeble response to Nazism would have been of real strategic value.

Fortunately, although Hitler could hardly have been aware of it, and as a disinterested, almost complacent, calm was maintained by the British people prior to the outbreak of war, threatening red warning lights did not go unnoticed by a few unorthodox men in the War Office and the secret services. Plans to counteract Germany's continuing policy of military and economic expansion were examined. They concentrated their experience and skills on counter-measures – even drawing up a worst-case scenario – the invasion of Britain itself.

With almost no encouragement from either the political or military establishment, they had to work in complete secrecy. In spite of inadequate resources on all fronts, their strengths were imagination – for none of them had previous experience of the reality of invasion – and a determination to ensure the survival of Britain's way of life. What they needed was time. And it was here that Neville Chamberlain was persuaded, or urged, or cajoled into the front line.

At best, appeasement might actually have worked. If not, it could at least create breathing space for the men and women who were likely to confront the enemy face-to-face when the threat materialised, and time to start the race to re-arm and modernise the British armed forces. Once looked at in the warm glow of after-knowledge, Neville Chamberlain can certainly be seen to have played his patriotic part in helping to secure the best interests of the British people.

Chapter Two

Intelligence:
A Fallible Craft

'Secrecy is our absolute stock in trade. It is our most precious asset.'

Sir Colin McColl, Chief of the SIS in 1993

'. . . imposture, subterfuge, trickery . . . hoax, ruse . . .'

From the definition of 'deception' in World Books Dictionary

In the 1930s and throughout World War II, the headquarters of the British Secret Intelligence Service (the 'SIS') was at 54 Broadway, London SW1, and the Chief – known as 'C' to his staff and a privileged circle in government and the armed forces – was Admiral Sir Hugh Sinclair, KCB, until his death in the autumn of 1939. His deputy, Sir Stewart Menzies, then took over as Chief of the SIS ('CSS') for the duration of the war.

It has been reported that the German Embassy monitored everyone passing through the front door of 54 Broadway, employing a newspaper seller on the opposite side of the street equipped with a remotely operated camera hidden in his news-stand. Meanwhile, to maintain the proper protocol between two potential adversaries, Sir Stewart Menzies and a diplomat from the German Embassy rode to the same pack of foxhounds. It was too cosy to last.

During the twentieth century the Secret Intelligence Service developed proportionately as the Empire expanded and British economic and political influence grew. The objective of the SIS was to collect and analyse the highest level of intelligence – political, military and commercial. It was intended to work in the national interest.

The collection of intelligence has been described as 'lying and spying'. It is a fallible craft. Conclusions are frequently wrong. The product is an assembly and assessment of insider information about the present activities and future plans of enemies, or commercial competitors – whether friend or foe – and the proposal of options from which a government may choose to base its policy. In practice, the remit goes much further.

The present-day Foreign and Commonwealth Office (during the war still two separate ministries, the Foreign Office and the Colonial Office) provides cover both for the budget – usually an undisclosed sum – and the unattributable activities of SIS agents. The very existence of these operatives, sometimes fully-fledged spies, was officially denied until recent years. In this respect, the overt deployment of personnel as passport control officers (PCOs), for example, benefiting from full or semi-diplomatic status at British embassies and high commissions abroad, was frequently an acceptable, if fairly obvious stratagem. One PCO who became a prominent figure was 'Little Bill' Stephenson, later Sir William, who, as the personal agent of Winston Churchill, exploited a vast network of American business contacts to the considerable advantage of Great Britain through much of WWII.

So comprehensively has the SIS developed its antennae that British diplomats and senior staff need a good, if not comprehensive understanding of SIS strategy, methodology and contacts – often at the same time providing cover, either wittingly or unwittingly.

The charter for the SIS concentrates on espionage abroad and, in certain circumstances, sabotage too, but this was not formally adopted as a policy instrument until the outbreak of WWII. The Security Service (MI5) is complementary, ostensibly holding a remit for counter-espionage within the United Kingdom and the colonies at that time. Inevitably in this underworld, such orderly spheres of responsibility are not cast in stone and overlap on occasion. While both agencies follow a dedicated policy of secrecy, the SIS is possibly the more deviously protective of the two.

It is not surprising that MI5 and MI6, when working to independent agendas, have sometimes come into bitter conflict. And it is a fact that paid informants may not be entirely averse to working for their own financial advantage by playing off one service against the other – even feeding similar information to the two agencies separately for double the reward. It is simply the market economy at work but it would be a serious mistake for fraudsters to see the secret services as a soft touch and try it on more than once.

At the time of WWII, the reputation of the SIS was probably the more gung-ho of the two, mainly thanks to the imagination of writers and researchers, amplified at times through leaks covertly encouraged by SIS mavericks – or the directorate looking for tactical advantage in the everlasting Whitehall battle for ascendancy. While Ian Fleming's inventive creation is a post-WWII phenomenon, there are realistic precedents for a type of James Bond dating from the early days of the twentieth century. One of the more remarkable was Erskine Childers who, in his 1904 book *The Riddle of the Sands*, described his small boat voyage along the German North Sea coastline to discover their secret preparations for the First World War. Some sources report that he was himself an agent for the SIS, although it was then hardly up and running as we recognise it now. Written as a novel, the narrative was intended to alert the British public and government to a growing German menace to this country's interests. This exposé is recognised now as a significant 'wake-up' call for WWI.

Childers, a Protestant and top-ranking official in the Home Civil Service, was later executed for illegally running guns to the Republican movement in Ireland. The intelligence world is indeed a complicated one and, yes, the severest sanctions may be imposed upon transgressors.

It is certainly a fact that the SIS, while more than adequately funded at times, has suffered at others from penny-pinching by its financial paymasters. This led to a quiet initiative, a dual-purpose development of SIS's own long-term businesses as cover for clandestine activity, together with a secondary objective – to build up a working kitty to see it through any bad times. In particular, import–export agencies and transport companies – by land or sea or air – are favoured. The spin-off here is contact with the business world, whose managers – by co-operation and secret participation – may benefit from useful commercial advantage over the opposition, especially foreigners who, while not necessarily excluded, are not first choice in this inner circle either. At the same time the businesses themselves provide standing agencies through which the SIS can operate in secret, and under ready-made cover with minimum cost. An exchange of selected intelligence is sometimes a mutual base point. A permanent link is therefore forged between the SIS and the City of London, for example. Equally durable relations are maintained with universities, to supply a reservoir of linguistic and technical expertise, and with the armed forces, for suitably disciplined manpower.

Absolute secrecy about objectives and technique is imperative for the safety of undercover field agents. As security back-up, the SIS maintains an ongoing policy of deception at all levels. Deception of 'friends' as well as the enemy is routine. This is calculated not only to prevent outsiders from discovering what insiders are up to, but also to leave just one controller holding all the threads at the top of any given operation, while both the field agents and their controllers are told only what they 'need to know' to achieve desired results.

Professor Christopher Andrew quotes the late Malcolm Muggeridge in *Secret Service*, as:

> . . . deriving from his years in British Intelligence, the lesson that nothing should ever be done simply if there are devious ways of doing it. Secrecy is as essential to Intelligence as vestments in a Mass, or darkness to a spiritualist séance, and must at all costs be maintained, quite irrespective of whether or not it serves any purpose.

It may, therefore be more calculation than coincidence that the SIS is popularly known as Section 6 of Military Intelligence – or MI6 – when it is principally financed and controlled by the Foreign and Commonwealth Office, and only indirectly connected to the structure of the Army's Military Intelligence department – which is separately funded by and directly responsible to the Ministry of Defence (or, as its Army component was known during WWII, the War Office). The Security Service (MI5), is nominally responsible to the Home Office, and follows a similar pathway of deception. Selected and possibly sanitised intelligence from all the secret services is now channelled upward through the Cabinet Office in Whitehall.

Dedication to both secrecy and deception is still demonstrable. But public accountability was rarely evident either before, or during WWII. One of the many important tasks undertaken by Sir Stewart Menzies and the SIS was code-named Ultra. This involved great secrecy and skilful deception. Successfully sustained throughout five years of war, the secrecy surrounding the Ultra programme preventing the Germans discovering that an ever-increasing amount of their secret radio traffic was being decoded and read by boffins at Bletchley Park in Buckinghamshire. This required the tightest security and most arcane of deception stratagems; these even included instances of calculated failure to take operationally appropriate counter-action when to have done so might have compromised this 'Most Secret' source.

The importance of protecting Ultra transcripts dated from 22 May 1940, just as the Dunkirk crisis developed. From then, although the product was intermittent and often incomplete, it gave Winston Churchill a very special advantage in outguessing Adolf Hitler for the remainder of the war.

The SIS was also in close liaison with, and maintained the influence of Stewart Menzies over, another secret service agency known as the London Controlling Section. World War I veteran, City stockbroker and MI5 officer, Lieutenant-Colonel 'Johnny' Bevan, MC, as head of the section, master-minded Allied deception strategy from the date of his appointment by the Chiefs of Staff in May 1942 until the end of the war. The LCS was given the personal backing and approval of Winston Churchill from an initiative of General Archibald Wavell in 1940.

A major task for the LCS was the operation mounted in 1944 to convince Hitler and the German high command that the cross-Channel Second Front was to be opened in the Pas de Calais region, rather than the beaches of Normandy. This involved the creation of an entirely fictitious American formation – the First United States Army Group or FUSAG – supposedly stationed in East Anglia and south-east England under the command of US General George Patton, with associated spurious radio traffic and dummy trucks and tanks on the ground for the benefit of any Luftwaffe spy planes. Bevan was able to draw profitably upon the 'double-cross' operation, conducted by a consortium of SIS and MI5 personnel, in which captured Abwehr agents were 'induced' to feed false information to their controllers in Germany.

So comprehensive was the secrecy defending this co-ordinated deception policy that, when one of the officers involved, Lieutenant-Colonel Peter Fleming, proposed to write an official chronicle on his own not inconsiderable role in strategic deception, Whitehall procrastinated for nearly four years before agreeing to release relevant official documentation. It was a supreme irony that Peter Fleming was to die soon after the release and, much to the undoubted satisfaction of the secret services, his book was never written.

While the SIS may rightly expect much of the credit for these deceptions, it was many years before the public was admitted into such secrets and then, generally, only in the case of successful operations. Deception was intended to ensure that neither friend nor foe discovered how clever the SIS had been nor, of course, how incompetent. Where revelations have emerged (such as a number of early publications about the Ultra programme), disclosure was sometimes simply unavoidable as participants' knowledge could no longer be lawfully suppressed. When exposure was 'official', it was often simply a tactic to gain political or financial advantage in Whitehall or Westminster.

Professor Christopher Andrew summed up his conclusions on page 500 of his classic book *Secret Service*:

> The simple fallacy behind the argument that total disclosure is the only alternative to total secrecy . . . escaped serious challenge for so long because the intelligence community acquired the status of an unmentionable taboo exempt from any process of rational public or parliamentary debate. Since 1924 successive governments have done their best to keep the taboo intact.

Another major SIS discipline is avoidance of visible triumphalism for its own sake. There is, however, no such embargo on back-patting papers for internal distribution, as we shall read later.

Well before WWII the SIS initiated several significant innovations, such as the development of a photographic reconnaissance unit (PRU) for aerial surveillance. Sabotage was also added to its non-attributable range of options. To implement the latter, the directorate created a new section, whose chief was known as 'D' (for destruction!). He reported directly to Sir Stewart Menzies, after his appointment as Chief of the Secret Intelligence Service. Section D – as the new unit was known – would have an immediate and profound effect on secret counter-preparations for an invasion of Britain.

It was one of the first government departments, perhaps even *the* first, to make a speciality of what would now be called terrorism. And it was from an initiative by Section D that the GHQ Auxiliary Units were spawned from this SIS maelstrom of secrecy and deception in midsummer 1940.

Although it was never recognised by, or confided to, the men and women at ground level, they were not only 'Most Secret', but part of a grand deception too.

In a way, they still are.

Chapter Three

Section D

'Great Britain's only successful experiment in Total War.'

Section D's closing report in August 1940

Anticipating the outbreak of war by nearly a year and a half, Section D, the first specialist dirty tricks department of the Secret Intelligence Service, came formally into being in April 1938. Its first title was Section IX.

After an interview with the Chief of the SIS, Admiral Sir Hugh Sinclair, Major Laurence Grand (later Major General) of the Royal Engineers, was seconded from regular army duties to become 'D', head of the new section. He was formally invited by Sinclair to 'cogitate on the possibilities of sabotage'.

Grand – described variously as 'chain smoking, of thin build, with a black moustache, and always carefully dressed', or a 'volatile dreamer', depending on the source – usually wore a red carnation in his buttonhole and that, together with his bowler hat, would automatically have qualified him for many a 'Present Arms!' as he approached War Office sentries. This standard Whitehall spooks' rig-of-the-day contrasted absolutely with his reported obsession with secrecy. Grand soon adopted the role and appearance of a classic mid-twentieth-century spymaster. He had an exceptionally persuasive charm which, together with natural energy, drive and initiative, made him a popular leader; as his empire expanded he was thus able to command comparable qualities and commitment from his subordinates. Although early recruits to this new section of the SIS were selected from the armed forces or the civil or diplomatic services, Grand also developed influential contacts in the City, the commercial world and universities to absorb men with specialist know-how or as advisers. No mention has been found that women were recruited too.

In the field, deeds would be done by undercover spies and saboteurs who, if caught, would be neither acknowledged nor defended by their government.

Grand's office was on the first floor of the SIS HQ, 54 Broadway. As the section expanded, it took premises close by in Caxton Street and, later, in the adjacent St Ermin's Hotel, off Broadway. Although working independently, Section D was always an integral part of the SIS.

Secondment from the regular army and into the SIS was not an easy option. Promotion – often in the forefront of an officer's mind – was a slow affair in peacetime. Although he knew precisely where he was in the pecking order, when, if ever, he could look forward to promotion and, in turn, work out his pension and date of retirement, his final years were unlikely to give job satisfaction. There was no real place in the War Office for men who made waves. In wartime, however, promotion – now being roughly proportionate to the number of names on casualty lists – was likely to speed along nicely. Within the SIS, however, wave-makers – while losing that plodding sense of War Office order – had much to gain. But there would be risks attached and some might even be life-threatening.

Secondment to the SIS therefore called for challenging personal decisions. Rather like joining the Freemasons, a man transferring would know very little of what he was joining because of the all-encompassing cloak of secrecy imposed on those already within this inner circle. It was not easy – and more likely an impossibility – to find someone to explain the rules before you joined, even off the record. Certainty about prospects was far from guaranteed. On secondment, an officer might *appear* to have been promoted, but his uniform would by then probably be cover and could, for the time being, even place him in any one of the three armed services. However, if he returned to formal duties, or was later called back on active service with his regiment, he would revert to the substantive rank recorded on his personal file. Although life in the SIS was more likely to be what officers call 'fun', it was not usually a job for life.

In spite of this list of potential drawbacks, once 'C' had outlined the charter already prepared for Section D, it seems likely that Grand jumped at the chance to take on the responsibilities the post offered. Sinclair had picked the right man.

The unconventionally open-ended charter described the section's objective as, 'to influence opinion in any part of the world as to be favourable to His Majesty's Government'. Such *carte blanche* authority was unprecedented and gave Grand the most wide-ranging scope for initiative and original ideas. Full-scale sabotage – a major innovation for the SIS – was not excluded although a non-attributable condition was always a clear understanding. Moreover, a truly formidable budget of £20,000 was his start-up fund, allocated from secret sources. There was nothing like this in the War House, as the War Office was often referred to in those days. The sky was indeed the limit for Section D. Great Britain had certainly tried nothing like these dirty tricks in its whole history – and the British public was not allowed to know much about it all for more than half a century.

With a burgeoning budget, Section D expanded cautiously but rapidly under Grand's energetic and imaginative leadership, spearheading the development of 'dirty tricks' and irregular warfare well in advance of a declaration of hostilities. The section was motivated into a state of total war by Adolf Hitler, 'who harnessed to his war chariot the four horses of treacherous diplomacy, lying propaganda, racial persecution and economic blackmail', as Section D's closing report put it.

A cadre of soldiers, mostly officers, was supplemented by the recruitment of likely lads from commerce, industry, universities and the City of London. This new blood was often a useful balance to the stereotypical thinking of former War Office personnel, familiarised as they were with progress in step with traditional red tape. To preserve the almost fanatical secrecy which Grand demanded, the process of recruitment was gradual, but comprehensive and continuous.

Section D soon had real clout. Grand was not only briefing 'C', often on a daily basis, but also meeting heads of the services and departments of state – such as the Foreign Office and, later, the Ministry of Economic Warfare. From these he assembled and collated potential targets of industrial or military significance to the enemy – clearly identified as Nazi Germany, though Italy and Japan were also in the gun-sights of Section D from early days. When war broke out in September 1939 the section was enlarged to the status of a self-sufficient department. Grand was soon a full colonel.

After the German Army had vanquished France in 1940, and in spite of his department's rapid progress, Grand complained that:

> Probably no department of war has more frequently been frustrated by the enemy's major operations or more domestically cramped by the diplomatic timidity with which we entered upon this Herculean struggle than this Section, if only because its activities by any standards other than those of total and lightning warfare are peculiarly disreputable.

When Grand had been selected to head Section D in early 1938, war with Germany may have appeared imminent but the precise date could not of course be forecast; indeed appeasement might still win the day. Strategic thinking within the section had to consider three eventualities.

First, and the least likely, was the success of the peace process. In that case Section D would be restricted to the creation and distribution of 'black' propaganda, with the intention of undermining both the German will to fight by exploiting a degree of resistance to war evident among the far from negligible number of anti-Hitler Germans, and covert industrial sabotage. The second option was a successful Nazi attack on, and perhaps occupation of, the Low Countries and France. Finally, the worst-case scenario was an attack on Britain, followed by partial or even complete enemy occupation. Either or both of options two and three would call for a response with a full catalogue of dirty tricks.

A great deal of work had to be done in a hurry. There was no precedent filed away in military or secret service archives, or very little suitable warlike matériel in the quartermaster's stores (indeed no quartermaster), no training, records or administration staff or facilities, and no agents in the field. It was not a promising start to a brand new secret service, but Grand tackled and unblocked these problems with vigour.

The start point was the selection of like-minded Army officers. Grand had some help from a list drawn up by a small, secret unit in the War Office, known at its inception in 1936 as General Staff (Research) or GS(R), which had collected a longish list – some reports talk of a total of 1,300 names – of serving, Territorial Army or Reserve officers who might be called upon as volunteers for irregular duty and who were not likely to be too hidebound by old-fashioned red tape.

With the vetting process complete, such as it was in those days, the selected officers were dispatched literally to all points of the globe to trawl for likely field agents, both local nationals and British expatriates, men or women. Contacts at high level were fed to them secretly through embassy and high commission channels, and from commercial sources. With little subversive-war industry at home, some emissaries also traveled, with a commercial front, to buy weapons, explosives, and ammunition. For this purpose, section officers, as these representatives were known, went on purchasing missions to the United States, Japan, Portugal, Spain and Italy, where some of the required paraphernalia was manufactured. Money was not a problem.

As recruitment continued, back at base camp in SW1 staff officers allowed themselves about three months to study the problems involved:

> Neither daunted nor tempted by so broad an horizon, we hurried slowly, recruited sparingly and limited immediate plans to the study of Germany's three most patent weaknesses – her dependence upon Sweden for her iron ore, her dependence upon Russia and Roumania for her petroleum and, in the political field, the bitter if latent distaste of Germany's middle aged and middle class for the Nazi Regime.

The net result was an almost instant, if far from perfect, world-wide espionage and sabotage agency under the command of 'D'. The collective total of their sharp-end experience was nil. Fortunately, they were quick to learn.

An early priority, as long as a precarious peace was still evident, was to identify sabotage targets, mainly industrial, to restrict Germany's economic capacity to go to war. Iron ore supplies from Sweden, for example, were essential for the production of heavy armaments of all kinds. Following the usual SIS maxim that everything must be kept a secret, the disaster which followed was not trumpeted by Section D, any more than their numerous successes. But, having recruited local agents and identified and prepared several opportunities to attack and interrupt this trade, flowing down the Baltic when the sea was free from ice, and through the Norwegian port of Narvik when not, the inexperienced agents, working to an equally inexperienced controller, were easily detected by what seems to have been routine Swedish police operations. Embarrassingly for SIS, they were then tried and imprisoned. Accompanying press publicity was not encouraged at home and the diplomatic fallout from both the Swedish and German authorities was minimised, more or less successfully.

Strenuous attempts were made to interdict Romanian oil production with advice and guidance coming to the section officers from our man-on-the-spot, the military attaché, Brigadier Sir Geoffrey MacNab. This project was a failure too.

Personnel within the section, probably supplemented with specialists recruited from outside the armed forces, went rapidly to work in the field of anti-Nazi propaganda. Their work differed from that of the Ministry of Information and other government agencies, in that it was brilliantly designed, and was printed and distributed in such a way that its origins were concealed completely, and usually successfully. Multiple deviation from fact was in order. This was 'black propaganda', 'scallywagging' of a new kind intended to deploy against the Germans the techniques of their own, unscrupulous state publicity machine headed by Josef Goebbels. Creation and distribution of the propaganda involved forgery on a massive and highly skilled scale, and – once the Germans had attacked and occupied the whole of western Europe, except Spain – 'risk to many men's lives'. Section D's experts regarded black propaganda, ostensibly indigenous, as infinitely more effective than leaflets dropped openly from British aircraft. It is recorded that such work in the field, while not as up-front as sabotage missions, was nevertheless considered both difficult and dangerous.

Section D sometimes incurred enmity from other active service departments, some no doubt envious of the funds and facilities which it commanded. Its operations also called too much attention to the work of the British secret services at times. As the overt package, a small, elite army of subversives and of saboteurs, passed into the control of Special Operations Executive later in 1940, the SIS drew a breath of relief. It could return to its traditionally independent, long-term, preferably covert role, supported by agents quietly put in place over many years.

A substantial legacy was bequeathed to SOE by Section D, and formed the foundation stone upon which much of it was built. In its short life, the section created research, development and production sub-stations, often in the Home Counties. The propaganda section was in the Old Rectory, Hertingfordbury and Station XVII at Brickendonbury, near Hertford, was used as a demolition school. These and the agent training school near Beaulieu in Hampshire were handed on to SOE, which was, as a result, able to make a flying start by the end of 1940.

*

The National Archives contain the Section D closing report to the CSS. Although undated this can, from the content, be dated as August 1940. Peevish, perhaps, at being disbanded but confidently recalling all the section's successes, it is a remarkable catalogue.

As so little about Section D is similarly in the public domain, the content must be approached with caution. Is it, for example, intentionally deceptive and misleading for future research? Why is there this isolated example of open exposure, and why was it not available for public scrutiny until 2002? Did it find its way into the vaults at Kew by accident? Should it instead have been put in a file marked 'for shredding'?

The only name appearing on the paper is that of Colonel Grand, and although he is written about in the third person, the content must either have been his, or at least assembled and compiled with his approval. There is no reason to trust this document without maintaining a cautious circumspection but, where it is possible to check, some facts at least can be confirmed. It is of significance here that some of the content is directly related to the GHQ Auxiliary Units. Depending upon the format, there are some forty pages in typescript.

The contents describe how Section D developed from researches made between April and June 1938; how it worked closely with the SIS but organised its own supply of materials and communications; how an agents' school was created; how the section was organised for sabotage and contributed to the war effort in valuable ways outside its immediate terms of reference; how it developed relations with some thirty-three foreign political organisations and, on sixty or more recorded occasions, sabotaged railways, factories, works, aircraft production, food stores and other military objectives; and how the section saw the part it had still to play in winning the war and building the peace.

The report does not spare any detail: 1,920 tons of wheat had been destroyed or contaminated, together with vast quantities of oil, hemp and timber; factories, buildings, power houses, railway bridges, dumps of petrol and ammunition, railway trucks and trains – all were reported 'sabotaged or destroyed'. There is a specific claim that 770 train bearings were 'melted' on average *every* month and 14,645 railway axle boxes destroyed in all. Research covered the general principles of sabotage methods, targets, devices, processes of manufacture, methods of camouflage, sources of supply and methods of packing. It embraced particular investigations into such subjects as time fuses, adulteration of metals, petroleum and lubricating oils, contamination of foodstuffs and raw materials, destruction of rolling stock, permanent ways, fire stations, ships, submarines, barges, aeroplanes, crops, forests and, last but not least, persons. If this was all true, Section D had set a spectacular pace for the exploitation of dirty warfare and seemed more than satisfied that it had made a good job of it.

After summarising achievements in the field of propaganda, the account really puffs itself up, positively glowing with pride at the work of the experimental communication department, where 'The Officer' (not identified), in just one year, invented:

> a) The D-Phone, a telephone which left scrambling far behind by encoding and decoding the human voice; and
> b) The Duplex Transceiver – described as a wireless telephone using a wavelength too short to be picked up by any other known receiver. This instrument was designed for communications between agents operating in foreign countries. Its range was strictly limited.

Any student of the activities of the Special Duties Section of the GHQ Auxiliary Units will be in no doubt that this transceiver was not just used abroad – if at all. A few surviving SDS radio operators, once subalterns in the Auxiliary Territorial Service (ATS – the women's section of the Army) and a few one-time agents in the British countryside, will be in no doubt that it was a design used by their network – which disappeared from the face of the known world at the end of World War II.

The summary of 'Special Achievements' is of particular interest although, admittedly, not directly relevant to the Auxiliary Units. For example:

> *Diamonds.* In her last hour an Officer of the Section left England and brought out of Holland £500,000 worth of Industrial Diamonds.
> *Gold.* Another officer of the Section also left England, and under the nose of German bombers, embarked £84 million in gold bars in the last French cruiser to leave the quay at Bordeaux.
> *RAF Targets.* In the course of his routine smuggling of arms and ammunitions and explosives into Norway, an Officer of the Section had been able to provide detailed contemporary knowledge of new targets, some of which have been used to great effect.
> *General De Gaulle.* The only officer who had so far lost his life in the service of the Section did so when leading an expedition by air in an attempt to rescue from German occupied territory in France the family of General de Gaulle.

This report summarises two further, and even more significant, Section D achievements under Laurence Grand's leadership. They provide an answer, almost certainly *the answer*, to questions which hitherto have mystified researchers into the origins and provenance of the GHQ Auxiliary Units – as well as the enduring secrecy which still surrounds them. They are:

MIR

Early in 1939 Colonel Grand initiated the organisation and development of guerrilla warfare. What began as a sub-division of this Section has since been established as a branch of the War Department.

Home Defence

At our most forlorn moment when our army was pouring back from Dunkirk through gates we could never have shut against the invading enemy, Colonel Grand conceived the plan of organising through Great Britain a closely co-ordinated sabotage and intelligence network among the civilian population who would be left behind in any territories which the German armies might temporarily be able to occupy.

Some 30 Officers of this Section went to work at high pressure and completed this organisation and distributed in several thousand secret dumps throughout the country a vast quantity of incendiary materials. This organisation has now been taken over by the newly constituted branch of the War Office, the Auxiliary Units.

Fitting as well as it does with other records, this is strong and probably unassailable evidence on the origins of both the Operational Section of the GHQ Auxiliary Units *and* the Special Duties Section. It is also the clear response by Section D to the problems of the 'third option' which confronted their analysts as French defences were collapsing in May 1940 – how to prepare for an invasion of the British mainland. The Home Defence Organisation was their prompt answer.

However, the intriguing question of Section D's formation of a network of agents – which was absorbed as the Special Duties Section of the already existing Auxiliary Units from 19 July 1940 – is avoided. A number of D's officers are known to have moved along with the civilian agents, becoming, technically at least responsible to the Officer Commanding GHQ Auxiliary Units, the very organisation which superseded the Home Defence Organisation. The question is whether their prime commitment from that date was to their new commanding officer or, and more likely, still with the Secret Intelligence Service proper.

For the very first time it is now possible to put into place the final pieces of the complicated puzzle on the origins of the Auxiliary Units, a puzzle which has previously confounded both Auxiliers and the public, and defied anything more authentic than semi-informed speculation.

Chapter Four

The Home Defence Organisation

'. . . a closely coordinated sabotage and intelligence network . . .'

Closing report by Section D

'We shall defend our island whatever the cost may be; we shall fight on the beaches, we shall fight on the landing grounds, we shall fight in the fields and in the streets, we shall fight in the hills; we shall never surrender.'

Winston Churchill in the House of Commons, 4 June 1940

At 11.15 on the morning of 3 September 1939, the Right Honourable Neville Chamberlain announced on the wireless to a breathless nation that, as there had been no reply to the communiqué sent by His Majesty's Government to *Herr* Hitler, the nation must therefore consider that 'a state of war now exists between Great Britain and Germany'. It was an admission that appeasement had failed.

The communiqué had been an ultimatum for the withdrawal of German armed forces from Poland, which – under the pretence of 'frontier violations' – had been attacked without provocation on 1 September. Great Britain had both moral and treaty commitments to Poland and, as the German Army did not hesitate in its advance deep into Polish territory or the Luftwaffe to bomb civilian and military targets alike, the Prime Minister and his Cabinet were left with no alternative but to declare war. By this time the Germans had not only absorbed the small fry but also, by one stratagem or another, Austria and Czechoslovakia too, in their declared desire to reunite all German-speaking people within one state.

With the conquest of Poland soon completed, despite determined resistance by civilians and the Polish armed forces, and the destruction of much of Warsaw, Europe settled to the 'Phoney War' during the winter of

1939–40. The British Expeditionary Force (BEF) dug in along the western sector of the French border with the Low Countries, while the centre and east, directly adjacent to Germany itself, were protected by the formidable and allegedly impregnable French Maginot Line.

In spite of heavy breathing from the German Führer, Luxembourg, Belgium and Holland remained implacably neutral, hopeful that appeasement would keep them out of trouble. Assuming that the Germans were fighting within the Queensberry Rules, this negative policy – already well rehearsed by the British government – seemed to have much to say for itself. As small countries with commensurately insignificant defence forces, they knew they stood no fighting chance against the modern might of Germany. The alternative, they hoped, was that the aggressor would react kindly to non-provocation. The result was that both the Dutch and Belgian governments denied Britain and France the access across their borders necessary to prepare defensive positions against the fairly obvious intention of the Germans to attack them. These refusals – intended to avoid giving the Germans any pretext for declaring war, and seemingly sensible enough at the time – were to prove catastrophic for Allied defenders when the Wehrmacht launched its full-scale attack on 10 May 1940 through Luxembourg, Holland and Belgium. The arrival of the Allied forces was inevitably too late to save them.

With the Maginot Line by-passed, and the BEF under Lord Gort cut off, the British Army made its famous fighting retreat to the Channel and North Sea ports, followed by the mass evacuation at Dunkirk, and other points of embarkation still in Allied hands – organised and carried out by the Royal Navy and its co-opted fleet of small ships. Although hailed by some at the time as a great victory, the story of the British campaign in France has since been shot at by critical analysts from every quarter. The BEF was not after all, it is suggested, as unprepared as it suited some institutions, including the government and the media, to tell the British people at the time. In general, a hopeful public still believed all they were told. The Allies had been out-manoeuvred by a ruthless and entirely unscrupulous enemy who had never intended to fight by outdated rules of fair play, and whose forces were better equipped with the paraphernalia of modern war, who employed effective co-operation between air and ground units, and deployed mobile instead of static tactics on a hitherto unprecedented scale. In particular, the German armoured divisions had revolutionised modern warfare in one giant stride, their *Blitzkrieg* disposing for ever of long lines of entrenched combat and substituting instead Panzer mobility.

As the attack on France began, Germany was well on the way to completing the conquest of Norway, begun the previous month, despite a valiant defence by the Norwegian armed forces and the presence of British and French troops and the Royal Navy, Denmark had been 'absorbed' without resistance at the same time. With the defence of France at an end after the armistice signed on 22 June 1940 and the establishment of a compliant French regime under Marshal Pétain, the Germans held the western coastline of continental Europe from the North Cape of Norway to the Pyrenees, leaving Hitler free to consider the next move.

If Hitler's declared aims about German reunification meant anything – and of course we now know they did not – Great Britain was not on his target list at all. The British people were still plodding along at home, hardly aware that they were at war at all. Admittedly, there had been a few hit-and-run Luftwaffe attacks here and there, but nothing like the feared 'Blitz' which had already been witnessed in cities such as Warsaw and Rotterdam. The evacuation of children from vulnerable cities was a stop-start process, with many child evacuees hating life in the countryside and drifting back to parents still living in urban areas. Food rationing was gradually being introduced and luxuries like a bottle of whisky had become expensive and hard to find. Gas mask drill was introduced at schools and pillar-boxes painted in a dull, nondescript olive (using a formula designed to change colour if a gas attack took place) rather than the traditional red. Territorial soldiers were directed into the armed forces and industry started increasing production of materials of war. Many workers were exempted from the call to arms – protected by 'reserved occupation' status – such as farmers, coal miners, engineers and, surprisingly, in country areas, mobile retail salesmen and *hunt servants*.

It hardly seemed like total war. But after Hitler had made a well publicised if seemingly disapproving inspection of the Eiffel Tower in Paris, and been photographed on Cap Gris Nez looking meaningfully at the white cliffs of Dover, it seemed clear enough that he was changing the rules of engagement and that – German-speaking or not – Britain was next on his target list. Indeed, he was soon writing Directive No. 16 ordering his armed forces to prepare for just that campaign. Winston Churchill – now prime minister, having replaced Neville Chamberlain on 10 May – said to the House of Commons on 18 June 1940:

> I expect that the [land] Battle of Britain is about to begin. Upon this battle depends the survival of Christian civilisation. Upon it depends our own British life and the long continuity of our institutions and our Empire. The whole fury and might of the enemy must soon be turned upon us.
>
> Hitler knows that he will have to break us in this island or lose the war.

*

Invasion had long been a contingency considered in Secret Intelligence Service planning. Sir Stewart Menzies had already presented a worst-case possibility to the Chiefs of Staff, namely that Britain would be invaded and entirely taken by the German enemy. In such a case, he proposed that the only recourse was to develop a diplomatic and political strategy to victory – replacing the military option – by attempting to persuade a reluctant United States of America to declare war on Germany, and ride to rescue its English-speaking cousins. The SIS had also catered for a *partially* successful invasion by the creation within Section D, under Colonel Lawrence Grand's direction, of a unit with plans to operate behind the lines within the United Kingdom. This formation was to be the 'D' Home Defence Organisation, or 'D/Y'.

The daring part was its originality. Acting within their sabotage and spying remit and undoubtedly inspired by urgency, Grand's team had already drawn up blueprints for a stay-behind terrorism and intelligence-gathering unit within Great Britain but behind enemy lines. Where those lines might be was of course not clear. The originality of the scheme was that, although supervised by 'Regional Officers', both seconded Army and full-time professional SIS officers from Section D, the task in the field was to be undertaken exclusively by volunteer civilians. It had never before been attempted by British agencies and nothing like it had been *in situ* in WWII before German invasion in any of the occupied countries in Continental Europe.

In this way the rather loosely knit rules of warfare, and guerrilla warfare in particular, were disposed of in a single stroke. Broadly speaking, these rules ordained that in armed conflict combatants had certain rights.

Providing they fought one another in uniform and were properly enrolled in the armed forces (with a pay book or identification tags to prove it) they could give up the fight, when all else was lost, by laying down their arms and claiming internationally recognised prisoner of war status. This was enshrined mainly in various Hague Conventions on the laws and customs of war, and amendments drawn up through the League of Nations. The provisions were interpreted in different ways in different countries, and were legally far from precise, but the division between uniformed fighting men on one hand, and civilians in plain clothes was clear enough. Potential status as a POW was not available to civilians and if they engaged in acts of war they could promptly be executed.

D's decision to throw overboard this valuable life-saving convention was unprecedented for the British authorities in modern times. The proposition was revolutionary and set entirely new standards in the British conduct of all-out war. It can be argued that it was simply a logical response in a dreadful situation, following new rules set by Nazi Germany, and was the only possible course of action if Britain were to survive at all.

While the SIS was moving with the new times, there were still many influential British officers, as well as politicians, who uncompromisingly rejected the idea of 'dirty tricks' in any form. For much of the war, until the word 'total' was fully understood and the scope of Nazi atrocities more evident, there was much disagreement at high levels on such all-out techniques.

Therefore it was not just to bamboozle the enemy that Section D's plans were classified 'Most Secret' from the start; legal implications were involved as well. That same security classification (later amended to 'Top Secret') remains technically in place to this day, and affected all the men and women of the GHQ Auxiliary Units, whether or not they were War Office or Secret Service recruits.

*

With the full knowledge and approbation of the Secret Intelligence Service, Colonel Grand gave the go-ahead to activate the Section D blueprint for stay-behinds at the beginning of June 1940, some seven weeks after conception. The Home Defence Organisation would flourish and appear to die in its originally intended form in less than two months, but its significance cannot be overestimated.

Thirty regional officers were dispatched urgently around the United Kingdom. Although few of their names or their precise stop-off points have ever been released, it is safe to assume from later developments that they were not at the outset confined to vulnerable coastal areas of Great Britain. Indeed, so various were the possibilities for invasion – Scotland, or South Wales or East Anglia or the South-East according to the latest guesses, as well as the post-Dunkirk paranoia over an assault by parachutists – that they must have fanned out in every direction from London. Each officer's first task was to make contact with influential personalities. Regional commissioners, to whom they were technically attached, must often have been an officer's first call.

Regional commissioners were appointed by the Home Office as delegates, established in the provinces with virtual plenipotentiary powers, prepared in advance to take over formal civil administration and co-ordination with the military in the event of a breakdown of authority in central government. In other words, if the enemy took London, local control would automatically be delegated to those regional commissioners still clear of German occupation. They had fingers in local pies at every level – aristocratic, landowning, with universities, local authorities, police, the Church (of England it may safely be assumed), and armed forces' commanding officers. Professor Sir Will Spens was the Regional Commissioner for East Anglia and he was not at all pleased with the proposal to organise civilian stay-behinds on his territory. Indeed, shortly after being called upon by the regional officer, he complained about the stay-behind scheme, of which he passionately disapproved, both to the Commander-in-Chief Home Forces, Field Marshal Edmund Ironside, and again to Major Peter Wilkinson when he was in Cambridge on behalf of the GHQ Auxiliary Units.

Neither was left in doubt of Professor Spens's disapproval and well-justified fears that HDO partisan activity would provoke the enemy into taking hostages from the population for which he was responsible. Spens was not let into the full picture, it seems, because there were certainly outline plans for resistance on a larger and more significant scale than straight sabotage, as we will see. The officers confronted by Spens concluded that, like so many British citizens, he had yet to understand the full demands of total war.

In spite of such little local difficulties, regional officers nevertheless made rapid progress, first recruiting through old-boy networks the 'key men' for their intended operations. Researchers were initially confounded by 'key men' when their existence became known as associates of the Auxiliary Units, whose veterans had never heard of them. There was nothing on record to define a 'key man' and as far as is known no survivor has ever come forward. The puzzle is now complete enough to state with conviction that 'key men' (or women), were the focal point of each small cell of saboteurs set up by Section D throughout the country from June 1940. Some had undoubtedly been recruited well in advance. They were in direct contact with the regional officer.

Their role was secretly to find a small number of trustworthy and carefully vetted civilians in their own locality and co-ordinate them into a secret guerrilla group. The members were not to know one another; indeed, as cover for their secret activities, they were to appear to continue their lives entirely normally. The 'key man' had a store of explosives and weaponry hidden away and only he knew where it was. Time for training was short and it was useful if the 'key man' was familiar with the use of explosives himself – although it was not usually intended that he would risk divulging his identity by taking part in operations. It was also a help if another of the group was good with explosives, and so quarrymen or miners were favoured.

The task before 'key men' was to live as normally as possible within enemy-held territory and then to call upon individual members of the cell when specific tactical targets were identified and communicated to them by Army commanders. How this communication was to take place is unknown because at that time a short-range radio-telephony transceiver suitable for clandestine operations was not available; in certain cases it can be assumed that the regional officer himself would have attempted to cross the front line to convey the Army's instructions but it is obvious that there was a limit to the number of chances he could take to do so. He may have been able to arrange a likely runner to do the job for him. Whatever the method, it was never to be called upon during the short existence of the Home Defence Organisation and much of the planning bears the hallmarks of hurried improvisation.

It is on record that the regional officers' trawl for 'key men' included clergymen, gamekeepers, poachers, dentists, and road menders and – surprisingly enough – they were all induced to keep quiet about their enrolment by the secret service.

The strong point of the set-up was the rapid and seemingly effective distribution of dumps of explosives and incendiary devices for sabotage.

Confusingly, these were sometimes called 'Auxiliary Units'. One report claims that, by 22 July 1940, 200 'key men' had been provided with more than a thousand dumps. In the report, a free hand with facts is sometimes evident. Within its own inner circle, D was not a section to understate its successes and another report raised the secret dump total to several thousand. It was anyway a remarkable achievement. The 'key men', their cell members and the operations they were to carry out were disavowable. The SIS, Section D, the British government and the armed forces would deny all knowledge of them, if they were caught. The men and women behind the lines were out there on their own.

The Mark I 'Auxiliary Unit' was a cardboard container. These proved vulnerable to damp and had soon to be toughened as the Mark II. The materials distributed included standard War Department booby-trap mechanisms and timers, but were mainly the products of Section D's own experimental workshops built up to develop its original ideas. With the SIS predilection for deception never far from sight, their targets were known as 'the Obstruction' and the work itself 'Obstructing'. The means included bottles of sulphuric acid and enough petrol and paraffin to make 45,000 petrol bombs.

Supplies were also distributed as 'Small' or 'Large' watertight metal containers. The Small version was sized 9 x 6 x 4 inches. The contents variously included magnets for the application of high explosive to steel surfaces; plastic explosive (which had been developed by the SIS between the wars) and blasting gelignite; instantaneous, detonating and safety fuse; fulminate of mercury detonators; incendiary bombs – generally referred to as 'fire pots'; capsules for igniting petrol bombs; and paraffin incendiary flares. Some dumps are recorded as including a small rifle, a Colt revolver, and ammunition.

No fewer than 43,000 'Tyesules' were distributed too. Tyesule does not appear in the dictionary but it was the trade name of a tinned Shell Petroleum lighter-fuel product which, it is assumed, was adapted as an incendiary device – incendiarism usually being in the forefront of Section D's planning. The HDO also seems to have been included in contingency plans to burn crops – presumably within Great Britain after German occupation. At a more sinister level, the records declare the production of 'cigarettes and powder'. What these amounted to or how they were to be used is not stated, but between August 1939 and February 1940 Section D recorded the distribution of a total of 880 'units' – weight not specified – costing £50 including a 33.3 per cent overhead charge. It seems reasonable to conclude that their use would have provided a permanent solution to any German soldier's addiction to cigarette smoking.

Once the members of Section D were given full scope for initiative, they left James Bond stalled at the start line.

*

On 2 July 1940 a German High Command order stated that 'The Führer and Supreme Commander has decided that a landing in England is possible provided air superiority can be obtained and certain other necessary conditions fulfilled.' Two weeks later, on 16 July, the Führer's Directive No.16 outlined his instructions for the information of his senior Nazi confederates and armed forces planning staff:

> As England, in spite of the hopelessness of its military position, has so far shown itself unwilling to come to any compromise, I have decided to begin to prepare for, and if necessary to carry out, an invasion of England.
>
> This operation is dictated by the necessity of eliminating Great Britain as a base from which the war against Germany can be fought, and if necessary the island will be occupied.

Just two days earlier, on 14 July, the Home Defence Organisation in Britain was stood down – so what *was* going on? According to the closing report, the stand-down was taken calmly, although at first sight primacy appeared to have been conceded from the SIS to the War Office in the ongoing Whitehall/Broadway/Westminster power struggle. Section D as a whole went the same way soon afterwards.

However, for the two months since 23 May, transcripts of growing numbers – if far from all – of German coded messages were available at just the highest level from 'Ultra' decodes at Bletchley Park. Their dissemination was the responsibility of the Secret Intelligence Service. It is possible that clues were now available that Hitler's true intention was to attack Russia and that, for the time being, he was content to leave the conquest of Britain to the Luftwaffe – certain enough in the opinion of Hermann Göring – or even to seek a peace accommodation. Victory without invasion must have been an attractive alternative to a leader whose real preoccupation was living space in the East (*'Lebensraum'*) for his people and the destruction of the hated Bolshevik Soviet Union.

This is not an unreal proposition and if the SIS knew something of it from special insider sources it would of course have been content enough to stand down from pre-invasion plans within Britain and get ahead with the next stage of its agenda – something like persuading the United States to hurry along and help finish the job by force of arms. Moreover, the SIS and Section D knew that the bulk of D's resources were likely to go from the defensive to the offensive, forming as they would the substance of the emerging Special Operations Executive tasked by the War Cabinet with setting mainland Europe ablaze. This would certainly explain why D's closing report calmly accepted that all its work was apparently meekly to be handed over:

> Towards the end of July, however, we were informed by G.H.Q. that with the general improvement in the military situation, and the state of defence, the menace of enemy occupation of any part of the country had vastly decreased.
>
> If the enemy did, however, gain a foothold, the probability was that there would be no one left alive behind the enemy lines to take subversive action. It was, therefore, decided that so far as civilian obstruction was concerned, the organisation which Section 'D' officers had been forming, was no longer necessary and its place could now be taken by Auxiliary Units working openly and using as recruits uniformed L.D.V.s [Local Defence Volunteers, the initial name for the Home Guard].

A 'general improvement in the military situation' was not immediately discernible to those not in the know, many of whom were still busily filling sandbags and mixing cement for pillboxes. Indeed the Commander-in-Chief, Home Forces was replaced by General Alan Brooke on 19 July in order to speed up defence preparation with his new broom. Moreover, as late in 1940 as 7 September, the code-word 'Cromwell' was disseminated to formations in the south and east of England. This brought the troops to immediate readiness before the prospect of imminent invasion.

Clearly the SIS knew more than most and Colonel Grand was reconciled to the loss of his empire, on paper at least. Perhaps his consolation came with the termination of his secondment to the SIS, a return to regimental duties, and eventual promotion to the rank of major general? From a researcher's point of view, the stand-down report is the first clear and indisputable link between the SIS, Section D and the HDO on the one hand, and the GHQ Auxiliary Units on the other.

We are about to examine the full story of the GHQ Auxiliary Units, previously presumed to be the originators of plans and preparations for the conduct of behind-the-lines guerrilla activities within Great Britain. It is not possible to do so without knowing the background and role played by Section D and the Home Defence Organisation of the Secret Intelligence Service. If the analysis developed in this chapter is understood, it gives Section D a prior position as both the first in and first out of the field. It also gives some reason for the lasting 'Top Secret' security classification and deceptive drip-feed of information relating to the Auxunits – until recently, there has been little or none about the extent of SIS involvement through Section D and the HDO. However, as we shall see, it would be a mistake to assume that the Secret Intelligence Service had completely and compliantly opted out of home defence. And, it seems very probable too that some time bombs were left ticking for the Auxiliary Units to deal with later.

Chapter Five

Military Intelligence (Research)

'The Hidden Power Of Peace-Prone Britain'

Joan Bright Astley, The Inner Circle

As early as 1936, and with war now a real possibility, the Deputy Chief of the Imperial General Staff (DCIGS) directed the creation of a think-tank for the War Office – a research unit named General Staff (Research), code-designated GS(R). It was a half-hearted affair, rarely to be resourced at the same level as Section D of the SIS and specifically excluded, apparently on extraordinary and highly impractical political grounds, from examining any matter 'likely to refer to the dispatch of a British Expeditionary Force to Continental Europe'. In other words, full-scale war against Germany was not part of GS(R)'s terms of reference – and so, at first, the study of irregular warfare was automatically embargoed as well.

GS(R) was headed by a grade 1 staff officer and so could have wielded a certain amount of clout in the War Office but, being limited in scope, was very much a one-man band, at first operating with just the officer and his typist, producing recommendations for administrative improvements and only marginally relevant to the defence of Great Britain. Some indication that the role of GS(R) was about to change was announced on 9 March 1938 to the House of Commons, in imprecise terms, by the Secretary of State for War:

> When so much instruction is to be gained from present events the absence of any branch exclusively concerned with purely military research is noticeable, and a small section to study the practice and lessons of actual warfare will be established.

This was followed by the arrival in the winter of 1938 of Lieutenant-Colonel John Charles Francis Holland, DFC, RE, an officer with experience of the Balkans theatre of WWI, where he had served as an observer with the

Royal Flying Corps. He was both Mentioned in Dispatches and awarded the Distinguished Flying Cross for a daring, record-breaking raid on the Bulgarian capital, Sofia. After the Armistice he served with the Royal Engineers during the 'war' in Ireland and that experience, combined with later research into unorthodox military techniques and systems, gave him the credentials to lead a larger and more positively directed ideas team, working for the first time on all aspects of irregular warfare.

Holland's charter from the War Office was: 'Research into problems of tactics and organisation, under the direction of DCIGS. Liaison with other branches of the War Office and with Commands in order to collect new ideas on these subjects. Liaison with Technical Research branches.' The Deputy Chief of the Imperial General Staff himself noted:

> I have introduced a research section directly under me. This section must be small, almost anonymous, go where they like, talk to whom they like, but be kept from files, correspondence and telephone calls.

According to SOE records, the objects of the new section were then redefined as:

(a) To study guerrilla methods and produce a guerrilla 'Field Service Regulation', incorporating detailed tactical and technical instruction, applying to each of several countries.

(b) To evolve destructive devices for delaying and suitable for use by guerrillas, and capable of production and distribution on a wide enough scale to be effective.

(c) To evolve procedure and machinery for operating guerrilla activities, if it should be decided to do so subsequently.

MI(R) concluded that:

> Guerrilla warfare should, in favourable circumstances, cause such a diversion of enemy strength as eventually to present decisive opportunities to the main forces.

However, for the purpose of complying with this broad-based mandate and, it seems, with the compliance of the Directorate of Military Intelligence, Holland was soon liaising closely with Laurence Grand and Section D. GS(R) was formally identified from April 1939 as 'D/MI(R) usually with the abbreviated designation 'D/M'. The new and almost unlimited terms of working reference created the opportunity for co-ordinated load sharing between 'D' and 'Jo' Holland, even after the latter led MI(R) back to the halls of the War Office in September 1939. They needed one another – Holland to take advantage of the SIS pot-of-gold and the SIS freewheeling approach to the solution of problems, and Grand for access to the considerable resources of the War Office proper. Although the two chiefs were poles apart in personality, on balance the arrangement worked well – if not entirely without turbulence.

Holland and Grand were both exceptional individuals, although different in character. The distinguished author Joan Bright Astley – who, after recruitment by Section D, soon became Holland's secretary – described Holland in her book *The Inner Circle* as:

> . . . a chain smoker, his ashtray filled with flattened butts, a habit, he explained, from those days when cigarettes were scarce, sorties frequent, and the precious end waited to be re-lit on return to base. He drew heavily on his loves, holding in the smoke until the last wisp of nicotine had reached his boots, when it was expelled with full force as he seized on some point of discussion. He had an independent mind, an acute brain, a loving and poetic heart; he was quick, imaginative, and of a fiery temper.

To survive in D/MI(R), she discovered the importance of constant alertness to Holland's impulsive temperament and the advantage of nimble footwork. One day, as she interrupted his profound thought processes by entering without knocking, he hurled a book at her.

From March 1939 Holland's unit prospered both with funding and fresh thinking, backed by the unfailing enthusiasm of Laurence Grand, who never let a good idea pass if it could possibly be of advantage to the cause. Personnel were recruited and the 'think-tank' administered and housed by Section D with offices alongside it in Caxton Street, followed by expansion into St Ermin's Hotel. The HQ of the SIS at 54 Broadway was only a stone's throw away. The days of War Office stringency and conservatism were left behind. Holland soon enlisted three staff officers to cope with his expanding section – Commander Dymock Watson, Royal Navy; Major (later Major General) Millis Rowland Jefferis, another Royal Engineer; and Colonel (later Major General) Colin McVean Gubbins, DSO, MC, of the Royal Artillery. The wisdom of Holland's selection was soon firmly established with the evolution of new concepts, and their rapid conversion into tactical or strategic practicality.

*

In his classic 1968 book about the GHQ Auxiliary Units, the American author, David Lampe, concluded from the very limited – if otherwise well-informed – sources then available, that Section D 'produced a very strange and very ineffectual resistance organisation indeed', although conceding that Laurence Grand himself had much more to do at this time than he could possibly have been expected to cope with and subordinates who had been 'wished on him'.

Lampe, whose original source material was usually accurate enough, was not blessed with the corroborative evidence now available in the National Archives. On the one hand we find that Section D, while often derided by the professionals of MI(R) for impetuous and poorly structured schemes, and obsessive security, was on other occasions admired for the exceptional speed and quality of its achievements. The truth may lie somewhere between and the weak link in trying to determine the facts, as always with the SIS, is its obsession with deception. With Grand and Holland working literally side-by-side, this makes an intriguing challenge for researchers. However, D's claim to have 'initiated' the 'organisation and development of guerrilla warfare', although never previously so clearly defined, does appear to be reasonably justifiable.

It seems certain enough that, although Grand and Holland were both Royal Engineer officers, and got along well enough, they were incompatible in certain ways. Holland's officers regarded themselves as professionals while many of D's men were from an unrealistic outside world. Grand's fixation with secrecy was the subject of derision at times. It was, according to Joan Bright Astley, the mixture between 'true and false' which irritated Holland and made him dislike the set-up and its elaborate web of concealment. Section D did its best for the 'cuckoos in its nest' but, nevertheless, Holland and his team soon started plotting a return to the War Office. Perhaps the disparate and usually irreconcilable demands of attributable and non-attributable operations on the one hand and, on the other, the very practical differences for irregulars intended to fight behind the lines as civilians (for Section D) as opposed to those in uniform (for MI(R)), were too far apart from the outset. With the later creation of civilian armies abroad through

SOE, boundaries between the 'avowable' and 'disavowable' operations of the War Office and the SIS became blurred. This led to in-the-field overlap and, inevitably in turn, an ongoing feud at staff level, sometimes dampened down but never extinguished during WWII.

As soon as war broke out, Colonel Holland swept into action and within days D/MI(R) moved its filing cabinets and typewriters across Whitehall and into offices on the third floor of the War House. The section dropped the 'D' and became MI(R), structured within the Directorate of Military Intelligence under Major General F. G. Beaumont-Nesbitt. According to Joan Bright Astley, who was in the thick of all this, Beaumont-Nesbitt was: 'tall and polite, an erect, good-looking man, his crisp moustache brushed up. In his bearing he was a typical Guards officer, in his actions perspicacious and farseeing.'

From then, D and MI(R) sought similar objectives in their different ground-breaking ways. Although on paper they were now administered by separate Whitehall departments, they remained intertwined for the rest of their short, but massively important existences, with 'pots-of-gold' still available from the SIS when important MI(R) progress was restricted by lack of ready cash. Between them they were to engage, with energy and ingenuity, all the new challenges of irregular warfare on a scale never previously envisaged. In turn, their achievement would be acknowledged by American Special Forces who, later in the war, generously accepted that everything they knew came from the Brits!

*

Holland had been given secret instructions from the DCIGS to report on the 'possibility of providing British support for insurgency in any country of Eastern Europe overrun by the German Army'. As this was clearly in contravention of the government's current political directive, the work of MI(R) was immediately given the security classification 'Most Secret' to ensure that the product was kept not only from enemy agents but also from the Palace of Westminster. It set the standard for all the department's work until August 1940, by which time – after a slow start off the blocks – MI(R) was manoeuvred into a comprehensive tactical lead over Section D and the Home Defence Organisation by finding itself placed in an apparently superior role in plans for the defence of the United Kingdom. The status of MI(R) at this time may have been somewhat illusory, being partly the result of military urgency as the Nazis tore mainland Europe apart. Clearly it was time to look for short-term innovation and the employment of irregular tactics in a language the War Office could understand. It was here that MI(R) had a lot to offer.

Colonel Holland not only had the advantage of research and action papers already prepared by GS(R), he also had access to a list drawn up since the Munich crises of 1938 by the Directorate of Military Intelligence – and not at first, it seems probable, available to Section D. This list was compiled from a trawl of the commercial and professional world for executives, writers, explorers and linguists with specialised knowledge of foreign countries. General Beaumont-Nesbitt's intention was to select from the list the men he proposed to recruit into an Intelligence Corps – surprisingly not in existence between the wars – which he had determined would be critical to the coming conflict. This list proved invaluable as MI(R) moved rapidly into the field of unorthodox warfare, enabling him to take advantage of fresh thinking, uncluttered by the hidebound ideas of many senior officers, an inevitable product from twenty years of undemanding peace.

Colin Gubbins seems to have welcomed the opportunities opened to him as Holland's senior staff officer in this new unit. Among a plethora of ideas, Gubbins set to work on two major projects – the creation of instruction classes for new officers, and the compilation of three pamphlets on irregular warfare, based on both his own, and Holland's, collective experience and research. Technical input came from Millis Jefferis. The accent was on British-is-Best throughout. Selected civilians were absorbed and commissioned in the Officers' Emergency Reserve.

It was decided to hold irregular warfare classes at Cambridge for men selected by Gubbins – among them explorers, expatriate British businessmen and oil executives – and suitably qualified regular officers. It was during a visit to organise these that Peter Wilkinson was confronted with opposing ideas from Professor Spens, following approaches to Spens by a regional officer from Section D. Fortunately for MI(R), college authorities were more compliant than Sir Will. Following an interview by Major (later Field Marshal) Gerald Templer of the Military Intelligence Directorate and the Royal Irish Fusiliers, successful candidates were added to an expanding shortlist which in the end totalled more than a thousand officers. A further clutch of classes was held in Caxton Hall in London, now doubling as a training ground for secret service as well as the Registry of Births, Deaths and Marriages. Joan Bright Astley, who helped organise the meetings, chose the hall – in any case conveniently near her office – for the good security cover given to the 'small and highly secret groups of young men in plain clothes' by the constant comings and goings. In her book, she sums up the syllabus:

> . . . informed them about the organisation of the General Staff; the part played by the Intelligence branches within it; the probable strategic picture of the coming war; the tactical opportunities for guerrilla action and subversion; the use of clandestine wireless communications; and the co-ordination of local resistance and sabotage.

With War Office preparations for irregular war otherwise still at an early stage, it is clear that much of the syllabus must have been conducted by officers from the SIS. The set-up created an original introduction to new and secret irregular warfare.

It beat drilling on Horse Guards Parade or digging tank traps in East Anglia any old day.

*

Writing Field Service Regulations was one of the first tasks assigned to MI(R), and work which had already been started by Colin Gubbins for GS(R) was completed by him early in May 1939. The final product was three small brown-paper covered pamphlets, containing rice paper sheets of print stapled together.[†] With no title, or any other mark on the cover and the only writing inside the serial number of the strictly limited first issue, they were eventually translated into the language of every foreign country likely to work with the Western Allies in subversive operations behind the lines, or in enemy-held territory.

One was entitled *How to Use High Explosives*, written jointly by Gubbins and Jefferis. Much of the content – a classic introduction for the previously uninitiated – was nothing new to Royal Engineers, although the ingenuity with which the devices were intended to be used probably was. It is surely relevant that in the 'Technical Developments' sub-section of D's stand down report, the following, deliberately vague, claim is included: '200 copies of

† Originals of two of the three, thought to be the only copies in public hands, are with the Museum of the British Resistance Organisation at Parham in Suffolk.

the Brown Book of instructions on the use of explosives and other products have been supplied to the headquarters of the Auxiliary Units.'

As far as is known, no 'Brown Books' as such have been discovered, but it seems fair to assume that both these and *How to use High Explosives* were the work principally of Millis Jefferis, an acknowledged master of explosive substances and the development of booby-trap devices. Within the Auxiliary Units, other derivative books of instructions were to emerge in due course – camouflaged as out-of-date calendars or editions of the *Countryman's Diary*.

It has never been doubted that Gubbins was the main contributor to *The Art of Guerrilla Warfare* and *Partisan Leader*, which total sixty-two pages in all. The doctrine laid out was largely drawn from the British experience of the offensive with Lawrence of Arabia in the First World War, and on the defensive in Ireland, Palestine, the Indian North-West Frontier and Russia in 1918–19. In a short review in *The Secret History of SOE*, Professor Mackenzie states that they are hard to summarise and 'contain a compressed bible of general principles without much superfluous verbiage and without any illustration of specific cases'.

Without much verbiage' is a guaranteed Gubbins hallmark. The 'Nine Points of the Guerrilla's Creed' could be taken as a charter for the Auxiliary Units from their inception in June 1940:

(a) Surprise first and foremost, by finding out the enemy's plans and concealing your own intentions and movements.

(b) Never undertake an operation unless certain of success owing to careful planning and good information. Break off the action when it becomes too risky to continue.

(c) Ensure that a secure line of retreat is always available.

(d) Choose areas and localities for action where your mobility will be superior to that of the enemy, owing to better knowledge of the country, lighter equipment, etc.

(e) Confine all movements as much as possible to the hours of darkness.

(f) Never engage in a pitched battle unless in overwhelming strength and thus sure of success.

(g) Avoid being pinned down in a battle by the enemy's superior forces or armament. Break off the action before such a situation can develop.

(h) Retain the initiative at all costs by redoubling activities when the enemy commences counter-measures.

(i) When the time for action comes, act with the greatest boldness and audacity. *The partisan's motto is 'Valiant yet vigilant.'*

Without significant modification, these solid guidelines for subversive action underpinned the techniques developed, at first, for the GHQ Auxiliary Units, and then – during the rest of WWII – the underground forces marshalled to the Allied cause in the fight-back against Axis invasion.

*

The officers of MI(R) were sent into the field, if not into immediate action, as soon as war was declared in September 1939. In some cases, they followed pathways abroad similar to those already trodden by D Section's regional officers. Although it was originally intended that any action with which MI(R) was connected would technically be avowable by the British government, this policy was not to last for long. And so, in their quest for useful contacts they, too, could take advantage of existing British embassy facilities throughout Europe, notably military attachés. Contacts sought were men or women in target countries – neutral or not – with official or unofficial influence, who were reliably anti-German and could be called on to assist in the development of useful dirty tricks, and then work towards co-ordinated subversion if their respective countries became occupied. With only theoretical experience, MI(R) officers had to make convincing cases for this semi-official co-ordination with the British authorities – who were not always looked upon as the 'good guys' anyway.

Later events were to show that – working in a hurry or not – the officers generally made a pretty good job of it, although embryo, non-attributable plans (with, it seems probable, the co-operation of Section D) to sabotage those Romanian oilfields critical to the Nazi war effort, were betrayed. An MI(R) team waiting secretly to do the very dirty deed had to slip hurriedly from the country at the very last minute, after dumping cases of smuggled explosives into a lake.

MI(R) missions usually arose out of particular crises or for particular projects that did not fit neatly into the sphere of responsibility of any other War Office branch. The first quasi-official call on MI(R) resources came just *before* the outbreak of war, and was answered by Colin Gubbins who, following two recent trips to open contact with the Polish secret service, was appointed to the staff of British Military Mission No. 4 and set out for Poland with a posse of MI(R) personnel a week before Hitler attacked.

The next opportunity came in Finland, which was attacked in overwhelming numbers by the Soviet Union on 29 November 1939. With this attack, similarly vulnerable East European countries had to start deciding which side in the big-power manoeuvres represented their best interests, and which to join for their own security if they had to. With the Finnish government generally sympathetic to the Germans, British intervention, with broadly anti-Bolshevik motivation, had to be secret and diplomatically invisible, as the long-term intention of the Soviets was, at the time, both ambiguous and unpredictable. Certainly, they could not at that time be counted upon as potential allies. MI(R) also raised and trained a batch of British 'volunteers' for Finland – a fence-sitting, half-hearted cover for a non-attributable, quasi-military operation.

This was an opportunity for MI(R). A team of officers with ski experience, under the Arctic explorer Captain Andrew Croft of the Essex Regiment, an early recruit to the section, was dispatched as 'advisers'. The minuscule Finnish Army held out bravely until overwhelmed. This fierce, short war ended with the Finns conceding territory by treaty on 12 March 1940, and was narrowly preceded by the prompt re-location of Croft's team to Norway. By now, Britain realised that this country was also under threat and Germany duly invaded on 9 April 1940. Just days before this, using semi-diplomatic cover as assistant consuls and again headed by Andrew Croft, a number of MI(R) officers were posted to Norway, as an advanced reconnaissance team. They and others from MI(R) had significant roles in the otherwise disastrous campaign by British forces to assist the Norwegian defenders.

Colin Gubbins led five hurriedly-formed Independent Companies to Norway – themselves an innovation by Holland and MI(R) – accompanied by Captain Michael Calvert, Royal Engineers, and joined by Captain Croft. These Independent Companies were among the few Army units to acquit themselves with some distinction and, soon after their return to the UK, were re-graded to form the first British Commandos. Another MI(R) officer, Captain Peter Fleming, of the Grenadier Guards – already famous as an explorer and writer – was dispatched by Sunderland flying boat on a separate and highly risky mission to the northern port of Namsos, to establish whether the Germans were there first. Fortunately, they were not, and Fleming and two sergeant signallers with radio sets, were able to give the all-clear to British forces poised outside with the Royal Navy.

MI(R) was not specifically involved in the defence of France but by mid-summer 1940 it had been put to the test and was ready to take the inventive blueprints created on the drawing-board back at base on to the next rung of the ever-developing ladder of irregular warfare. These plans embraced entirely new concepts of warfare, most of which, although irregular at the time, have now become routine as acceptable, conventional methods of waging war. They included:

(a) The creation and development of commando forces.

(b) Involvement in the establishment of escape routes on the Continent for PoWs and survivors of aircraft shot down in enemy-held territory. This led to another section of the secret service, known as MI(9).

(c) Networks of clandestine communication with PoW camps, to collect intelligence on the deployment of enemy forces.

(d) Participation in the creation, training and supply of under-ground armies in enemy-held territories – to be called, from August 1940, Special Operations Executive.

(e) A full study of the means by which the enemy could be deceived about the size, scope and timing of any future military operation, and the selection of operational code-names for future use.

(f) And finally, selecting, equipping, training and providing with camouflaged hideouts, the men of Winston Churchill's secret army of civilian stay-behinds – the GHQ Auxiliary Units of WWII.

The task started almost immediately after the Dunkirk evacuation from France.

Chapter Six

'A Blaze of Wild Priorities'[†]

'Let us therefore brace ourselves to our duties, and so bear ourselves that if the British Empire and its Commonwealth last for a thousand years, men will still say "This was their finest hour!"'

Winston Churchill to the House of Commons, 18 June 1940

On 17 June 1940, just one day before the above inspired speech, a number of propositions requiring urgent top-level political decisions were placed before the Prime Minister and his inner War Cabinet. Following the collapse of France, and with Britain's defences in an inadequate and incomplete state, the nation's survival could well depend on the outcome.

The Cabinet had before it a paper presented by the Chiefs of Staff, written by 'Jo' Holland and MI(R), and passed upward with the approbation of the Commander-in-Chief, Home Forces, General Edmund Ironside. The paper proposed a radical and unprecedented addition: the selection, recruitment, training and equipping of *civilians* to come directly under General Headquarters with an operational role, but without a military presence or command structure in the field.

The job proposed for these civilians was to stay behind the front line after German invasion, and emerge at night from secret, camouflaged hideouts fully equipped with arms and explosives. Their mission was to create havoc and destruction among enemy supplies and communications. While never an integral part of the recently formed Local Defence Volunteers (LDV) – soon to be renamed and restructured on military lines as the Home Guard (HG) – suitable recruits could nevertheless be found in its ranks. Men with WWI service, and experience of arms and explosives, were seen as ideal material and so were men such as gamekeepers and poachers, who knew their locality well, were familiar with shotguns and adept at clandestine night work. To join this 'scallywagging' as some officers are on record as calling it – a minor police record was not necessarily a disadvantage.

† Nigel Oxenden's phrase, from his *Auxiliary Units – History and Achievement, 1940–44.*

The proposition had been placed before the highest elected authority in the land because the contents were arguably illegal under the international law on conflict – confusing and vulnerable to subjective interpretation as it was – and certainly against the recognised conventions of war between civilised nations. Guerrilla warfare was not of course unknown elsewhere and, indeed, much of the blueprint for action was based on the study of irregular forces throughout the twentieth century. In Britain's democracy a decision to fight 'dirty' and flout internationally accepted standards, could not be made by a military authority. Only a political decision would suffice. Members of Parliament, however, were never consulted. Neither was every member of the government itself.

After deliberation, the scheme to create what were to become known as the GHQ Auxiliary Units was agreed, with the caveat that the Prime Minister was to be kept regularly and fully briefed on progress. 'These men are to have revolvers' was his personal minute appended to Cabinet papers at a time when firearms were in seriously short supply and in high demand from the armed forces proper.

Also in the middle of June the War Cabinet approved the 'first use' of poison gas on British beaches as soon as the enemy landed, again in contravention of international agreements, and in July initiated the development of a civilian army on the Continent, to be organised by a new Special Operations Executive – another idea involving 'Jo' Holland. The whole package was classified 'Most Secret' from the outset and – although it was to prove impracticable to keep the *name* of the Auxiliary Units at such an elevated level – the *operations* they were intended to perform remained highly classified for the duration.

Immediately after this secret Cabinet approval, the authority to go ahead was moved back though the Chiefs of Staff, to the Commander-in-Chief, who appointed Lieutenant-Colonel Gubbins of MI(R) to command the Auxiliary Units. General Ironside would have had no doubts that he had selected the best-qualified man for such a daunting assignment.

*

Colin Gubbins's military credentials were impeccable. A Celt, the son of a consular official in the Foreign Service, he was educated at Cheltenham and trained for the artillery at Woolwich. As a young gunner in WWI he was awarded the Military Cross. In 1919 he was selected by Ironside to join his military mission to Archangel, as staff officer, in support of the doomed White Russians in their last-ditch fight against the Red Army. It was in this fluid campaign, with ill-defined front lines, that he first witnessed the effectiveness of irregular operations. Gubbins was shortly in at the deep end again with a posting to Ireland, where he served with the British Army from December 1919 to September 1922, that is throughout both the Irish War of Independence, and the subsequent Civil War. These formative years enabled him to study every aspect of the irregular warfare waged by Republican volunteers, which forced the British into brutal retaliatory measures, largely carried out by the notorious Black and Tans and the Auxiliaries, specially recruited from among former British soldiers left otherwise unemployed since the end of WWI. The burning and looting carried out with official eye-closure brought down worldwide condemnation upon the Lloyd George coalition government and, according to some historians, finally forced both sides to the conference table. It was certainly in these entirely 'irregular' conflicts that both Holland and Gubbins came, perhaps independently – although their periods of service in Ireland overlapped, it is not recorded that they worked together – to the conclusion that a dedicated, well-disciplined group of irregulars, properly led, could engage disproportionately large numbers of conventional forces.

Gubbins described his time in Ireland, as '. . . being shot at from behind hedges by men in trilbys and mackintoshes and not allowed to shoot back!'

No assessment of the development of irregular warfare is therefore complete without some knowledge of Michael Collins, the leading protagonist in the battle against British rule, and the effectiveness of his Irish Republican Army in the early 1920s. Collins was Irish by birth, a passionate Sinn Féin politician, and a ruthless practitioner of the republican cause. On record as a man of irresistible charm for those who fell for it, he could also be overbearing and truculent to those who did not. He joined the Irish Republican Brotherhood, the precursor of the IRA, while working as a clerk in London. But in 1915, fearing he would be conscripted into the British Army and, learning the ground rules of treachery, he told his employers he was volunteering for the Western Front. After receiving a gratuity for his loyalty, he hurried back to Ireland where he took a minor part in the 1916 Dublin rebellion, being interned by the British authorities as a result. Released in 1917, he was soon charged again, this time with making a seditious speech. After jumping bail, Michael Collins was now a wanted man.

Following the declaration of an Irish Republic in 1919 – prematurely anticipating British acknowledgement of the horrendous Irish casualties incurred on the Western Front in WWI – Collins started and largely directed the IRA campaign against British forces. He was adjutant-general, director of organisation, and director of intelligence; and also minister of finance to the Dáil Éireann, the Irish Republican 'government' which, with a loan of £375,000 – much of it raised by Collins's army from unwilling Unionists as the price of safety – had established its own ministries and courts of justice. He cycled every day from the ministry of finance office to his intelligence HQ, and continued to dine in public. Sitting with a revolver on his desk, he was adept in avoiding capture. He was on the 'wanted' list all this time. As combined head of IRA intelligence and operations, and being his own paymaster too, he organised an extensive network of spies, armed volunteers, and assassins – known as 'The Squad', equipped with 'trusty Parabellum automatics'.

To allow all this to go on, the Royal Irish Constabulary (RIC) and the British command at Dublin Castle must have had a great deal to learn about the ruthless tactics of irregular war – not least that Collins had his own informers everywhere, including officials in the Castle itself. Collins's spies passed details of RIC and British troop movements, and the barracks where they were billeted. Using devious tactics, the irregulars then ambushed soldiers and policemen alike, and set their buildings on fire. They even managed to incinerate the offices of the Inland Revenue in Dublin. They assassinated traitors to the republican cause and took and murdered hostages to further political objectives. The British reacted, often to their own international disadvantage, with counter-barbarity.

All this was a fertile indoctrination for Gubbins and Holland. They must have been impressed that Collins lived in freedom long enough to become a principal negotiator in drawing up the subsequent treaty, when Britain conceded home rule and dominion status to the Irish. However, separation of the six northern counties proved to be one step too far for republican dissenters with even more extreme objectives. Collins was ambushed and murdered by them in 1922.

The campaign was undoubtedly fundamental to the development of Gubbins's strategic and tactical thinking while planning later techniques of irregular warfare in WWII, and setting standards for many of the Allies' guerrilla operations. In turn, it should be acknowledged that these British officers owed much of their considerable expertise to lessons learnt from Michael Collins, the master Irish tactician,

Armed with this experience, and equipped with detailed MI(R) studies of other irregular conflicts, Gubbins was nearly ready for war. After working with him in these bustling, formative days, Joan Bright Astley recorded in *The Inner Circle*:

> . . . quiet-mannered, quiet-spoken, energetic, efficient and charming. A 'still-waters-running-deep' sort of man, he had just enough of the buccaneer in him to make lesser men underrate his gifts of leadership, courage and integrity. He was a man-at-arms, a campaigner, the fires banked up inside him as glowing as those round which his Celtic ancestors had gathered. He was dark and short, his fingers square, his clothes immaculate and in peacetime he wore a carnation in his button hole.

During the months before the official declaration of war in September 1939, Gubbins made secret trips for MI(R) to friendly Baltic countries, as well as Czechoslovakia and Poland. His task was to contact intelligence services and open opportunities for future co-operation if those countries – and by then it seemed more and more probable that they would be – were attacked and overwhelmed. Gubbins's diplomacy and integrity in developing these contacts were eventually to prove fruitful as, one after another, they fell either to Germany or Soviet Russia – sometimes to each in turn.

More immediately, however, they led to Gubbins's first wartime assignment – as chief of staff to Military Mission No. 4, headed by General Adrian Carton de Wiart, VC, whom he described meeting when they fought together in the 1917 campaign on the Western Front: 'He was already a legendary figure with his Victoria Cross, his black eye patch, his stump of an arm and his formidable bearing.' Carton de Wiart headed this mission under flimsy cover, described variously as 'Liaison' or 'Agricultural'. In fact it was largely an MI(R) effort to develop clandestine contact with the Poles, and Gubbins was a principal figure among the score or so of officers involved. Their work was hampered from the start by the rapid collapse of Polish defences and they finally had to beat a perilous retreat across the border and into Romania.

There is, however, strong circumstantial evidence from abroad, notably the United States, that Gubbins brought off an outstanding coup, possibly almost single-handed, in securing from the Polish intelligence service details of the ways and means they had already developed to break Nazi war codes transmitted by the infamous Enigma machine, which the enemy mistakenly believed throughout the war to be unbreakable. And that, again with Polish assistance, Gubbins was physically instrumental in taking a working Enigma machine, modified from its original commercial status into a vastly more complex encoding type, through Romania and, initially, on to France. As France fell, these secrets were hurriedly evacuated to the Government Code and Cypher School (GCCS), recently established at Bletchley Park. Although the various reports of this coup – significant enough to affect the whole course of WWII in the Allies' favour – are convincing enough even for the greatest sceptic, corroboration from British authorities is limited, with the possibility that much of the story was edited from later reports or biographies on Gubbins. It does seem sure enough, however, that during this adventure, he was trapped in German-held territory for up to a month after the final capitulation and, together with Polish 'friends', was lucky to escape at all.

He had no serious respite, even during the Phoney War, for he was promptly put in command of newly-formed 'Independent Companies' when Norway was invaded by Germany on 9 April 1940. These Independent Companies, another innovation sponsored by Holland and MI(R), comprised specially trained and well-armed Territorial Army volunteers. Intended to be mobile and largely self-supporting, they were sent to Norway tasked to take advantage of the unique, fjord-probed coastline, to travel up and down in commandeered fishing vessels known as 'puffers', harassing the enemy as waterborne marauders.

Much of the campaign was a disaster for the British forces. Thanks to a staff decision, about 1,000 men of the Independent Companies were debarred from their intended mobile role, but fought skilful delaying actions. Gubbins achieved a certain notoriety by following a written instruction from General Claude Auchinleck, the local C-in-C, to 'remove any officer of any rank who you think is not resolute, willing to fight or not fit to command, and replace him at your discretion'. On 23 May, following some uncertainty over seniority, Gubbins relieved Lieutenant-Colonel T. B. Trappes-Lomax of command of 2 Company, 1st Battalion Scots Guards. From then, some say, he was a condemned man with the Brigade of Guards. Whatever the long-term effect on his turbulent military career, the immediate outcome after a successful evacuation in the first days of June, was top-level confirmation of the development of Independent Companies into the Commandos. The C-in-C gave the following verdict about him:

> The swiftness and efficiency with which the evacuation was carried out reflects great credit on Brigadier [his acting rank] Gubbins and his Staff. Gubbins has, I think, been first-class. Should be a divisional commander or whatever the equivalent may be in the New Army.

Gubbins was awarded a DSO. The citation explained:

> Lieutenant-Colonel Gubbins displayed sterling qualities of leadership in the handling of his troops operating in a strange and difficult type of country. On several occasions he personally led troops which were fighting a rearguard action in contact with the enemy. His courageous example of devotion to duty, though greatly overworked, was an inspiration to his men and their safe withdrawal was due to his inspiring leadership.

He arrived safely back in Scotland on 10 June 1940. After a few nights' sleep and now a substantive colonel, a revitalised Colin Gubbins was ready to tackle another command, the brand new Auxiliary Units.

*

The first of many priorities was to appoint senior staff and establish an Auxunit headquarters. The HQ problem more or less solved itself with the provision of quarters in QMG House, a temporary overspill for the War Office and GHQ, in Whitehall Place, Westminster. The rooms were cramped and, apart from having no nameplate on the door, far from anonymous. However they had to be tolerated until the Luftwaffe stepped in and blitzed the building in the autumn of 1940. Gubbins then dispatched one of his senior aides, Major the Honourable Michael T. Henderson, younger brother of Lord Faringdon, to scout the country for a more suitable, long-let alternative for the Auxiliary Units. The preferred location would be somewhere in central England, with good travel links but as clear as possible of vulnerable invasion areas and further targeting by the Luftwaffe, and have adequate training space and accommodation, both for staff and Auxiliers under instruction.

Deploying the right connections and exploiting short cuts provided by his own old-boy network – hallmarks of those urgent, early days – Henderson soon discovered that Coleshill, the country estate adjacent to that of his brother, was qualified in all respects. The owner, the Earl of Radnor, was away at another of his homes, it seemed, leaving the forty or so rooms inhabited only by the earl's two Pleydell-Bouverie sisters and their dogs. By commandeering the house, situated in Oxfordshire adjacent to the county boundary with Wiltshire, and with a rail link at Swindon, the problem of a new HQ was promptly dealt with – to the great satisfaction, no doubt, of the Radnor estates' manager who, with such an elderly, expensive house and grounds to run with a war on, must have been hard put to balance the accounts. The benefit that war brought more than equalled the sacrifice made by the earl's sisters who, after a comfortable life far away from even the Phoney War, were now assailed by the crash of army boots, shouted orders and explosions through much of each twenty-four hours. Their dogs must have found it worse than Guy Fawkes' night.

For senior staff officers, Gubbins chose Major (later Brigadier) Geoffrey H. R. ('Bill') Beyts MC, a career officer from the famous Rajputana Rifles, Indian Army, as head of operations and training, and Major (later Sir) Peter Wilkinson, of MI(R) and the Royal Fusiliers, responsible for administration and liaison. Both set off in the fast track to keep pace with Gubbins. The immediate work load was enormous.

With only outline, generalised instructions and innovating as he went along, Beyts was sent into the field, as Gubbins and Wilkinson – while setting up an efficient administration – worked out how to create an instant army of civilians from almost nothing. They had to raise funds, find weaponry and explosives (all in desperately short supply), write a training programme, establish rapport with Army commanders, equip their HQ, and soothe the feelings of anyone whose feathers may have been ruffled by the energetic Beyts, who was out there searching for the right men and right places, and desperately trying to wind up the unwilling to an awareness of urgency. At an early stage it was agreed, and then hardly changed throughout the life of the Auxiliary Units that, as a strategic rule, operational patrols (as they were to be called) would be placed mainly in rural spots within twenty or so miles of coastlines vulnerable to invasion, rather than inland; and that, in general, towns would be avoided. Hit-and-run sabotage attacks as they envisaged (Wilkinson later described then as 'flea-pricks') were, it was believed, less likely to succeed in built-up areas. Indeed that was where the Army proper might expect to be fighting. It was impracticable to have Auxunit patrols in places too remote to get to in a hurry when the balloon

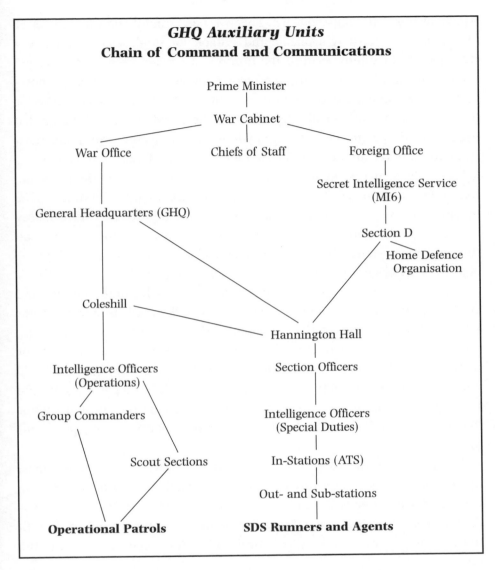

GHQ Auxiliary Units
Chain of Command and Communications

Prime Minister

War Cabinet

War Office — Chiefs of Staff — Foreign Office

General Headquarters (GHQ)

Secret Intelligence Service (MI6)

Section D

Home Defence Organisation

Coleshill — Hannington Hall

Intelligence Officers (Operations)

Section Officers

Group Commanders

Intelligence Officers (Special Duties)

Scout Sections

In-Stations (ATS)

Out- and Sub-stations

Operational Patrols   **SDS Runners and Agents**

went up, or too far from areas likely to be selected by the enemy as their headquarters, their tank laagers, aircraft dispersal sites, ammunition and petrol dumps, and communication centres.

Working with the best available intelligence which, by today's standards would be looked upon as little better than imaginative guesswork, the first counties to be dealt with, as the most likely to be invaded, were Kent and Sussex, and then those of East Anglia. So indifferent was the intelligence assessment that a significant body of expert opinion persisted in putting East

Anglia as top of the hot-spots' list. This was based mainly on the number of ideal beaches ostensibly available and suitable for small boat landings, but this failed to take into account the hazards of the long sea voyages to get there. With the enemy having to employ converted – rather than purpose-built – vessels and the concomitant certainty of debilitating sea sickness for the troops, their vulnerability to attack by the Royal Navy, and the limited number of deepwater ports for unloading vital stores and munitions, East Anglia was never an ideal target area for invasion. Moreover, in spite of its acknowledged success in supporting German ground troops, the Luftwaffe had so far failed to achieve air superiority over mainland Britain, and slow moving convoys of unhappy German soldiers would have been at the mercy of the Royal Air Force. The German command was only too aware of all this, and preferred the shortest sea route possible, commensurate with prime objectives. Kriegsmarine captains were even more sceptical.

With Beyts working away from home for much of his time, Gubbins and Wilkinson were no less fully occupied and at full stretch to find the right men for the next phase of the developing Auxiliary Units' operation. Using their own old-boy networks, and the pre-hostilities War Office shortlist of names, they set about recruiting suitable officers to follow Beyts into the field and take over responsibility for creating the actual fighting patrols, selecting their leaders, finding stores and equipment, overseeing the construction of 'hidey-holes'– and all this without an instruction manual or any precedent to follow.

It was at about this stage, that Gubbins absorbed a little gem, a prototype upon which to model his future force. It was called the XII Corps Observation Unit, and was already commanded by one of his own MI(R) officers – Captain Peter Fleming of the Grenadier Guards. This turned out to be both the very first operational Auxiliary Unit and a vital stepping-stone into the future.

Chapter Seven

First into the Field

'. . . those were serious, burdened, rushing days, and the holes in the dyke called for all the fingers in our hands.'

Joan Bright Astley in The Inner Circle

On 25 May 1940 Colonel Holland took 'the opportunity to shake off the fluff of the Secret Service'. With a remit to train LDVs to fight behind the lines, Captains Peter Fleming and Michael Calvert were temporarily detached from MI(R) to XII Corps.

XII Corps, under its GOC, Major General Andrew 'Bulgy' Thorne of the Grenadier Guards, had responsibility for the defence of Kent and Sussex, the counties nearest to France and therefore critically vulnerable to attack. With only one fully trained division, and an almost complete absence of modern fortifications, XII Corps was on a hiding to nothing once Hitler decided to invade – as General Thorne must have explained to Winston Churchill at Chequers, the official country residence of the Prime Minister, where they had a private lunch towards the end of June.

The stop-line drawn by General Ironside along the North Kent Downs and around London depended more upon the exploitation of natural and man-made features – such as high ground, broad natural waterways, canals, railway embankments and cuttings – than prepared defensive positions. Forced to acknowledge the likelihood that his flimsy crust of beach defences would soon to be overwhelmed by a Wehrmacht assault, Thorne planned an organised withdrawal northwards and then, turning to face south from the Downs' stop-line, a counter-attack to drive the German army – now with lines extended, and limited armour and supplies – back to the sea.

It was an imaginative scheme and, with his limited resources, probably offered the 'least-worst' option – on paper at least. The problem was lack of troops, armour and artillery to do the job. Elderly cannon were being positioned around the white cliffs of Dover and on sites such as the Napoleonic Wars' redoubt at Dymchurch – specially protected from enemy

The main elements of General Sir Edmund Ironside's defence plan,
June 1940. (*Mick Wilks*)

fury by a small detachment of troops under the command of Lieutenant Richard Todd – well before he ever thought of becoming a celebrated actor. Although Royal Engineers and civil contractors were furiously at work building pillboxes and tank traps, and with his soldiers hurriedly being retrained in the light of recent battle experience, General Thorne knew he would need an extra ingredient if his plan was to have any positive effect against an implacable enemy, already on a 'high'.

Thorne therefore created the deliberately nondescript XII Corps Observation Unit. It has been suggested that the idea came from his pre-war post as military attaché in Germany where, during a visit in 'Eastern States' he was told that – being without a proper army, the 'Princes' had created stay-behind parties to make life as difficult as possible for any invader. Having no access to specialists for such a task, for there were none in the British Army, Thorne formed a small detachment, a score or so of his own NCOs and other ranks, intended to work within enemy-held territory from concealed hidey-holes, mainly in the Weald of Kent. They were to emerge with stealth to delay a German retreat after the British counter-attack. Then, with the advantage both of height and concealed prepared positions and with the enemy vulnerable and unable either to move forward to Canterbury or back to the sea, expose them to the mercy of the artillery and such hull-down tanks as could be mustered. The other ranks of the Observation Unit depended upon the two officers from MI(R) to prepare them for a mode of war never previously employed by the British Army and for which they had no instruction manuals. General Thorne's plan rested on these two officers; fortunately Colonel Holland could hardly have chosen more wisely.

Peter Fleming had enjoyed a privileged life. He was a grandson of the financier Robert Fleming, elder son of Valentine – who was killed in action on the Western Front in WWI – and Evelyn Fleming, and brother of the more sporty Ian who, after a WWII career in Naval Intelligence, shot to celebrity status as the creator of James Bond. Sometimes a sickly child, Peter was academically gifted. Educated at Durnford School, Swanage; Eton – where he developed a skilful capacity for appeasing bigger bully boys; and Christ Church College, Oxford, he absorbed material quickly and without apparent effort. He was soon recognised as both an outstanding writer and actor.

After an unhappy time apprenticed to a stockbroker in New York, he came back to the United Kingdom and was appointed deputy literary editor of *The Spectator* magazine. He also travelled widely, writing best-sellers along the way. In spite of resistance from a class-conscious mother – who considered that, coming from a middle-class family, she was not a good prospect – he married the famous West End stage and film star, Celia Johnson. It seems that, with the exception of a developing aversion to the German enemy, and an addiction to the slaughter of thousands of game birds during the shooting season, Peter Fleming was without a single destructive thought either for man or beast.

Fleming had a useful aptitude for making lifelong friends with older, influential men – among them were Generals Carton de Wiart and Wavell, and the editor of *The Times*, for which he worked as a travelling correspondent and editorial writer. In the autumn of 1938 he returned to England to work at Printing House Square but was 'uncomfortable' with *The Times* – which was still supporting appeasement – a policy, according to Duff Hart Davis, Peter's biographer, that 'strikes posterity as barely credible'.

Well before the declaration of war, Fleming was in touch with MI2, part of the Directorate of Military Intelligence. After an interview with General Beaumont-Nesbitt, Fleming noted that 'MI are going to give chaps like me a preliminary canter soon.' In May 1939 he joined the Grenadier Guards Officers' Reserve. In June and July he trained with the regiment and immediately went to work for MI2. In any event he was now, with the initial rank of captain, more or less ready for secret war.

Before war broke out, at first still also working long hours at *The Times*, he was absorbed into MI2 and, shortly after the third week in September, into MI(R) proper. Joan Bright Astley tells just how selection from the shortlist worked:

> I was sent over to the War Office to make a preliminary sorting and then to pick out those whose qualifications seemed most suited to training in irregular warfare. Those selected – men like Peter Fleming, Geoffrey Household, Peter Wilkinson, Tommy Davies, Malcolm Munthe, Douglas Dodds-Parker – we sent invitations for interview in the War Office. Major Gerald Templer of the Military Intelligence Directorate did the interviewing. I made notes and soon we had a core.

*

Captain Michael 'Mad Mike' Calvert was on the MI(R) core list too. Born in India in 1913, he was educated in England and – after joining the Royal Engineers – at the Royal Military Academy and Cambridge University, where he obtained an honours degree in Mechanical Science. Calvert became one of the legendary figures of WWII, winning two DSOs, the American Silver Star, both the French and Belgian Croix de Guerre, and as CO of the Special Air Service Brigade achieving the rank of brigadier. Calvert was also credited with having killed more Japanese than any other Allied soldier.

It was in the Norwegian campaign of April 1940 that Calvert and Fleming first went into action with MI(R). The German invasion started on 9 April, shortly *before* Britain planned to make pre-emptive moves in the same direction and shortly *after* Neville Chamberlain had misleadingly claimed that Hitler 'had missed the bus'. Amidst scenes of utmost confusion in London, the government unwisely despatched a seriously ill-equipped and under-trained expeditionary force to Norway. Colin Gubbins and the Independent Companies, and Mike Calvert went in with it.

Under the command of General Carton de Wiart, the force earmarked to land at Namsos from a Royal Navy convoy of ships was dangerously hove-to outside the approach fjord without adequate charts or pilots, and no idea whether the port itself was already in enemy hands. In the absence of any useful intelligence or shore contact, and in order to resolve the logjam, Fleming had little difficulty in obtaining command of a reconnaissance party.

He explained later in a radio broadcast that, before they flew out from the RAF seaplane base at Sullom Voe in Shetland in a Sunderland flying boat on 14th April 1940: '. . . someone very obligingly stayed up after hours [in the Bank of England] packing a small fortune in Norwegian currency into a suitcase, rather as if they were cutting sandwiches for a picnic.' The Sunderland crossed the North Sea at low altitude. On the last lap, Captain Fleming proposed a gung-ho diversion to bomb any enemy troops they could find. This was firmly vetoed after a signalled reprimand from the cruiser HMS *Glasgow*: 'Essential observe complete secrecy.' Having found the right fjord, they roared 'between the steep, white jagged hills that ran down to the dark green water', passed Namsos, a little huddle of coloured wooden houses, and landed in another arm of the fjord. A dinghy came out to meet them 'sculled with such frenzy that it looked like an epileptic water-beetle'.

When Fleming stepped ashore at Namsos, he was the first British soldier to land in Norway. The two RAF signallers in his reconnaissance party notified the waiting task force that Namsos was clear of Germans and, during the short night, three destroyers slid into the harbour and disembarked the first wave of the expeditionary force. The Germans had been deceived but the secret British presence was detected by a Luftwaffe reconnaissance aircraft, after which the enemy bombed and completely destroyed the small township. The expedition became increasingly futile and Carton de Wiart, hanging grimly on, sent Fleming back to London with a personal report for Military Intelligence. The *Daily Sketch* had already reported him killed in action.

Immediate plans were laid to extract de Wiart's soldiers with maximum damage limitation – meaning at once! Captain Fleming was ordered back to Namsos with new orders, and remained on the general's staff until the Royal Navy successfully evacuated the expedition early in May.

The strange presence of two airmen/NCO signallers that Fleming had with him contributes to the mystique surrounding his true secret service allegiance. While to all intents and purposes working directly for Colonel Holland and MI(R), he carried with him a degree of influence well above that of the usual serving captain. It is also a fact that the Secret Intelligence Service was continually on watch over its own interests and, to do so, may well have 'planted' its own personnel.

If MI6 had any speciality at all it was in the field of radio communications. It is confirmed that RAF signallers were with Fleming at least until the autumn of 1940, during his time in the south-east of England with XII Corps Observation Unit, and also that this was a unique embellishment to his resources, not seen anywhere else in the Auxiliary Units at any time. It is hard to take at face value Fleming and his signallers' claim that they had no idea of the station destination for their transmissions but it would be no surprise if the critical Namsos signals were sent through Station X of the SIS, the principal W/T centre for worldwide MI6 communications 'somewhere in Buckinghamshire' and then re-routed to General Carton de Wiart at sea off Namsos. If so, Fleming's primary allegiance could always have been to the Secret Intelligence Service. In his biography it is reported that 'their [the RAF operators'] role was not clear to anybody else'. He did later work on strategic deception in the Far East under Colonel J. H. 'Johnny' Bevan, head of the very special and secret London Controlling Section, in liaison with the SIS.

When Fleming was next seen back in the MI(R) office in London, Joan Bright Astley noted:

. . . he walked in as imperturbably as he had walked out of MI(R) for Namsos that evening many months ago. It was always good to see his square face with its wide smile and to straighten out one's own fevers and uncertainties against his calm acceptance of events and tolerance of human frailty. He was a four-square, basic, solitary sort of person, immune to luxury, to heat or to cold, with a rocklike quality which made him the most staunch of friends and a kindness which made him the least vindictive of enemies. He was in his way a famous figure, not only because of his early and romantic success as explorer and writer, and his marriage to one of our best actresses, Celia Johnson, but also because he kept his own brand of personality intact and dignified, dealt with all men as equals, and used his pen honestly and well, based on logic and spiced with satire.

After winter warfare training, temporary Captain Michael Calvert had also been picked for Norway and sailed as adjutant, Royal Engineers, with a convoy scheduled to land troops at Andalsnes, the southern jaw of a planned pincer attack on the strategic port of Trondheim – the northern half being the expedition at Namsos. It was soon apparent that this plan was futile too and, with winter weather still prevailing and after some initial, tentative advances inland, Calvert and his RE NCO, were placed with solo motorcycle transport between the lines to cover an organised retreat back to the port of Andalsnes and home. Setting charges in defiles and under bridges, with makeshift material, called for eyeball-to-eyeball confrontation with a steadily advancing enemy, and last minute match-ignition of fuses while the sergeant, with the engine on his single-cylinder Royal Enfield already in gear and at high revolutions, crouched poised for Grand Prix lift off as the enemy appeared round the corner.

After ten days or so in action behind British lines, out of petrol and only narrowly in advance of the Germans, they coasted downhill to find the port with not a single British soldier or ship in sight. To their eternal relief, an RN destroyer soon hove into view with vague orders to rescue some relation of Norway's King Haakon – if he was there – and the captain, after just a few moments to ensure there was not a royal in sight and to glance at Calvert's identity papers, swung ship and headed for Scotland at full speed ahead.

Calvert was soon appointed explosives' instructor at the newly established Special Training Centre (STC) – sometimes recorded as the Irregular Warfare

Training Centre (IWTC) – for Commandos at 'The Big House', Inverailort in north-west Scotland. It is said that he first acquired the nickname 'Mad Mike' there, because of his confident, casual expertise with explosives. After six weeks – taking him to mid-June 1940 – in the stimulating company of Lord Lovat, who was later acknowledged as an outstanding Commando leader, and David and Bill Stirling who went on to great things with the SAS – he was annoyed to be dragged to the War Office, away from his friends, and report to one of 'the lesser known sections' of the Military Intelligence Directorate as part of the 'core' of MI(R) no doubt. He recorded with relief that, 'Evidently this was something special.'

After his briefing, he met Peter Fleming, up from Kent for the occasion, under whose command he was to work. First they had to reconcile their counter-productive rank differential. Fleming, a full captain but an inexperienced part-time soldier from the Reserve, had technical seniority over Calvert, a regular with temporary captain's 'pips' who was only a substantive lieutenant. As soon as the irregular nature of the task before him was explained and the job-descriptions outlined, they headed for Bilting in Kent – where Fleming had established his HQ – to develop the XII Corps Observation Unit for General Thorne.

*

In mid-May 1940, Peter Fleming had set energetically to work with a score or so of newly irregular troops. Calvert followed less than a month later. While Fleming mustered, quartered and trained the squad, later divided into the East and West Kent Observation Units, Calvert prepared and placed mines under piers and port facilities, as well as on bridges and in culverts on roads leading north from the coast – vital conduits for an enemy; and tested innovative explosive devices. With the mines in position, the men of the Observation Unit would emerge from underground hides and detonate the charges, and then disappear again. In theory the German invading army would thus be unable to advance or retreat; the British could then counter-attack from land, sea and air and set about their annihilation.

An Observation Unit headquarters was established in a typical half-timbered house in its own grounds and with suitable training areas, just off the A28 trunk road from Ashford to Canterbury, 'The Garth' at Bilting. The older part had the upper floor removed and was known to Calvert as 'the Barn'. It was soon stacked to the ceiling with explosives in crates, and whatever weaponry Fleming could muster. This was not an inconsiderable amount and, as the office and dining areas were in the Barn too, a certain understanding was necessary among the personnel. The only lighting was candlepower and this flammable correlation with crates of explosives sometimes led to firmly articulated protests from uninitiated visitors. Cigarette smoking was discouraged.

A dozen or so steel crossbows were included in the armoury; Fleming had witnessed crossbow accuracy and the efficacy of their silent killing power during pre-war travels to remote places, and now he considered the possibility of attacking petrol dumps with flaming arrows. Perhaps these were the very devices developed by Section D and referred to in Colonel Grand's stand-down summary of achievements?

History has credited Fleming with an all-encompassing, secret service mystique, not far short of James Bond himself. It is a fact, however, that he was both inexperienced in warfare and had come to Kent with the briefest 'brief' imaginable. He was free therefore to innovate and improvise from the start, with no precedent to follow slavishly and, it seems, little or no supervision from above. Although he was later to describe his own efforts and their likely effect as futile, he and Mike Calvert did make extraordinary progress in establishing their own version of a small stay-behind army from nothing.

So widespread was the scope of their inventiveness that they soon needed reinforcements and they secretly enlisted civilian volunteers – possibly LDVs – for the first time. According to David Lampe in *The Last Ditch*, weapons and explosives were dumped throughout Kent and Sussex on an almost random basis, with little attention to long-term security or control, and little or no time for screening. Can there be any doubt that these dumps were the work of Section D's regional officer? It is no surprise, consequently, that opinions vary on the potential of the Observation Unit, its soldiers, and civilian 'pressed' men. In his 1964 book *Fighting Mad*, Mike Calvert described the civilians they recruited as:

> Mostly farmers or farm workers, solid chaps who were not likely to lose their heads under the sort of pressures that occupation brings. But there were other people as well, quite ordinary types in normal, everyday jobs. People who were entrusted with our secrets. There were even one or two country parsons among them! . . . None of them knew who the others were.

If this was the beginning of Britain's resistance army, they were not told the rest of the 'Calvert theory', which he explained during a post-war radio broadcast. His own perception was that the men of Kent were unprepared for war, were more concerned with the harvest than fighting the enemy, were not willing to blow up precious historic bridges, and that, although landowners were sometimes prepared to send their sons to the front to die, they were not willing to give up an inch of their land for the war effort. He suggested that subversion by civilian saboteurs would have been needed so that the incensed Germans would have been provoked into acts of retaliation, hostage-taking and executions. Only then, he believed, would Kent rise *en masse* against the invader. The greater cause would therefore be served by the sacrifice of individuals. This proposition is not, as far as can be determined, on record elsewhere. but the current attitude among some civilians may have been typified in *The Englishman's Home*, a poem by Howard Graham:

> I was playing golf the day,
> The Germans landed.
> All our troops had run away,
> All our ships were stranded.
> And the thought of England's shame
> Very nearly spoilt my game!

One of Peter Fleming's many useful assets was a family contact between the Flemings and Lovats in Scotland, which he exploited to secure a number of Lovat Scouts, headed by Lord Lovat's younger brother Robin, to improve the quality of the OU training programme. In his book *Harvest of Messerschmitts: The Chronicle of a Village at War*, Dennis Wright included an eyewitness report from Mary Smith of Elham, a village north of Folkestone in Kent:

> Lord Lovat . . . was up to his tricks at Elham during 1940. He arrived wearing a major's uniform with a tam-o-shanter and, after inspecting the Home Guard, was closeted for a long time with Major Kingsley Dykes, to whom he presumably outlined his plans for the formation of special squads. These units, in the event of a German invasion, would stay behind on Romney Marsh or in the hills, hiding during daytime and creating havoc behind enemy lines at night. For these special suicide squads, he was looking for men who had special qualities and knew the ground like the backs of their hands.

After this visit, a number of Home Guards were not seen again with the local platoon. Nobody asked questions but 'the little underground bunkers with camouflaged steel lids still exist . . .'

So Lovat himself was on the spot too, in 1940, it seems. His men, inter-war Territorial soldiers, all normally working on his estate as ghillies, foresters, shepherds or gamekeepers, were experts in stalking, field-craft, camouflage, night work, and all-in fighting. Calvert also suggested that, as provocation, they were prepared to shoot German soldiers in the back 'and that sort of thing' but, again, this is not corroborated elsewhere. What is certain is that both Fleming and his successor, Norman Field, were to find the men of the Lovat Scouts of inestimable value.

Peter Fleming and Mike Calvert left the Observation Unit in November 1940, by which time it had been detached from XII Corps and placed directly under GHQ command within the Auxiliary Units – although still asserting an independent identity by continuing the local use of the OU name as cover. Several sources record (possibly apocryphally) that, before they moved on, the two founder officers brought off a significant coup when Andrew Thorne was replaced as CO of XII Corps by General Bernard Montgomery. During one exercise, they successfully penetrated his HQ building at night, placed a small explosive charge *on* his sleeping duty officer, and hid time-fused thunderflashes in decorative flower tubs on the terrace. These duly went off as planned the next morning while the general was explaining to them just how effective his HQ security was. According to Calvert, the general – after an outburst – took it well. However, his claim that 'Monty' then invited them to have a drink with him sounds imaginative! The fate of his duty officer is not recorded but it seems less than likely that he was Mentioned in Dispatches.

In a small but perhaps significant way, early confidence in the coastal defence of Britain might have depended upon the effectiveness of the XII Corps Observation Unit. As an invasion never happened, this remained untested; and General Thorne, already sixty years of age, was soon marginalised. He was later labelled the 'Forgotten General'. And although the soldiers of his Observation Unit were certainly the first stay-behinds in the field, it was only by the very shortest of heads.

Chapter Eight

Second Place

'Now it has come to us to stand alone in the breach and face the worst that the tyrant's might and enmity can do. To carry ourselves humbly before God, but conscious we are ready to defend our native land against the invasion by which it is threatened. We are fighting by ourselves alone, but we are not fighting for ourselves alone!'

Winston Churchill in the House of Commons, 14 July 1940

Although perhaps not blessed with birth under quite the same privileged sign of the silver spoon as Peter Fleming, Andrew Croft was a remarkable achiever. With the exception of Colin Gubbins's adventures in Poland as war with Germany broke out, Captain Noel Andrew Cotton Croft, formally a 34-year-old officer of the Essex Regiment Reserve, was the first of the core MI(R) officers put into the sharp end of irregular warfare. He remained there for the duration. On the way he achieved colonel's rank. Fleming and Croft have rightly been recorded as two of Gubbins's more colourful officers.

In *The Last Ditch* David Lampe described Croft's background and pre-war chronicle of achievements as:

> . . . the Head Boy at Stowe, an Oxford MA, holder of the Polar Medal after taking part in the 1933 British Trans-Greenland expedition, aide-de-camp to the Maharajah of Cooch Behar, leader of an Oxford University Arctic Expedition, secretary to the Director of the Fitzwilliam Museum in Cambridge, and a traveller to Lapland with a team of ethnologists. Croft could fly a plane, was an expert skier, and could make himself understood in ten languages.

With this background, and after attending one of Gubbins's indoctrination courses earlier in the year, Croft was put in charge of a small, diplomatically invisible group of MI(R) officers sent as advisers to the Finns after they were attacked by the Soviet Union at the end of November 1939.

Croft's team smuggled substantial quantities of munitions into Finland, in preparation for the arrival of British 'volunteers' and a provisionally planned, more official expeditionary force. Both adventures were aborted when Finland and Russia signed an armistice on 12 March 1940.

Croft's relocation was last minute and he next surfaced as one of a number of MI(R) officers on a quasi-official reconnaissance mission to Norway only days before the German invasion. He actually witnessed the start of the invasion from his hotel window. A second timely relocation, this time from enemy-held territory, seems to have followed for, early in May, he was Gubbins's intelligence officer with his Independent Companies in the Battle of Norway.

Croft sailed to Mosjöen, arriving on the night of 5 May. At the end of the month, during the last-minute evacuation from Bodö, he was left behind to destroy petrol dumps, vital supplies for an approaching enemy. His third timely withdrawal, after the rest of his force had left, was an escape by fishing boat to Narvik, a trip of more than 100 miles, where the Allies still had a foothold in some strength. His final departure from this theatre of war was from there.

If it were at all significant to determine the first British officer to set foot in Norway, Andrew Croft would probably have a lead on points over Peter Fleming, for much of his munitions' smuggling to the Finns originated from within Norway. It all depends on the start date selected. Fleming may just, however, have led by a nose into the Auxiliary Units, although this was a photo finish too. Suffolk Auxilier Herman Kindred, the best independent eyewitness available, placed Croft's arrival as some time before August 1940, while Croft himself recorded that he first went to East Anglia in mid-June. Before Suffolk, he had already set up the embryo Auxunits in Essex; but he cannot have preceded Fleming's mid-May arrival to command the XII Corps Observation Unit in Kent.

Croft's allocated task in East Anglia was to select, interview and get security clearance for the leaders of the scores of Auxiliary Unit patrols that he envisaged; then to assist in the selection of six-man teams of civilian guerrillas and start training at an elementary level; and finally to supply all the weapons and explosives he could lay his hands on and hide these in temporary Operational Bases (OBs). Initially these were simply hidden dumps such as his own – in his father's coach shed in the garden at Kelvedon in Essex. As his father was the local vicar, his son may have counted both upon the blessing of the Almighty himself and cover for these very unorthodox plans from the very highest possible authority.

The first extemporised hides were simple structures such as old shepherds' huts on wheels dumped, unobtrusively, in the depths of woods. New recruits were next encouraged to dig more secure hides for themselves. The do-it-yourself product was usually a rectangular hole in a wood, just deep enough to roof over with railway lines, sleepers or timbers, lined with corrugated iron sheets and covered with a layer of earth. Materials available locally were used, rather than official War Office issue. The powers-that-be had grander problems to think about in 1940. Usually with just one access tunnel, the whole thing was likely to be damp and certainly inadequately ventilated – then soon abandoned as entirely unsuitable for even short-term habitation. As Croft left East Anglia, replacement bases were being rapidly installed from a standard working drawing. Surviving members of each patrol may therefore quite genuinely recall three, perhaps even four sites for their stay-behind hideouts because in many cases this first standard version had to be abandoned too, after inadvertent discovery by small boys bunking off from school, or courting couples, or poachers ferreting for rabbits.

The task of logging all OB sites with accuracy proved such a problem that the War Office never bothered to try; later surveys, locally and by the Defence of Britain project, have all produced imperfect – sometimes controversial – results. In time, this led to a certain degree of bewilderment for researchers – who found themselves directed around from one collapsed earthwork to another by veterans, farmers, or one-time small boys, all confidently offering useless guidance in the best of good faith. Rather like patrol members of the Auxiliary Units, only a few OBs are still around.

Although Croft must have set himself some targets and favoured particular locations, the selection of both men and sites for the bases was often dictated by elements of opportunism. With time pressing and no local shortlist to work from, he had to depend upon recommendation and his own instincts. He needed enough men to do the job and not too many to endanger security or overwhelm his limited training and supply facilities.

Before he left the Auxiliary Units in the autumn of 1940, Croft had established a network of patrols which was to form the basis of the southern East Anglian stay-behind irregular army until stand-down in 1944. From the limited records available – mainly a nominal roll (the existence of which was firmly denied by the Ministry of Defence until it finally released it to the

Public Record Office in 1996/7) – Essex finished up with over 200 men in 31 patrols, grouped at Colchester, Bures (overlapping Suffolk), Kelvedon, Witham, Danbury, Dengie and Southend. The Suffolk area was split, the northern half being linked with Norfolk. However, Croft's area probably included the patrols grouped at Ipswich, Woodbridge, Framlingham and Metfield. The unofficial looking nominal rolls, sometimes typed, sometimes handwritten, lacked uniformity and appear usually to have been compiled during 1942/3 to individual Intelligence Officers' specifications. It is unlikely that the whole network could have been completed in Croft's few months in East Anglia, but the groundwork of the Essex and South Suffolk Auxiliary Units can definitely be attributed almost completely to his efforts.

And, while he was at work, the pattern was being replicated around all the vulnerable coastlines of Britain. By the autumn of 1940, a force including somewhere in the region of 3,500 'civvies', many recruited directly from the Local Defence Volunteers and the Home Guard, had grown from these small nuclei with unbelievable rapidity. Women had been absorbed, too. All were volunteers for a suicide mission – but how well did they understand all the risks likely to be involved?

Croft next went to war in some style. Lampe's record shows that he served with (although not necessarily in) 'airborne forces, the Special Air Service, the Long Range Desert Group, the Commandos and Special Operations Executive'. With SOE he commanded a small-boat unit working a clandestine ferry service for agents between the island of Corsica and mainland Italy and the south coast of France. It is safe to say that he became a master of irregular warfare. Croft was awarded both the DSO and an OBE.

Before he died, 'National Registration No. TXAN/51/5, Sergeant Herman W. Kindred' (as the nominal roll shows) of the Stratford St Andrew Patrol near Saxmundham, remembered Croft as a stickler for security, emphasising that the lives of stay-behinds depended upon secrecy. Croft himself wrote later that, although nearly everywhere he served he met 'Coleshill trained men' (that is Auxiliers), they never mentioned their service in the Auxiliary Units. And neither did he!

*

One of Gubbins's final achievements for the Auxiliary Units was to create GHQ Auxiliary Units Scout Sections, using regular Army personnel. Their primary task was to train civilian saboteurs. Gubbins was probably aiming to re-create mini versions of his Independent Companies. Although he was not directly involved in the creation of XII Corps OU, it was also something of a model for the Scout Sections which, as well as being equipped to train their amateur comrades, were similarly provided with Operational Bases in which to stay behind themselves. By creating AU Scout Sections – comprising suitably trained regular 'irregulars', Gubbins established a vital nucleus of experienced personnel many of whom were later dispersed into line units and special forces such as the SAS in time for D-Day.

The origin of XII Corps OU itself, while probably benefiting from the tacit blessing of Winston Churchill was, it seems, little more than an expedient by General Thorne – hurriedly activated by Captains Fleming and Calvert. A professional soldier, Captain Norman Field (later Lieutenant-Colonel, OBE) took command of XII Corps Observation Unit in Kent from November 1940.

Field, a Royal Fusilier, was wounded in May 1940 with the BEF at La Panne, near Dunkirk – the worst hours of his life were 'on that beach waiting for evacuation, under constant gunfire and bombardment from the air, and without adequate weaponry to retaliate'. While convalescing, he was visited by a fellow Fusilier, Peter Wilkinson, then a major and GSO2 (General Staff Officer Grade 2) to Colonel Gubbins. With no real idea where Wilkinson was serving but sensing that it was to do with something 'hush-hush' and might give him a chance to get into action against the enemy, Field suggested that Wilkinson might bear him in mind for something suitable as soon as he was fit again. Although he got no positive response or sign of encouragement from his enigmatic colleague, he was soon directed – even before being passed fit for service – for interview with Gubbins at the Auxiliary Units' HQ. Wilkinson and Field had no further contact with one another until well after the end of the war.

After an interview alone with Gubbins in the vast servants' hall at Coleshill, Field agreed to join as soon as he was fit. Gubbins said 'Leave that to me!' and Field soon found himself before a medical board and passed fit for duty 'within the United Kingdom'. As it seems unlikely that Field was on the MI(R) core list, his personal connections and active-service experience must have identified him as an ideal replacement to take over the Observation Unit and remodel it on more orthodox lines. And so, although the Auxunits were never to expect any War Office trophies for administration, this maverick OU now needed an injection of at least a

A historic photograph of the Staff and Intelligence Officers taken on the steps at Coleshill House in January 1942. Colonel C. R. Major, then the CO, stands in the centre of the front row with Major Geoffrey ('Billy') Beyts on his right. Between them Junior Commander Barbara Culleton (the 'Battling Bantam') can be seen in the second row. Her Senior Commander, Beatrice Temple, is the only other lady present (front row). Major Maurice Petherick stands between her and the CO. *(Eric Gray)*

In this photograph, Captain Stuart Edmundson stands at the left of the second row; his colleague and family friend, Captain Ian Fenwick – later killed in action with the SAS behind the lines in France – stands tall in the centre – of the top row. *(Miss E. M. Wilmott)*

Mabel Stranks 'vetted' Auxiliers on their way to Coleshill at this former post office in nearby Highworth. *(Ann Warwicker)*

Coleshill House was the Headquarters of the GHQ Auxiliary Units from 1940 until stand-down in 1944. *(BRO Museum collection)*

General Sir Edmund Ironside, C-in-C Home Forces, appointed Colonel (later Major General) Colin Gubbins as the first Commander of the GHQ Auxiliary Units. *(BRO Museum collection)*

Colonel (later Major General) John F. C. ('Jo') Holland headed the secret pre-war 'think tank' – MIR – which developed a blueprint for the Operational Patrols of the GHQ Auxiliary Units. *(BRO Museum collection)*

Colonel (later Major General) Laurence Grand was put in charge of Section D of the Secret Intelligence Service before the outbreak of WWII. In July 1940, following the dissolution of Section D, a number of officers from the Home Defence Organisation were posted into the Special Duties Section of the Auxiliary Units. *(BRO Museum collection)*

ABOVE: Under the overall command of Colonel Millis Jefferis, Colonel Stuart Macrae was responsible for many 'dirty tricks' developed in 'Winston Churchill's Toyshop'. *(BRO Museum collection)*

ABOVE RIGHT: Colonel Frank Douglas, the final Commanding Officer of the Auxiliary Units, had undoubted secret service connections. *(BRO Museum collection)*

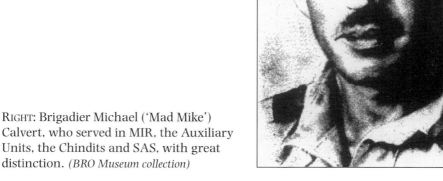

RIGHT: Brigadier Michael ('Mad Mike') Calvert, who served in MIR, the Auxiliary Units, the Chindits and SAS, with great distinction. *(BRO Museum collection)*

RIGHT: Peter Fleming. After active service in Norway with MIR, Captain (later Colonel) Peter Fleming, Grenadier Guards, was appointed to command General Andrew Thorne's XII Corps Observation Unit in Kent. He remained on secret service in the Middle and Far Eastern campaigns for the rest of the war. *(BRO Museum collection)*

BELOW RIGHT: The late Joshua W. S. ('Stuart') Edmundson, TD, formally opening the Museum of the British Resistance Organisation at Parham, Suffolk, in 1997. *(Author's collection)*

BELOW: Captain (later Lieutenant Colonel) Norman Field as a young officer in the Royal Fusiliers. He was wounded in action at Dunkirk, before becoming the Intelligence Officer of XII Corps Observation Unit in Kent, effectively the first 'stay-behinds' of the Auxiliary Units. *(Lt Colonel Field)*

Colonel Noel A. C. ('Andrew') Croft, DSO, OBE. After his return from Finland, where he had been an adviser to the defence forces, and Norway with Colonel Gubbins's Independent Companies, Captain Croft's next assignment for MIR was to set up the Auxiliary Units in Essex and south Suffolk. From the autumn of 1940 he was in SOE, notably running a small-boat unit trafficking between Corsica and the enemy-occupied mainland of France and Italy. *(Julia Korner, née Croft)*

Captain J. W. S. ('Stuart') Edmundson, RE, (seated centre) and, on his right, Lt John Dingley, DCLI, with their staff, responsible for creating Auxiliary Units Operational Patrols in Devon and Cornwall.
(Lt Colonel J. W. S. Edmundson)

This model Auxunits truck was made from issued materials – such as palliasses and trip wire spools – by Devon Auxiliers for the second birthday on 2 September 1941 of Will Edmundson, their Intelligence Officer's son. *(Dr Will Edmundson – photo: Ann Warwicker)*

Brigadier Geoffrey ('Billy') Beyts, in charge of training at Coleshill, who developed courses there on close quarters combat and irregular warfare. *(C. Jack Grice)*

A post-war image of Nigel Oxenden, with one of his stable of racing motorcycles and sports cars. *(Joy Oxenden/BRO Museum collection)*

Major Nigel Oxenden's memorial stone, erected in Jersey with subscriptions from his Norfolk Auxiliers. *(Joy Oxenden)*

Group Commander Lieutenant T. H. Denny, with his Leiston, Suffolk, Operational Patrol, after the issue of rifles. Note the random distribution of serge battledress and an uncertain discipline with forage caps. *(BRO Museum collection)*

South Essex Group Commanders – Rayleigh, Hockley and Rochford patrols. (left to right) 2nd Lt R. Baptie, Captain C. G Ford, Lt W. G. Heath. *(Donald Handscombe)*

Unique photographs of the Sandford, Somerset, patrol under training. Obviously well led, the Auxiliers were formally dressed; well equipped with weaponry; carrying Army gas mask cases; and practising left-handed shooting. However, the officer giving training in the underground cave is wearing polished leather gaiters, more suitable for the parade square than irregular warfare. *(By kind permission of Nora Trego)*

A Scout Section was stationed at the Mill House in Cransford, Suffolk. Personnel were volunteers from the Suffolk Regiment. The secrecy under which they operated led to the local belief that they were not only 'special' but also superhuman. The myth still persists. *(Geoff Bowery)*

XII Corps Observation Unit was absorbed into the Auxiliary Units as a Scout Section in the summer of 1940. This is a rare picture taken under their third commander, Captain G. R. MacNicoll, London Scottish, (seated centre) wearing a beret, usually in those days a sign of either rank or membership of a 'special force'. Field Service caps for ORs were still an issue, and peaked caps usually a private purchase. In the middle row, the rakish G.S. cap is evident – unsuitable in many respects but cheaper to produce. The last two Lovat Scouts, inherited from the early days of Captain Peter Fleming's command, can be identified in the front row, wearing Glengarries. *(Lt Colonel Field)*

The Cransford Scout Section on a hardening-up cycle cross-country during the bitter winter of 1940/41. This picture was taken in defiance of strict rules of secrecy. *(Geoff Bowery)*

Identified only as 'Bottles' Worby, this regular soldier of the Suffolk Regiment, was a stalwart of the Scout Section posted to Cransford village. *(BRO Museum collection)*

Perranporth Auxilier Trevor Miners, pictured here outside the entrance to his Operational Base, once underground and now exposed by erosion. *(Andrew Miners)*

The Museum of the British Resistance Organisation in Suffolk has a full-scale replica constructed after surveys of a number of local Operational Bases. *(Ann Warwicker)*

The escape tunnel in the replica at Parham leads to a well-concealed emergency exit. *(Ann Warwicker)*

The escape tunnel from the OB at Holton, Suffolk, is still intact. *(BRO Museum collection)*

Interior of an OB at Staplefield, Sussex, and the entrance to the culvert pipe escape tunnel, a type often found in that area. *(Stewart Angell)*

Erosion has exposed the escape tunnel and ventilation pipe at this Operational Base in Yorkshire. *(BRO Museum collection)*

Veterans return to their underground – and sometimes underwater – Operational Base on Romney Marsh, Kent. *(Edward Carpenter)*

semblance of orthodoxy – without losing an iota of its spirit of adventurous innovation and irregularity.

After just a couple of days' briefing at Coleshill, Field was posted to replace Peter Fleming – now on his way to Cairo, Greece (from where he later made a lucky escape), and all points east, with MI(R). Field gradually established some formal control of these essentially informal stay-behind soldiers and their civilian volunteers who, by then, had all been absorbed into the Auxiliary Units. He first arrived at 'The Garth' with Colonel 'Bill' Major who, although taking command of Auxunits, had no previous experience of irregular warfare and needed to see what it was all about. Although the two officers were in time for lunch, the meal was delayed until an injured Luftwaffe pilot, recently shot down, could be removed by ambulance to Canterbury Hospital from his supine position on the dining table, which now replaced the explosives' packing case previously in use. The hand-over took place all too hurriedly but Field did learn something of the ropes when he attended Fleming lectures to assembled Auxiliers during a weekend enlivened by periodic explosions in the massive fire place at 'The Garth' and outside the open windows 'whence he had tossed live fuses with detonators and, perhaps, timers'.

Left behind in the mess was a copy of Peter Fleming's latest book – a short novel, written during a week on the sick list in March – called *Flying Visit* in which, with great prescience, he mooted the idea of an arrival by parachute – somewhere in Britain – of the Nazi Führer Adolf Hitler himself, on an appeasing mission of peace. Within months of this book's publication, The Deputy Führer, Rudolf Hess, did just that in real life. It is no surprise that people found something surreal about Peter Fleming. His inscription in *Flying Visit* was: 'To the Officers' Mess, XII Corps Observation Unit. What Officers! What a Mess! P. Fleming Scripsit.'

Captain Field inherited a miscellany of soldiers. Several officers, apparently Fleming's friends and accomplices, simply disappeared during the four- or five-day handover. The Lovat Scouts' platoon had already departed, leaving just two NCOs, Sergeant MacDonald and Corporal Mackenzie. They proved invaluable. No one knew who paid them. Among the miscellany was a Royal Engineer corporal, and one RAF cipher clerk and his radio operator, inherited from Fleming. Word was that they had been placed with the Observation Unit by Lawrence Irving (said to be the grandson of the famous actor), an RAF ADC to General Thorne. The responsibilities of the RAF men were never made clear to Field, who was nominally their CO, but they appeared during field exercises, strung their aerials between trees, and transmitted twice daily in enciphered Morse to an unspecified destination. It now seems likely that their paymaster was the SIS.

Field also had a clerk who produced an official-looking XII Corps Observation Unit office stamp which Fleming seems to have had made at a local stationer's shop. There was a war on and, of course, the imperative was to get things done in a hurry and with a minimum of red tape. The stamp was a useful asset with which Field produced 'official' passes for Auxiliers, to enable them to check through Home Guard and Army road blocks and, for a few selected wives, to help them escape the area after invasion. Within restricted areas it may also have helped them do the shopping.

With the arrival of Captain G. R. MacNicoll of the London Scottish, Field split the OU into East Kent – with soldiers raised from the Buffs depot at Canterbury and stationed at 'The Garth'; and West Kent – with a subaltern and men from the Royal West Kent Regiment based at a gamekeeper's cottage at Angley Wood, near Cranbrook. Their plan of action in the event of invasion was to lie low by day, leaving a couple of scouts to see what was going on. Their intended targets by night were fuel and ammunition dumps, communications, supplies, and parked vehicles and aircraft. After their training, these were regarded as easy to deal with.

Milk churns and waterproof bags were stored in outbuildings at 'The Garth'. As long as Calvert was encouraged to follow his 'containment of the enemy' strategy, these were filled with either guncotton or ammonal, and modified into home-made mines, prepared with delay switches and water-proof fuse. The bags – standard Royal Engineer issue – and not unlike a modern supermarket freezer bag in size and shape – were made of heavy rubber material. The 'open' end was secured and made watertight by two rectangular sections of hardwood, about nine inches in length, which clamped tightly together with wing nuts. A prepared, easily sealed hole took the time fuse. The complete mines would then be concealed under bridges and culverts for the stay-behinds to activate.

Field also discovered stored camouflet sets. Camouflets are small mines containing an explosive powder charge. Field and his men found these useful for creating instant grenade practice pits and also to disguise the visibly chalky soil dug from new OBs. A labour-saving technique was developed by dumping piles of spoil in a line and about 50 yards apart, then blowing them

KENT HOME GUARDS
(L.D.V.)

THIS IS TO CERTIFY that the bearer

C. G. Stears

is a member of the above Force.

Commanding No. .... Platoon.
.... Company.
.... Battalion.

Signature of Holder:

C. G. Stears

"KENT MESSENGER," MAIDSTONE.

An Auxiliers' Identity Pass, printed at the local newspaper office and signed – some time after XII Corps Observation Unit had been absorbed into the GHQ Auxiliary Units – by the Intelligence Officer, Captain Norman Field under an 'official' stamp purchased through a local stationery shop.

up with camouflets. The result, for any enemy spy plane to see, was a series of craters resembling a stick of jettisoned bombs. This was a great help for the section of Welsh miners – part of a tunnelling company – that he managed to have seconded from XII Corps to dig new OBs and an underground explosives' store at his HQ.

Fleming had already constructed a number of ingenious hideouts for his stay-behinds, including sophisticated, camouflaged trapdoors giving surreptitious entry and exit. Later, Field demonstrated a 'front-door bell' to General Montgomery, which subsequently gained media notoriety. Dropping a small marble into what appeared to be a mouse hole in a bank operated the device. In fact it was the end of a length of gas pipe, down which the marble ran before dropping with a clatter into an empty biscuit tin. 'This was an effective way of requesting the troglodytes within to open up for a friend without', wrote Captain Field.

The best hideout legacy was undoubtedly the 'forme', a strange, boat-shaped depression in a wood on the Kentish Downs. Its original measurements were 60 x 30 feet, with a depth of 30 feet when originally excavated in the First World War as the landing and tie-down site for a small airship, used to reconnoitre the Straits for the famous Dover Patrol. When Fleming handed it over to Field, the depth had been reduced by ten feet or so and it had been roofed and covered with a layer of earth, creating an unusually large hideout instead.

Field's understanding of Fleming's reasoning was that no one would suspect that, beneath this strange-shaped hole, another would lurk. Access was by a vertical shaft and a tunnel about 25 feet in length. The entrance was under a heavy tree trunk mounted on rails and counter-balanced. It opened – if you knew precisely where to press – with mere fingertip pressure. This hideout, a shelter for men on the run, was equipped with food and water, and an adequate air supply for about fifty men.

A mundane advantage for his soldiers had accrued from Fleming's 'professional' association with his brother Ian, who was in Naval Intelligence. Much to the satisfaction of XII Corps Observation Unit, Ian 'sequestrated' and delivered to 'The Garth' a pile of white RN-issue soft woollen blankets to replace their brown and decidedly hairy WD issue.

On another occasion, Ian was said to have brought a suitcase to 'The Garth' and to have left in it a full Luftwaffe officer's uniform. This kit was prepared for his 'ditched pilot' project to recover a current German naval cipher book. The plan was, it is said, to fly a recovered German aircraft, with heavily armed British troops hidden aboard, toward France and ditch it in the Channel within sight of the coast and certain rescue by a patrol boat of the Kriegsmarine. The rescue boat would then be overwhelmed by a fusillade of sub-machine gun fire and sailed triumphantly back to England by Ian himself, complete with the latest German codes. It seems fair to assume that this imaginative plan was abandoned because of a shortage of spare, fully working but disposable German aircraft. Although he had a distinguished record on the staff of the Director of Naval Intelligence, the impartial observer blessed with hindsight may conclude that Ian's talents found a more appropriate outlet after the war.

On 6 November 1941, having been ordered to rendezvous at 'Crossroads, Map Reference 4569', Field demonstrated to a sceptical General Montgomery, one of the Unit's Observation Posts above the village of Charing, overlooking (through rabbit holes) a major junction on the A.20 trunk road below. The OP was entered through a concealed hatch activated by pressure on a nail head in the floor of a cattle trough. The media have since done much to exaggerate this visit by the two officers into some sort of Whitehall farce. It was, in fact, an example of the ingenuity which developed, first among the Observation Units in the south-east, and then Auxiliary Units in other vulnerable parts of Britain. As Captain Field opened up the secret hatch and entered the hide below, General Montgomery's scepticism was soon replaced by unexpected enthusiasm.

Field was quick to recognise the effective unconventionality of much that he inherited from Peter Fleming, and then to adapt and innovate his own command. There were still surprises in store, as he found during another VIP visit, this time as late as 29 August 1941 when, according to his diaries, General Alan Brooke, C-in-C Home Forces:

> Left at 8.30 a.m. to spend a day with the auxiliary units in Kent and Sussex. These units comprise two main elements – one an information one equipped with wireless and another a sabotage one equipped with explosives and weapons. Both are intended to work behind the enemy in the event of an invasion. They are therefore organised into small patrols and have prepared some 'hide-outs' in the woods where they can live and hide their weapons. These are beautifully concealed and could be walked right over without ever detecting them. I was impressed by the type of man, both regular and home guard employed in these units. The latter were the best type of yeoman farmers.

The fact that wireless sets were being operated in his area, by personnel perhaps listed somewhere in the Auxiliary Units, came as a total surprise to Captain Field. So secret was the intelligence-gathering network that its existence was kept absolutely separate even from the Officer Commanding operational Auxiliers. While conducting General Brooke's visit to several of his OBs, Captain Field was mystified when, asked to stop outside a cottage in a wood, he noticed that the general was met and taken inside by two subalterns in ATS uniform. Only later did he discover that they were radio operators for the secret radio network set up by the Special Duties Section of the Auxiliary Units, and that the cottage was one of their Control (or 'IN') Stations.

Unlike the patrols of all-male saboteurs, the SDS was a spy network of both men and women – first created by Section D of MI6 and now an integrated, but independent, part of the secret 'Scallywags'. As an example of the tight security imposed from HQ, the operational Auxunits of Kent had at that time no knowledge of the SDS scheme and radio network, which had already been operating in the locality for some twelve months.

Interest in XII Corps' OUs and the front-line Kentish Auxiliary Units has hardly declined after all these years. One rumour recycled by the BBC, for example, is that a secret army of 3,000 men was ready and waiting on Romney Marsh in the summer of 1940. Apart from the obvious logistic absurdity, Field quietly reports that – yes, by July 1941 (twelve months later) – he had been able to establish *three* Auxiliary Unit patrols on the Marsh, totalling just 24 men. Another myth, regularly recycled, is about plans to explode toilet seats in buildings likely to be occupied by German officers – but this deserves no further comment.

Much as he enjoyed his job at 'The Garth', Captain Field's time there came to an end in November 1941 when, after a chance meeting with General Montgomery, he was given, a junior staff job until being selected for the Staff College some six months later. He then served continuously with the Parachute Regiment until the end of the war, for a time in joint planning with the US Army. He was Mentioned in Dispatches and awarded both the American Bronze Star and the OBE. Still living not too far from 'The Garth' in 2007, he is a patron and respected adviser to the Museum of the British Resistance Organisation at Parham in Suffolk.

Chapter Nine

Evolution, Revolution and Reaction

'... it was decided to hold four weekend courses. Coleshill House was considered suitable ... the HQ staff came down on Fridays from Whitehall Place, laid on the programme ... and returned to London on Sunday evening. The first course was on August 22nd 1940 ... Early in the Blitz the offices at Whitehall Place were damaged by enemy action and the contents were brought down to Coleshill, which thereafter became HQ.'

Major N.V. Oxenden, MC, in his report to the War Office in 1945

Colonel C. R. ('Bill') Major, of the Royal Irish Fusiliers, was appointed to succeed Gubbins as CO of the Auxiliary Units in the autumn of 1940, taking over on 9 November. He was fortunate to inherit the product of five or six months' frenetic activity by his predecessor and his group of outstanding officers.

The task was now more clearly defined. While invasion was still ostensibly anticipated at any moment, it was to continue and consolidate the selection and training of a hard core of hard men, mainly taken from the Home Guard. Having been provided with firearms and explosives, and with development of skills in their use well under way, they were to stay behind in hidden Operational Bases. Once the enemy had passed by, they would emerge, preferably at night, and commit mayhem among his armed forces. The objectives were both tactical and defensive. The constant 'pinpricks' of these guerrillas (who would today be called terrorists), as envisaged by the Auxunits' GSO2, Major Peter Wilkinson, were intended to hit the Germans at their weakest – assuming they had managed to elude the Royal Navy during the protracted Channel or North Sea crossing in a hastily improvised fleet – and now in unfamiliar territory, still debilitated after the hazards and discomforts of the voyage and beachhead battles, unsupported by the full weight of their armour, and with dependable support from the

Luftwaffe minimised by the increasingly successful counter-aggression of the Royal Air Force.

It was never intended that Auxiliers were to compare with the men and women of the European resistance movements or those recruited for service abroad with the Special Operations Executive who were meant to operate in harmony with the orders of a centralised command structure. These were clandestine armies-in-waiting, prepared to assist an Allied counter-invasion of their homeland. Comparisons with the Auxiliary units are pointless, for these were seen only as a short-term, expendable, harassing force intended – with the blessing of the British high command – to be of some useful influence in local battles. There is no evidence that they could have operated in effective synchrony even with local Army commanders.

Colonel Major already had a name for his command – the GHQ Auxiliary Units. Widespread speculation on the choice of the 'Auxiliary Units' title is also pointless for, although minutes of whatever meetings there were have not been released, on the balance of probabilities the name was simply nondescript War Office cover for activities intended from the outset to depend upon secrecy at all levels. Wilkinson was emphatic that the name was neither chosen by him nor, so far as he knew, by Colonel Gubbins. In any case, the word 'Auxiliary' was in high demand at the beginning of the war. There were Auxiliary firemen and policemen, the (women's) Auxiliary Territorial Service, even Auxiliary static water tanks. The most favoured and least likely idea is that Gubbins chose the title as a reminder of his days in Ireland.

The Auxiliaries of the early 1920s were recruited from former British officers, as back-up to the Royal Irish Constabulary, who were in danger of being overwhelmed by the Irish Republican Army. In doing so, 'Auxiliaries' stood shoulder to shoulder with the hated Black and Tans. They wore uniform, had rank structure and were, of course, paid for the job. None of these characteristics bears serious comparison with the GHQ Auxiliary Units. Indeed, the Auxiliaries in Ireland, provoked by IRA incineration of their barracks, the murder of their personnel, and in reprisal for hostage-taking, retaliated with counter-barbarism on an unprecedented scale. They shot on sight, often without identifying the victim first, and specialised in the indiscriminate, often random, destruction of houses – whole villages on occasion – and the dairies which were the working people's lifeline. They brought worldwide condemnation upon the British government. If there is any valuable comparison to be made, it is clear enough that the Auxiliary Units were modelled more on the provocateurs, that is the IRA itself, than the Auxiliaries.

The most likely explanation for the War Office decision on a name for stay-behind units is therefore a simple adoption of the earlier use by Section D of 'Auxiliary Units' for the boxes of weaponry and explosives which had been dumped around the country on behalf of its Home Defence Organisation.

The 'GHQ' in the name linked them directly with the top echelon of military direction – bypassing local Army commands which, while usually aware of the presence on their ground of unidentified and unspecified numbers of underground Home Guards, were to have little or no effective operational control over them. As the men in the Operational Bases were isolated from the outside world, including the military one, it meant that the only order they could follow was the last one given by their Intelligence Officer before he withdrew – something like 'Mount an operation against the enemy every night until you are killed, captured or relieved by counter-attack.' We do not have to go far to see that this was unworkable and why Wilkinson described the likely effect of Auxiliary Units' operations as pinpricks. The issue of a fortnight's rations gives some idea of the survival prospects. With lots of luck, and a little bit of stealing and poaching, a life span of thirty days to six weeks was just a possibility.

It seems less than fair that, as civilians, the men doing the job were, under the accepted conventions of modern warfare, vulnerable to execution without trial once detected and captured by the enemy. Could this be another reason why the authorities decided to keep it all quiet until more than fifty years after the war was over?

*

Auxiliers were led locally by Intelligence Officers issued with staff cars and drivers. These were very special symbols of influence and authority in otherwise stringent times. The men being driven around, usually of modest captain's rank and without any special marks of authority, often showed less than expected conformity with normal War Office protocol, and seemed to have less respect for authority than was proper. In some cases, this amounted to none at all, as Captain J. W. Stuart Edmundson, Auxunits' IO for Devon – and only recently a lieutenant on the Reserve – demonstrated when he told a full general to mind his own business. 'As I was being led away to the Tower of London, I had the good fortune of Colonel Gubbins's intervention, followed by prompt release.'

Colonel Major also had an up-and-running HQ at Coleshill House in Oxfordshire, the first premises in Whitehall Place, adjacent to the War Office, having been evacuated well before the end of 1940 as both inadequate in size and unserviceable after an enemy air raid. The original set-up must have depended much on harmonious relations between the incumbents, for these were small offices. Not only did they come to house Gubbins, Wilkinson and Beyts, but also the soldiers of 'Winston Churchill's Toyshop', officially styled MD1 – Lieutenant-Colonel Millis Jefferis (later Major General Sir Millis Jefferis, KBE, MC) and Major (later Colonel) R. Stuart Macrae. Coleshill, a great leap forward, was something really different.

The Coleshill Estate is now managed by the National Trust. It is still possible to visit the full-scale model OB built during the war, but there is little else of WWII historical interest to see today. The fine Roger Pratt seventeenth-century Italianate mansion was burned to the ground in 1952, after a carelessly handled blowtorch started a fire in the roof. The outline of the footings survives in the form of a box hedge, and the steps where groups of officers were photographed are now just crazy paving. The stables – where visiting 'students' were accommodated – although now falling into dangerous disrepair, still show the sign on the Camp Commandant's office door and the hatchway into his typists' office. Now musty and dusty, it was once upon a time ablaze with life and action.

Auxiliers arrived for training either at the nearest railway station or, if they could muster road transport (with petrol coupons provided by the area IO) at nearby Highworth post office to be vetted by the postmistress or her young ladies. A telephone call to 'Highworth 85' would, for sensible reasons of basic security, then arrange Army transport displaying GHQ insignia – an heraldic lion rampant and the identifying unit number 490 – for the last lap into the estate.

The role of Mabel Stranks, the postmistress at Highworth, has been seriously overplayed by the media. As well as being a practical help to Auxiliers, she was a useful security cut-out at an everyday level. Her service to the Auxiliary Units has now been recognised by the local council, which has erected a blue plaque on the outer wall of the old post office. Mabel Stranks was not, however, a personal agent for Winston Churchill and did not hide a loaded Tommy gun under her counter – as some commentators would like us to believe.

The final approach passed a blockhouse guardroom which, now festooned with graffiti and detritus collected over the years, is also still standing. Behind a wall near the main road it is just possible to discern the outline of three huts, occupied from about 1942 by Auxiliary Units (Signals), specialists in constructing, adapting, and servicing the radio transceivers operated from secret locations by SDS agents and ATS subalterns.

Once commandeered, the house and grounds of Coleshill were systematically redeveloped for Auxiliers, Scout Sections, and Group Commanders' training – camouflage, night stalking, the use of firearms and explosives, map reading – usually during weekends. These were the only opportunities for Auxiliers to get away from full-time jobs and their families. Dummy tanks, aircraft and lorries were littered around for explosives training. There were hand-grenade and shooting ranges for light machine guns, rifles and handguns.

Other ranks staff included typists, RASC drivers, batmen, Royal Engineers, and former burglars. Instructors were usually, but not always, officers. Lurid stories abound, particularly on the subject of close quarters combat (CQC) – an art form at which Auxiliers were required to excel. Were or were not professional criminals specially released from Barlinnie Prison in Glasgow to demonstrate their skills at Coleshill? Was one of the CQC instructors a white Russian émigré? Did one physical training instructor – having picked a well-built but simple looking Welsh Auxilier from the valleys upon whom to demonstrate his martial arts machismo – find himself humiliatingly thrown and held by a 'catch-as-catch-can' national champion? Did the infamous duo of former Shanghai Police Department Assistant Commissioners, 'Dan' Fairbairn and 'Bill' Sykes, visit Coleshill to demonstrate their advanced fighting-knife techniques in person? In a way, David Lampe, in taking at face value a variety of overplayed rumours in *The Last Ditch*, did the authorities a favour by deceiving seriously interested researchers and re-channelling their energies to pathways of irrelevance and often untrue trivia.

Coleshill House was the home of three Auxiliary Unit COs. Colonel Major was the first, and he was followed by Colonel Lord Glanusk from the Brigade of Guards, and Colonel Frank W. R. Douglas, Royal Artillery. Douglas remained until the final whistle was blown in January 1945.

Not every Auxilier had his training at Coleshill but as many as possible were crammed in. The record shows that, in the four years of active occupation, 100 Home Guard weekend courses were held; 25 for Patrol Leaders, 19 for Group Commanders 15 for Scout Sections, 11 for new intakes, 5 for Scout officers, 4 for RE corporals and 3 for IOs' HQ staffs.

None of the records shows how well the Pleydell-Bouverie sisters survived it all! But, although by 1945 the estate was in a bad way as a result of more than four years' modifications by the Auxiliary Units, it can only be hoped that the official War Compensation Scheme provided useful consolation for this aristocratic family at a time of serious austerity, baggy 'demob' suits, and food and fuel shortages for the great majority.

*

A final bonus for Colonel Major was the work done by the staff assembled by Gubbins. Gubbins's second-in-command was Major Beyts and his GSO2 Major Wilkinson. The foundations laid in their early days with the Auxiliary Units would remain in evidence for the duration.

Geoffrey Herbert Bruno ('Bill') Beyts, (later Brigadier Beyts, MBE, DSO, MC), was born in India. His family had Dutch origins. At the age of seven he was sent to school in England and after completing his education at Wellington College he was a King's Cadet at the Royal Military Academy at Sandhurst.

He chose a career in the Indian Army as an officer in his father's regiment, the 6th Rajputana Rifles. He was awarded a Military Cross in 1932 for counter-insurgency operations during the Burma Rebellion, emerging from the jungle after nine months, and only after his unit had caught or killed the 100 men on a wanted list. It was this battle experience that brought him – and a dozen Indian Army colleagues – to stiffen the inexperienced Independent Companies in Norway in 1940. Most of the early officers selected by Gubbins for the Auxiliary Units and SOE were 'friends'. Having further proved his fighting ability and courage in the Norwegian campaign, Beyts was appointed second-in-command of the Auxiliary Units. With extensive experience of active service, skills in close quarters combat, sniping, night and silent movement, as well as having a formal Army background, he was the ideal man for training and operations.

Under both Gubbins and Major, 'Bill' Beyts displayed the most extra-ordinary dedication and energy. Initially, he travelled the country advising units' set-up teams in the field. At the same time he prepared operational guidelines for Intelligence Officers, lecture notes, and training schedules and facilities at Coleshill. Although he never admitted to it, he had further responsibilities for the Special Duties Section, for whom he made broadly based advance scouting missions – including flights to reconnoitre the northern Scottish Isles. He claimed that on one occasion he fired his revolver from cliffs surrounding a sheltered bay at U-boat crew members taking the air on the conning tower while their submarine had stealthily moored to re-charge batteries. He was satisfied to see the U-boat steam promptly to sea and later to hear that it never returned.

Beyts remained with the Auxiliary Units until August 1942, when he returned to India as chief of staff to SOE forces (later renamed Force 136 in this theatre) in South-East Asia. After his return to regimental duty at the end of 1943 he was in constant action against the retreating Japanese, winning the DSO and promotion to the rank of brigadier. Although he was not entirely in accord with Colonel Major's plans to abandon the cellular system of secrecy, hitherto sacrosanct for the security of the patrols of the Auxiliary Units, and other changes which the new CO had in mind, he loyally and energetically developed a training schedule which stood hardly unchanged through their whole lifespan.

Peter Wilkinson (later Lieutenant-Colonel Sir Peter Wilkinson, OBE, DSO) is described as 'a brilliant linguist with a rapier mind'. Urbane, self-confident, and six feet tall, he was a man with influential connections in high places and always looked the part. Moreover he had the clipped accent of the British officer class and a prestigious Clarges Street flat in London's West End.

MI(R), it will be recalled, had run a series of special courses on irregular warfare even before war broke out, and these continued at least until March 1940. It seems certain enough that the agenda and organisation of these fell largely within Wilkinson's remit. Two small courses of about thirty carefully selected men were held in London in May and June 1939, but plans for more had to be limited when war was declared. However, with breathing space during the initial stalemate on the Western Front, Gubbins and Wilkinson (and, separately, General Ironside) visited Cambridge to arrange 'Politico-Military' courses, a proposition warmly welcomed by the university authorities. Officer cadet training was arranged for chosen men and the first Cambridge course, whose students called themselves 'The Gauleiteers', lasted from 15 January to 9 March 1940, later being continued under more formal management by the Directorate of Military Intelligence.

In his post-war book *Setting Europe Ablaze*, Brigadier Sir Douglas Dodds-Parker, himself a 'Gauleiter' and one of the men selected for MI(R) on Joan Bright Astley's core list, who rose to senior rank with SOE in the Middle East, wrote that one of the useful qualifications for the course was specialist knowledge of foreign countries. Candidates were favoured who might be available for 'action rather than Intelligence'. Instruction was comprehensive – from international law and economics, to varieties of sabotage, both physical and commercial. He acknowledged that he learned more in his time at Cambridge, enjoying the great hospitality of the cellar at Trinity College, than during all his younger years as an undergraduate at Oxford University.

It was a gathering of the elite, many of whom led the field and performed heroic feats for the Allied cause in Britain's ruthless counter-campaign of irregular warfare and especially secret service against an implacable enemy. Peter Wilkinson must qualify for a share of the credit.

Wilkinson served with MI(R) and Colin Gubbins in Poland and Czechoslovakia and, before the French military collapse in 1940, he co-ordinated the early subversive activities of their escapees and intelligence officers. With the Auxiliary Units he was nominally responsible for administration and liaison or, as he put it himself, 'Plans and Organisation'. The job-description was open ended. With Gubbins, he moved to SOE in the autumn of 1940. Colonel Major could certainly count the benefit of his groundwork.

At SOE Wilkinson remained in contact with Czech intelligence and was responsible for supplying the munitions used by its agents who assassinated Reinhard Heydrich, Czechoslovakia's feared, fanatical Nazi 'Protector'. Wilkinson served in SOE with distinction at home and abroad, both before and behind enemy lines, and is credited with involvement in the formation of the 'Jedburghs', effective, three-man liaison teams parachuted into France at the time of D-Day to co-ordinate the numerous resistance organisations there. Wilkinson joined the Diplomatic Service in 1947, attaining ambassador's rank and, finally, was appointed security co-ordinator at the Cabinet Office in Whitehall. Although he went blind in later life, he kindly sent a message of support to an Auxiliary Units' reunion held in 2000 – the year of his death.

After his transfer to SOE in 1942, Beyts was replaced by Gubbins's cousin, Nigel Oxenden, MC*, also educated at Wellington College and, until then, Auxunits' Intelligence Officer in Norfolk. A WWI veteran of the Welsh

Regiment and, from 1916, the Machine Gun Corps, Oxenden made a great impression on the Norfolk stay-behinds. His combat experience, pragmatic attitude to the task for which they were volunteers, the example he set and a robust hatred for the aggressor were not forgotten and, after learning of his death after the war, men not normally emotional, collected enough funds to prepare a memorial – adapted from a Jersey Cider press millstone – to place at his home on the Channel Island of Jersey. It was inscribed: 'In Memory of Our Beloved Major N. V. Oxenden, MC. Presented by Norfolk Aux. Units.'

Other founder members of Auxunits' HQ Staff were Major the Honourable Michael T. Henderson, 16th/5th Lancers, the quartermaster who, it will be recalled, as the brother of Lord Faringdon and Gubbins's personal plenipotentiary, had opportunely identified the availability of Coleshill in the first place; and Major Edward Beddington-Behrens, Royal Artillery, in charge of recruitment. Beddington-Behrens had a distinguished WWI career, being awarded the Military Cross in August 1917 and a Bar in June 1918, for 'conspicuous gallantry and devotion to duty'. He was gazetted major in May 1940. Peter Wilkinson described how, the following year, Beddington-Behrens demonstrated a continuing capacity for bravery when he seized the chance to join the echelons of the mythically unforgettable:

> He was a fairly ebullient character and he was selling the idea [of the Auxiliary Units] to the Commanding Officer of Eastern Command and he pushed his way into the General's room and, seeing an open French window, he plucked out of his pocket a Molotov Cocktail – which was a mixture of petrol and goodness knows what – and hurled it through the French window against a brick wall opposite, demolishing, or rather incinerating, in a flash the General's favourite peach tree. And once again, the General, whose name I'm afraid I've forgotten, was not at all amused and poor Colonel Gubbins had to spend the whole of the next morning trying to pacify him!

Wilkinson also recalled the Fleming/Calvert night exercise against General Montgomery's HQ in Kent. His received memory of Monty's reaction, as seen from Auxunits' HQ, was a shade different from that recorded by Mike Calvert: 'I may say that the General hadn't a very strong sense of humour when the joke was on him, and he was not particularly amused!'

Major absorbed officers from the Brigade of Guards, the House of Lords, and land and thoroughbred horse owners. Once the heat was off the invasion scare, they were instrumental in introducing unlikely subjects such as arms and foot drill to training and competition schedules. While this may have served to smarten up the singularly unmilitary student Auxiliers, it definitely did not fit their self-image as ruthless guerrilla fighters. While some took well to a new, formally militarised role, at times proudly displaying parade-ground prowess with the Home Guard, the majority milled around in dispirited confusion. Morale and enthusiasm were adversely affected, leaving the second batch of IOs with increasingly de-motivated volunteers.

Several of the first IOs and Scout Section officers turned out to be valiant warriors. Donald Hamilton-Hill served with distinction both at home and abroad with SOE. Ian Fenwick, Roy Bradford and Dick Bond fought and died in action with the SAS. Peter Weaver survived SAS Operation Bulbasket (discussed in Chapter Fifteen). Peter Mant Macintyre Kemp, also from Wellington College and a veteran of the Spanish Civil War, fought with the Commandos behind the lines in both the European and Far Eastern theatres, being awarded the DSO and achieving the rank of lieutenant-colonel. Fleming, Mike Calvert, and Andrew Croft, already on board as Colonel Major walked up the gangplank, were about to jump ship and join other special forces. Some original Intelligence Officer initiates remained at work in the Auxunits' field. Replacement IOs were generally of lesser calibre than the originals.

Each of those first IOs who had assembled in Room 365, 7 Whitehall Place, promptly at 1100 hours on 13 July 1940 were, after briefings from Wilkinson and Gubbins, allocated an area of personal responsibility. This might be a single county or a larger area like East Anglia or Devon and Cornwall. At the time, all held – or were immediately promoted to – the rank of captain. They were:

> Devon and Cornwall: J. W. Stuart Edmundson, Royal Engineers.
> Lincolnshire: Donald Hamilton-Hill, Seaforth Highlanders.
> Forth and Tees: Eustice Maxwell, Argyll and Sutherland
>   Highlanders.
> Dorset and Somerset: Lord Tony Ashley, Grenadier Guards.
> Forth, Berwick and Northumberland: Hamish Torrance, Highland
>   Light Infantry.
> Sussex and Hampshire: John Gwynn, Grenadier Guards.

A Scottish borders area, under Captain Peter Forbes, and the north-east of England, partly headed by Captain Anthony Quayle (later Sir Anthony, the post-war film and stage star) became operational a little later. Once fully organised there were more than twenty command areas for Intelligence Officers, each with a small administrative staff.

Orders for new IOs were to recruit reliable local civilian men to go to ground in small patrols and then, following invasion, to attack enemy forces from within. This was a complete revelation to officers such as Stuart Edmundson – until then a mere RE lieutenant in the Territorial Army Reserve. He was, moreover, without the benefit of a previous MI(R) course in irregular warfare. Edmundson was never told why he had been picked out but, after a diversion to see how Fleming had gone about it in Kent, he took to his new challenge energetically, if not effortlessly, operating first from Plymouth (where a lorry load of explosives preceded him) and, later, the village of Lydford. He was also astonished to be issued with a coveted staff car and driver. He remained with the Auxiliary Units, latterly in the Special Duties Section, until he was transferred to the Far East in 1943 to join SOE and, later, the staff of Earl Mountbatten, the Supreme Commander South East Asia, at Kandy in Ceylon.

Other units more-or-less *in situ* for Colonel Major were the Auxiliary Unit Scout Sections. The need for local training had become apparent as travel to Coleshill became, in many cases, a virtual impossibility. Exploiting an almost unique talent for combining tact with authority, Gubbins overcame opposition from local Army COs and solicited some of their best subalterns, NCOs, and soldiers and, in each area, set up (usually) two Scout Sections of a dozen men each.

Often selected from the local county regiment, these sections were billeted in some secrecy in the same locality as the civilian patrols they were instructing. Since they were lacking experience of irregular warfare themselves, their own training went in parallel but just ahead of their trainees. They were also intended to stay behind when the balloon went up and many of them – particularly in Norfolk – spent most of each day digging, first their own Operational Bases and then others for Auxiliers. Elsewhere this was not so, with the civilians making their own efforts to prepare the original secure hides.

Scout Sections provided standard Army training in map reading, the use of weaponry and explosives, close quarters combat, sniping and night cross-country work. A Royal Engineer NCO was usually included and he tended to teach whatever speciality he had – sometimes the use of explosives or the construction of booby traps. In central Suffolk, where the Scout Section under Lieutenant 'Mac' McIntyre was billeted in 'The Mill House' at Cransford, near Framlingham, the RE corporal proved his value in the construction of ingenious trapdoors to cover camouflaged hatchways leading down to OB main chambers. Giant home-made concrete counter-balances with gas-pipe pivots, the hallmark of his special interest, can still be found at the bottom of collapsed OB shafts and escape tunnels.

Once absorbed into the GHQ Auxiliary Units, the first *de facto* Scout Section was the XII Corps Observation Unit in Kent. The rest were similarly constituted, although not identical. Every Scout Section member was aware that he would be a stay-behind when the invasion emergency came and two OBs were prepared, each for six men. These soldiers represented something of a threat to the security of the civilian warriors for they knew where the latter were hidden, having often helped to dig their OBs and in any case, trained with them. This was a particular weakness for, in early days at least, Auxiliers knew little or nothing of any other stay-behind unit and could therefore give nothing away if captured and interrogated under torture. Until Scout Sections appeared, this secrecy had been absolute and fundamental.

With that exception, Scout Section and Auxilier stay-behind plans replicated one another in most ways – their weaponry, booby-trap devices and explosives were similar. Scout Section training included extensive map reading, and frequent cross-country forced marches to harden up and familiarise the soldiers with the landscape and match Auxiliers' local knowledge. This was in keeping with guidelines for outwitting the enemy recorded in Gubbins's *Guerrilla's Creed* – until Colonel Major came onto the scene.

Several Scout Section subalterns, and some of their other ranks went on to serve with special forces. Roy Bradford, for example, a pre-war architect and Territorial Army soldier, and one of Edmundson's Scout Section subalterns in Devon, was later promoted to captain and installed as the Intelligence Officer for Sussex. By 1944, he had been inducted into the Special Air Service, for which he led a parachute drop into the Morvan area of France in Operation Houndsworth soon after D-Day. He was killed in action while ambushing a convoy of German soldiers on 20 July 1944 near Lucy-sur-Yonne.

*

The end of 1940 was a critical time for the Auxiliary Units and it came to a head with the arrival of Colonel Major. Starting from virtually nothing and under pressure from the mounting fear of imminent invasion, the HQ team and the Intelligence Officers had rapidly improvised from pre-war blueprints and scrambled together a formidable number of partly trained saboteurs or guerrillas to stay behind and harass the enemy. Each unit was isolated from others for important reasons of self-preservation. Auxiliers were still usually operating in their working clothes. Khaki denim overalls were sometimes on offer but Stuart Edmundson later stated that he never trained a man in uniform.

Under Gubbins, there was no time for nominal rolls or formal administration. Records were in the minds of the IOs or, at best, scribbled on the back of an envelope. This was tight security. Colonel Major set about standing all this on its head. In some ways, his period in command represented a high point for the Auxiliary Units: there was still a threat of invasion; weaponry, equipment and stores were more in evidence; and uniforms not only became available, but were issued and required to be worn during training and at 'stand to' times. Some sort of formal affiliation to the Home Guard, previously top of the vetoed-at-all-costs list, was introduced; HG flashes were issued; even joint participation in church parades was not unknown. With these changes much of the absolute secrecy previously demanded from every participant in these highly secret units was thrown away and replaced by War Office standardisation. The pretext, if there was one, was that security was actually enhanced with the issue of uniform. If wives could see their men-folk cycling away from home in Home Guard uniform, carrying a Lee-Enfield rifle, any local suspicion that they were not pulling their weight for the war effort would be disposed of. Moreover, in such unglamorous cumbersome gear, it was less likely that they were off to see a lady friend either.

Perhaps some senior official in the Adjutant-General's department of the War Office had belatedly concluded that, if they were in uniform, civilian stay-behind volunteers might just acquire some rights to prisoner of war status once captured. If this was so, it was not communicated to the men themselves who, generally, never fully understood the legal weakness and the threat to their lives that existed in such an irregular role.

The most dangerous change of all was the introduction of a group system. This called for joint operational training between all the patrols in a given location – usually six or seven in number – under one Group Commander. He was a liaison officer with a Home Guard commission. This produced another link with the open world and left the secret army with virtually no secrets at all. The GC, always an older man and often a WWI veteran, was originally intended to stay behind with his men, who were themselves now given formal rank – sergeant for the patrol leader, corporal or private for the rest. It soon became clear, though, that a hard life below ground, especially in winter, was not for the middle-aged, and the GC was relegated to a more administrative role. But because he knew where the patrols were located, and the identities of participating Auxiliers, irreparable damage was done to cellular security.

It says much for the dangerous operational weakness of the group system that it was abandoned soon after Colonel Major departed from Coleshill in February 1942, to be replaced as CO by Colonel Lord Glanusk. Although a stalwart of the Brigade of Guards himself, Glanusk quickly shook his new command free from much of the inadequacy of the group system. That experiment was deemed a failure.

In his 'History and Achievement' report to the War Office, Major Oxenden summarised the changes in 1942:

> *1942. Simplicity Spells Success*
>
> The greatest service that Lord Glanusk did for the unit was to throw doubt upon the wisdom of the elaboration, both in essentials and details, that had grown up. Once the matter was seriously questioned it became increasingly obvious that the auxilier had been in some respects over-rated, and that such a policy [the group system] would inevitably mean confusion and inefficiency in action.
>
> Tests of cross-sections of the unit here and there showed that, after two years' training, less was known about the use of explosives than in 1940, that many of the 'toys' since issued would never, and could never successfully be used, and that liaison between patrols was little more than wishful thinking, and of questionable use at that. At one stroke our policy had been cleared of much hampering undergrowth. From now on the patrol was self-contained and would fight alone; from now on the rank and file would not be asked to think.

With that resounding denunciation, the group system was trashed. Oxenden's rather strange conclusion that 'the rank and file would not be asked to think' meant, perhaps, that a small group of men, working in isolation, and properly equipped, could again be trained to react *spontaneously* to any operational challenge, based on their local knowledge, their training, and pre-prepared charges and weaponry. Moreover, the leader would no longer be expected to wait for orders and co-ordinate his plans with others – equally untrained to do so – in some quasi-military fashion. An additional bonus soon developed as Auxiliers' skills were released. They rose to the occasion, sometimes developing 'toys' even more innovative than those of the professionals. Home-made booby traps were one of their specialities.

But, while the soft core of aristocratic overlords prospered in some comfort and exercised their thoroughbreds at Coleshill, prepared lectures and demonstrations on boot polishing, saluting procedure and rifle drill, and yearned for the old days – their real world on Horse Guards Parade – the civilian hard core shivered in OBs and crawled their way through waterlogged ditches. Fortunately, they also had some practical, first class instructors on hand too.

It is time to see what they were all about.

Chapter Ten

The Operational Patrols

'If we had received an order to kill a collaborator, would we have done so without compunction? Yes! Without compunction.'

Donald Handscombe, Essex Auxilier

Soon after the collapse of France and the evacuation of BEF personnel from continental ports and beaches, the imperative for stay-behind action on Britain's mainland – based on pre-emptive MI(R) planning – could no longer be delayed. With a cadre of officers, hurriedly collected and trained, headquarters' administration and provisional training schedules in place, and 'go-ahead!' authority from the highest political level, the result was the GHQ Auxiliary Units Operational Patrols – the very first experiment involving British civilians in irregular warfare.

Captain Duncan Sandys outlined their charter in a memorandum to his father-in-law, Winston Churchill, dated 8 August 1940, from draft papers by Gubbins:

> They are intended to provide, within the framework of the Home Guard organisation, small bodies of men especially selected and trained, whose role it will be to act offensively on the flanks and in the rear of any enemy troops who may obtain a foothold in this country. Their action will particularly be directed against tanks and lorries in laager, ammunition dumps, small enemy posts and stragglers. Their activities will also include sniping.

Until Scout Sections came into the picture in the autumn of 1940, the men selected and invited to volunteer for this uniquely dangerous undertaking were exclusively civilians. Colonel Holland's blueprint for action, now being developed under Colin Gubbins's energetic command, did not involve soldiers, although some, but not all, Intelligence Officers *assumed* they would join their men in Operational Bases behind German lines. It is clear enough now that no direct order was given to them and, as so often happened, IOs were left to make their own decision. From the outset, the selection of patrol leaders, the extent of local training, and the clarity of warnings about the risks involved, were also each IO's exclusive preserve. As most had little or no practical experience, nearly everything depended upon their imagination and capacity to absorb the training schedule outlined by Gubbins and amplified by Beyts and then pass it on lucidly.

No one gave a moment's thought to involving women, no matter how qualified they were. Even with a war on and the collapse of the British Empire and way of life an ever-threatening possibility, middle-class standards had to be maintained and the likelihood of women joining a bunch of unshaven men in a confined space underground – let alone sharing unisex toilet arrangements, where they existed – was a consideration which never once intruded on the 'men only' scheme of things.

Don Handscombe was an early and not untypical volunteer. Aged twenty-two when war broke out, he was his father's farm manager, running horticultural greenhouses at Hockley in Essex on the large family arable holding and two further farms supervised for the War Agricultural Committee – which had been established to maximise food production and minimise the volume of imports along vulnerable shipping lanes. Don's work on the land exempted him from conscription. Exemption from military service was a first essential in choosing men for the Operational Patrols. Ideally they were resourceful, hardy, patriotic and flexible, able to master elementary military training with firearms and explosives and in map reading, and could show ability to live off the land when stores ran out and to survive in harmonious close proximity with their comrades. All this was pointless unless they were free from compulsory induction into the armed forces proper.

The initial manpower supply-base was therefore usually from WWI veterans – although they proved too middle-aged to take the strain of a hard life underground and were soon stood down or promoted. Others usually well suited were farmers or farm workers, miners and quarrymen, foresters and estate workers. A criminal record was no absolute bar to enrolment and young men under the legal age of military service were often welcomed. Poachers and gamekeepers, both with built-in stealth, an ability to live off the land, and experience of taking good care of themselves in outdoor conditions, were valued candidates.

As a general rule, intellectuals or academics were less in evidence. However, in some areas a supply of white-collared, 'educated' men was typical rather than the exception. With them, some rather unconventional patrols emerged. Qualities similar to the robust mainstream were still of importance but the men selected tended to come from specialised centres of employment, such as the Admiralty Buildings at Bath and the Marconi factory at Chelmsford in Essex. These Auxiliers did not, therefore, necessarily have their Operational Base underground and out in the countryside, where the majority were located. In early studies they were, for the purposes of distinction, called 'urban' patrols by researchers, although there is no corroboration of that title in official records.

There has also been confusion with other non-conformist stay-behind units using the same, or similar, instruction manuals as Auxiliers but, apparently, under the direct supervision of the secret services. It now seems more than likely that these – and the urban patrols – were not directly under Gubbins's command. Indeed it is probable that they had specific, one-off targets of potentially strategic significance, identified by Section D of MI6, rather than the local roving commission of their more rurally situated comrades. Some of these maverick mavericks had specific training as assassins.

Most Auxilier veterans insist that they had nothing at all to do with the Home Guard. It is often true that, from the moment of their enrolment in the Auxiliary Units, any connection they had with the HG was severed; some had their HG enrolment forms torn up before they were released into the Auxunits. But it is now known from available records that LDVs and HGs were specifically regarded as the principal selection ground. Reasonably enough, following their special training and tight conditions of secrecy, Auxiliers came to look upon themselves as a superior force – and so did their officers. Right at the end of their war service, Colonel Frank Douglas was still reporting that: 'To compare the Auxiliary Units with the Home Guard is like comparing the Brigade of Guards with the Salvation Army.' He was undoubtedly right and it was a point of view proudly and steadfastly maintained by many Auxiliers themselves. But it is clear that more often than not, they were looked upon as 'Home Guard patrols' at Coleshill and by soldiers of the Scout Sections.

Don Handscombe was in no doubt about how his own selection derived – not from a direct call to meet Captain Croft, or his successor, offering him patrol leadership, but from his early voluntary membership of the LDV ('with an armband and ragged sort of training, and using our own shotguns') and then, as the Volunteers were formally absorbed in midsummer 1940, the Home Guard:

> Strangely, although we lived nearer to Daws Heath and Rayleigh than Leigh-on-Sea, we were actually in Leigh postal parish area, and I had to join the Leigh-on-Sea Home Guard.
>
> Because of the danger of invasion, it was a Restricted Area. People were persuaded to leave. The roads were empty and a lot of people went inland. There were restrictions on movement and those with motorcars had a special licence and plate so it could be easily recognised and that they were legally in the Area. Trains and bus services were stopped or at least subject to being stopped and questioned by police.
>
> On the north side of the Thames the beaches were done with defences, scaffolding, tank traps and barbed wire, mines and pill boxes.

Don's extensive domain of glasshouses was miraculously left undamaged by the air Battle of Britain overhead – and he never heard even a local murmur about the Auxiliary Units while serving with the HG. However, during the winter of 1940, he was approached in the local pub by a chap he knew vaguely, Fred Harris, who told him something of his special group – it turned out he was with the Thundersley Patrol – and invited him to join. As Don wanted to do anything possible to assist the war effort he agreed to do so but, first, was asked to meet a civilian cut-out called Marion Green from the nearby town of Hockley. He passed Don along the line for interview with Captain C. G. Ford, Commander of Group 8 (Southend) Auxiliary Units. After a talk, Captain Ford told him he would let him know whether he had been accepted.

Within five days, and presumably after character checks of some sort, he was informed that he was in. Don had not been interviewed directly by his Intelligence Officer, Captain R. F. H. Darwall-Smith, and nothing has been discovered to indicate the extent of the vetting process in those early days. The names of later entrants, however, were passed through the records of MI5, Special Branch and the local police before clearance was given. Some Auxiliers are reported to have put the chief constable on their personal black list: knowing their names as he did, he represented a threat to safety and would have been among the first weak links to be disposed of. Most, however, placed him among the 'powers-that-be' and, with such a special rating, exempted from potential execution.

Don soon discovered a second tier of the vetting process; it existed within the patrol itself. Although final decisions were made by the leader, the members had a say, too. While it was primarily intended to arrive at a consensus on operational matters – a procedure later endorsed by the SAS – it also covered new entrants. Unless they pulled their weight, and turned up for training in foul weather as well as fair, they were rejected by core members of the patrol who, being hard men themselves, left the reject in no doubt of the physical risk he would run if any of their secrets were let out of the bag. No court martial or resort to King's Regulations was called for. Several potential members of the Thundersley Patrol were stood down in this way because they lacked commitment. If they failed in training how could they be expected to perform reliably in action? This accounts for much of the high quality of their security both during and after the war, and the fact that the patrol was rarely up to full strength.

This authority from within was common. In the Castle Rising Patrol in Norfolk, for example, two successive leaders were 'disposed of' similarly, after the rank-and-file had determined that their allegiance was in doubt – one was even suspected of holding secret pro-Nazi sympathies.

Don himself had been subjected to filtration-selection under the cellular system, a vital ingredient for the patrol's safety. It incorporated a cut-out procedure before joining and, in most cases, the destruction of any identifying papers in Home Guard records. Only then did the recruit get to know all the other members of his own patrol. It was intended that not a single local person (other, perhaps. than the chief constable) would know the names or even the existence of adjacent patrols, and certainly not the whereabouts of their Operational Bases. The application of this fundamental policy of secrecy provided an almost comprehensive guarantee that no one could disclose, either inadvertently or under forceful interrogation from the enemy, the identity of more than, say, the half dozen members of his own patrol.

With local variations, this circuitous and secret introduction and enrolment into the Auxiliary Units Operational Patrols was going on in many parts of Britain, in particular those areas thought most likely to be invaded by an enemy poised just across the English Channel.

In Sussex, for example, Bill Webber, leader of the Firle Patrol, was recorded as joining Auxunits from mid-June 1940 – two weeks or so *before* they were officially in operation. It is a clear indication in otherwise spectacularly unclear records, that he joined the Home Guard first and that date remained as a record of his admission to the Auxunits. These points may seem academic now but they did lead to several cases of drawn-out injustice fifty years later, when Auxiliers were at last allowed to apply for the 1939–1945 Defence Medal and had to establish three years' service to an initially implacable and unhelpful Ministry of Defence Army Medal Office.

The Cooke family of brothers and cousins living in Sussex were admitted to the Icklesham Patrol *en bloc* – and in 1942 would win the All-England training competition at Coleshill. Alex Rogers was called into the Ugborough Patrol in Devon and Walter Tucker to Coad's Green in Cornwall. Hampshire, Dorset and Somerset were well under way. Across the Bristol Channel, a dozen or so patrols were created in Pembroke. Surprisingly far from any invasion beaches, patrols were set up in Hereford and Worcester. These were maverick units in many ways. It now seems probable that their purpose was not to cover inland areas behind invasion beaches, but specifically to protect the surrounds of Worcester where a last-ditch defence of the royal family and the government was at the planning stage.

At Cymmer, near Part Talbot in South Wales, where WWI veteran and local Scoutmaster Wally Thomas was searching for the right type of man, he co-opted senior Scout Roy Coleman as soon as he was seventeen and old enough to join the Home Guard. In due course Roy achieved the perfect cover for his secret enrolment into the Auxunits, being issued with two complete sets of battledress – one with 'GHQ 202 Battalion' shoulder flashes and the other with 'F Company, Home Guard'. The downside was that, in addition to a full daily shift in the local pit, he had to parade with both the local HG *and* the Auxunit to keep up the pretence.

With very few exceptions, the men taken into the Auxiliary Units were selected from the Home Guard. The link is undeniable.

*

From August 1940, with the selection of personnel well under way, Colin Gubbins moved along to the next stages – training stay-behinds and providing their hideaways, as Operational Bases were known for a short while (until the title was seen to have a negative, non-belligerent context).

The Coleshill HQ and its officer, NCO and other rank staff remained the focal point for training throughout the existence of the Auxiliary Units.

Major Beyts was in control and responsible for the high standard of the programme. With both targets – in the form of old cars, dummy aircraft and tanks, and oil drums filled with noxious contents – and ranges for firearms and hand-grenade practice in position, it was time to assemble the 'students'. From the earliest days it was obvious that not all Auxiliers could get there. They still had to make a living; transport was a problem; their cover duties in the region of their home – varying from Home Guard parades to service as air raid wardens or in the Royal Observer Corps – were essential commitments too; and although Auxiliers themselves never thought to take advantage of their status as unpaid, part-timers even the Army was reluctant to subject them to the full displeasures and often archaic disciplines of King's Regulations.

The first courses started as early as August 1940, with the staff – before the building was 'blitzed' – coming down from Whitehall Place each weekend to set up the programme, the targets and the catering. Incredibly, the provision of food was – before the arrival of the Army Catering Corps – in the hands of Major Beyts's wife who, it seems, made this her immediate contribution to the war effort.

Training patrol leaders and their deputies was the first priority; Scout Sections followed along, as they were shortly to set the lead out there in front-line areas. A pattern was established for students to arrive at Coleshill on Friday evenings, followed by a meal in the servants' quarters. Then, after a briefing there would be night exercises in the estate grounds and overnight accommodation in the stables – mercifully if basically adapted for human habitation. The weekend would continue with full-scale weapons and explosives training, close quarters combat (both man-to-man and with fighting knives), camouflage practice, manoeuvres, more night exercises, and lectures; and departure for home on the Sunday evening. Later courses were also conducted to a model OB built in the estate grounds. It is still there for guided tours by National Trust visitors.

For some of the Patrol Leaders it was a first in many ways. Not all had previously stayed away from home overnight and wives were suspicious. (At a presentation for the Museum of the British Resistance Organisation in Suffolk sixty years after stand-down, a widow came forward to announce that the '202 Badge she had just been shown' was the first indication she had ever had of her husband's WWII Auxiliary Unit service.) None had fired a Tommy gun or thrown a No. 36 Grenade; none of them had previously enjoyed Army rations; and very few had given a lecture themselves. Now they were all required to do so, if only for five minutes or so. This was an initiation into the importance of their role as patrol leaders. While they were to run a democratic unit, with collective discussion encouraged, final decisions would be theirs. As this included selecting targets, and how, where and when to attack them, a leader's decision-making aptitude was of major significance if the patrol was to survive for any useful time.

There is unanimous agreement among veterans of the efficacy of the courses, the thoroughness of the practical instruction and the indelible impression made upon them by this introduction into the sharp end of Army life. Not a moment was wasted, it seems. Major Beyts's contribution was subsequently acknowledged with the award of the MBE.

Don Handscombe, the newest entrant in the Thundersley Patrol, thought that he was both too busy and too junior in Auxunit service to be the Patrol Leader, but agreed to attend one of the first, but not *the* first, Coleshill course some time in 1941. Together with Fred Harris, the man who did soon take over the patrol, he travelled from Benfleet to Fenchurch Street in London, then by Underground to Paddington, and on to Swindon on a rail warrant. Both were in uniform, displaying an Auxiliary Units' flash, although in local training they still usually just wore Army denims over their working clothes. They carried revolvers in standard webbing holsters, Army haversacks with a few personal belongings, and gas masks; with so many other men travelling in uniform, they attracted no special attention.

He is unsure how he got from Swindon to Highworth but remembers presenting himself at the Post Office there:

> The two of us went in and the postmistress was selling stamps. She said 'Yes?' We said quietly who we were and that we had come to Coleshill. Without looking up she asked for our names, which we told her, and she said 'Wait outside by the post box.' She evidently checked up with Coleshill and within ten minutes an army truck pulled up outside.
>
> We had rail warrants but some of our people travelled the whole way directly from their patrols. We were checked in. Our billets were bunks with chicken wire in stables out the back. There were 20 to 25 men on the course. We had good food and mixed freely, using our own names.

We had an opening address and a lecture on communications instructing your patrol on how to select a target and how it would be carried out. The course was intensive and very efficient. We didn't have much time to condense the programme and went at it all the time.

The students worked in syndicates, in turn taking the part of patrol leader. Don's instructors were carefully selected and, after his own lecture on target selection and *modus operandi*, they took it to pieces and encouraged discussion on his ideas and performance. He was sent back later on a refresher course and found it almost identical in content, but equally convincing.

With this scant but vital experience, the Patrol Leaders returned with a lot to tell the other Auxiliers. But, obviously enough, such limited know-how was not in itself sufficient to prepare them all for the real thing. It was here that the Scout Sections, still often only just a nose ahead of their Home Guards, filled the gap between Coleshill and the enemy. It was they who, with full-time application, set the standards for cross-country marches and night navigation; for demonstration and practice with weaponry, explosives and grenades; and all of this on an ever-escalating scale as supplies and equipment became increasingly available.

Scout Sections were just one of a number of improvements brought about as the Auxiliary Units became steadily more sophisticated. And, by the autumn of 1940, updated intelligence assessments affecting the general military situation influenced the direction of their progress, too. The intelligence community more or less agreed that the Germans would be unable to mount a cross-Channel invasion during the winter months. The principal factor was simply the weather. There was not the remotest prospect that the German high command would consider launching unsuitable troop-carrying craft, mostly commandeered from continental canal fleets and hastily modified for sea conditions. Even allowing for the energy and ingenuity which German engineers were showing in the conversion process, it was obvious to everyone that the chances of surviving a Channel crossing in winter, and then setting up a chain of supply craft, were non-existent. It is also likely that decryption of the enemy's signals was revealing at least something of Hitler's intention to leave it to Göring's Luftwaffe to crush Britain, while developing his own preoccupation with the attack on Soviet Russia.

In turn, this reduced-threat breathing space for Britain undermined the potential usefulness of stay-behinds, exposing them to criticism from opportunistic military non-believers and leaving their continued existence in the balance. In the draft of his final report to the War Office (the report itself has never seen the light of day), Major Nigel Oxenden recorded:

> Rumour had it that [the Auxiliary Units] final abandonment was avoided by a timely dinner at the Cavalry Club. In any case, the Commander set about strengthening its position, as well as its striking power, by the permanent attachment of regular personnel.

'The Commander' was, of course, Colonel Gubbins and the 'regular personnel' the men of the Scout Sections, begged, borrowed and sometimes stolen from Army COs, not always aware of why they had agreed to the detachment of some of their best soldiers. Such diplomatic manoeuvring – a Gubbins hallmark – was seen again when he was confronted by multiple international challenges in his later job as the head of the burgeoning and, in many quarters massively unpopular, Special Operations Executive.

Auxiliary Units' Scout Sections became the private army of the area Intelligence Officer and were used by him in different ways. First of all, however, he had to train these regulars to train the Auxiliers. It required un-learning conventional disciplines and certain modifications of standard military manuals. In many cases, Scout Sections' conventional training was adapted to demonstrate to the civilian patrols how the soldiers themselves proposed to fight behind the lines. It was a new concept both to IOs and Scout Sections but, generally, they amassed useful skills, both in the field and as demonstrators and lecturers.

In Essex, following the first of his two courses at Coleshill – with his IO showing foresight by training him not as the deputy but as patrol leader in case Harris was killed in action – Don Handscombe continued his training with one of the Essex Regiment Scout Sections stationed in Rivers House at Earls Colne, a dozen miles west of Colchester. This was too far for the men to march and all five Southend patrols were taken there several times by Army truck. They were billeted in the open or, during really bad weather, in outhouses and each course took two or three days. With a river running through an area of sandpits, it proved ideal for weapons and explosives training and demonstrations.

During one visit, 'Private' Handscombe demonstrated an explosion under a simulated railway bridge, for the benefit of a visiting 'General and his Staff officers': 'I set it up single-handed with him and his Staff watching me, but it went alright and he was very pleased with it. It actually blew one of his Staff officers off his shooting stick!' The 'General' was later identified as Colonel Lord Glanusk, CO of Auxunits at Coleshill for a year from February 1942.

Joint patrol, night-attack manoeuvres were also arranged. The targets were aircraft positioned at nearby Marks Tey RAF airfield. Each patrol made a simulated attack, sometimes with Auxiliers from other patrols joining the regular RAF guard units as defenders: 'I believe we had two goes and on one occasion we successfully laid our simulated explosives on several planes and withdrew without trouble. But I think the second time we were captured.'

Duncan Sandys had assured the Prime Minister that 'their activities will also include sniping' and the Thundersley Patrol had a .22-inch rifle, equipped with both a silencer (or 'sound-suppressor') and telescopic sight. The members were all good marksmen and needed no special instruction. Taking it in turns to keep the weapon at home, they were in no doubt of its intended use: 'It was an assassination weapon and we were aware of, but not issued with, a list of collaborators.'

Scout Sections in Suffolk were in regular operation with their 'Home Guards', as they insisted on calling them. The Scout Section under Lieutenant 'Mac' McIntyre was billeted at the Mill House in Cransford, near Framlingham. Not only did they take every opportunity to train and toughen themselves as well as their Auxiliers, they also prepared two OBs for themselves and set fine standards of night patrols in the spring by stalking a nearby mansion house, clandestinely removing its daffodil crop undetected, and transporting it in a 15 cwt army truck to be sold on the black market at Ipswich.

In Norfolk, Scout Sections spent most of their time digging OBs both for themselves and their Home Guard patrols. Strong evidence exists, however, that the Wroxham, Norfolk, Scout Section was unique in that one of its two OBs held a radio for the local Auxunits' Special Duties Section, a link which existed rarely, if ever, anywhere else. Undoubtedly each Scout Section very much reflected the ideas and inventiveness of its individual Intelligence Officer, in spite of the stream of directives originating from Coleshill. This also, perhaps, goes some way to establishing that the officers and men in the field had been well selected in the first place.

It is an interesting fact that Scout Sections simply disappeared as they were stood down from 1943 onward. If secrecy was to be preserved by dispersing the men it worked well. Witnesses and records have been few and far between. David Lampe's otherwise well-informed book hardly mentions them at all. It would not be a surprise if some subalterns were transferred into other secret services. As usual, however, a few papers, dated during Gubbins's days as Auxunits' CO, did find their way into the National Archives and, at the end of the 1990s, a couple of eloquent NCOs were brave enough to show themselves above the barricade of secrecy.

Chapter Eleven

The Crest of a Wave –
And the Trough?

'This would mean that their remoter ones [i.e. Operational Patrols] would have to travel considerable distances, possibly devoting a night to the journey, neglect any targets of their own that might crop up, fight on ground that was utterly strange to them, and spend a third night getting back.'

Major Nigel Oxenden

This appraisal of Colonel Major's group attack innovation from the officer who, in 1942, became head of training at Coleshill, demonstrates the lukewarm reception this new plan must have received from some veterans, particularly those with experience of irregular warfare – a qualification lacked by the new CO of the Auxiliary Units himself. At the beginning of 1941 when this change of strategy was implemented, Major Beyts was still in charge of Auxunits' training and his veteran status was beyond question. His opinion about group attacks is not recorded. Indeed he may have been the fountainhead of the whole idea. However, there seems a strong possibility that the staff at Coleshill were, at best, divided from the outset.

Professional loyalty prevented any sign of these doubts being communicated to Auxiliers as they came to Coleshill, or lined up for nighttime and weekend instruction with Scout Sections somewhere near their home OBs. There is not the slightest clue that this change of basic policy, abolishing as it did their main safety net of cellular secrecy, was ever made known, or even understood in detail, by the stay-behinds, to whom the added risk factor would surely have been significant once embroiled in action. According to Don Handscombe in Essex, the new scheme was never formally explained to his patrol. It was, instead, introduced in stages, sometimes under the pretext that one undermanned patrol could help out another, instead of remaining entirely in isolation. Certainly, available firepower could be enhanced – although, it will be recalled, direct confrontation with the enemy had always been discouraged. Until now, Gubbins's 'Guerrilla's Creed' had taught the merits of living to fight another day by leaving full frontal conflict with the enemy to conventional troops.

Colonel Major came to the Auxiliary Units from the Military Intelligence Directorate (and appears to have returned there after the war), whereas Gubbins, Beyts and Oxenden had all seen active service. With a formal military background, it has to be asked if Colonel Major was the best man for the job, arriving as he did with no previous knowledge of the Auxiliary Units and without having been a party to the irregular activities blueprinted and initiated by MI(R).

Oxenden described the new CO's arrival at Coleshill, when he '. . . made his debut at a weekend course disguised as a Home Guard, both to learn much that he probably didn't know, and to see the unit from a viewpoint that would never again be accessible to him.'

This covert induction to fieldwork may, in some respects, appear to have had merit. It is anyway a clear indication of a man who, without the benefit of appropriate practical experience, could never lead from the front. While this was not necessarily an all-encompassing prohibition on good leadership, Colonel Major's new posting was not in any way normal or formal. Once the balloon went up his decisions could mean life or death for both operational Auxiliers and Scout Sections. And herein lies the weakness of his group attack idea.

On paper, the new plan may have been intended to develop some useful advantages. It fitted more closely within formal military practices, for example; it would be better understood by local Army commanders; and helped compensate for the chronic manpower shortage persisting in some areas. But the extended job-description for the group attack system was entirely contradictory to the localised, silent and individual commitment first outlined by MI(R) and firmly followed under Gubbins. It certainly called for dramatic changes to Auxiliers' training.

No longer working as individual patrols under the sole command of their leader – now with the quasi-formal rank of sergeant – their training would involve attacks in conjunction with other patrols, under a Group Commander – now called a lieutenant or captain but recorded as a commissioned officer neither in the Army nor the Home Guard. Don Handscombe, still not a Patrol Leader but one of the many Auxiliers showing above average dedication, was next offered such a 'commission'. However, with consuming commitments to the family business, he again turned down the offer although, in a private arrangement with his GC, it was agreed that, in the absence of the appointed leader, he would take command of his patrol as soon as 'Action Stations!' was called.

Researchers endeavouring to slot the Auxiliary Units into some sort of recognisable official pigeonhole run a huge risk of being confused by this informality.

When in the uniform which increasingly took the place of denims over working clothes, 'pips' or 'stripes' were now displayed. Auxiliers became less and less like a band of secret saboteurs and, although still under the command of their IO, more like just another arm of the Home Guard.

Some Group Commanders were selected from outstanding Patrol Leaders. They needed practical experience for their new tasks, or imagination in lieu, and also time to learn about administration. The final total of GCs and assistants 'commissioned' in Colonel Major's time exceeded 200; Coleshill provided nineteen courses for them in nearly four years.

GCs tended to come from the educated, better-off, and older former Patrol Leaders. Patrol reshuffles followed, with corporals being upgraded to leaders, or 'sergeants', and new entrants trawled to keep up the numbers. By this time it was clear that young men coped better than older ones with the hard life underground and were consequently preferred as trial replacements. Some outstanding GCs came to the fore, of course. In central Essex, fruit farmer Keith Seabrook distinguished himself with a large command, and this was recognised with the award of an MBE at the end of the war. In south-east Essex, Captain Ford also commanded the thorough respect of all his Auxiliers.

His time in the Auxiliary Units left a lifelong impression on the late Deryck Neville who, in a declaration to the Ministry of Defence in support of his application for the Defence Medal more than fifty years after stand-down, remembered every detail of the set-up:

> I commenced working for J. W. Garner and Co, farmers, at Rising Lodge, King's Lynn on Monday, February 10th 1941. During that week both Mr Garner and myself received Notices from the Ministry of Labour directing us to report the next Sunday to enrol in the Home Guard.
>
> We paraded at the Chemical Works Sports Ground, South Lynn, and were drilled and marched and told to report again the following

Sunday. We were then given uniform but before the parade we were approached and asked if we would join something special – where there would be no drilling, etc.

We agreed to join the Auxiliary Units and were told that we would cease to exist as far as the Home Guard was concerned. Lieutenant Newnes said that he was the only person to have any record of our joining. The two of us were taken straight from the HG Parade. If asked we were to say we were in another branch.

In spite of an overwhelming case and abundant collateral, Deryck Neville's medal application was refused.

Neville had joined the Auxiliary Units during the life of the group system. The only record shows that 'Private TBBS.64/3 Neville D. G. H.' was in the Castle Rising Patrol in Norfolk. In March 1943, he transferred to the Middleton Patrol ('part of Group 8 – whatever that was' as he admitted), whose OB was on land where he worked for the War Agricultural Committee. He remembered Captain J. L. Hardy, DSO, MC, taking over as GC, with Lieutenant M. Newnes as assistant. The patrols in the group at the time were Castle Rising, Mintlyn, Gayton, Narford, Downham and Middleton, and the originality and professionalism of Captain Hardy's instruction 'made a good impression on them all'.

If the balloon went up, the intention was that Group Commanders would stay behind to co-ordinate their patrols but many commanders were unsuited – some very much so – and a trend developed to employ them more as administrators and less as action-men. For often hard-pressed Intelligence Officers, the bonus was a useful reduction in work.

All this helps to highlight the confusion, never resolved, over the role of the IOs themselves as the enemy approached. Were they to stay behind with the Auxiliers or not? Some IOs definitely intended to do so. Captain Norman Field in Kent, for example, not only trained his staff to operate from underground with him, but also created two OBs, 'Big Kate' and 'Little Kate', for his HQ squad. Whether or not an IO intended to remain in the field, the creation of the group attack system did nothing to overcome the never-clarified problem of communications between Auxiliers behind enemy lines and the nearest British Army CO. The role for Group Commanders was no clearer.

Before he moved on from the Auxiliary Units on 2 July 1942, four months after Colonel Major's replacement as CO by Colonel Lord Glanusk, Major

Beyts tried to sort out the problem by defining a positive course of stay-behind action for the IO. There is no record of a nationally implemented decision, however, and the uncertainty remained. Much depended upon an IO's understanding with local Army commanders, whose authority at this stage seems to have over-ridden that of Coleshill. The local CO's wish was paramount and led to a lack of standardisation. Some IOs would stay with their men; others intended to cross the front line regularly with orders for the Group Commander to disseminate to his patrols.

This was the highest risk strategy imaginable. The danger of capture during clandestine crossings, possible exposure to gunfire, either friendly or unfriendly, and the complete absence of radio communications as an alternative way of conveying instructions to the men in their OBs would all have militated against any understanding by the patrol leader of his best course of action in support of the British defence force in his area. The capture of an Intelligence Officer could have forced from him the whereabouts of his Group Commander and all their patrols down the line.

Somewhere in the middle of all this stood Group Commanders. Too old for irregular active service, they were dangerously aware of the whereabouts of six or seven patrols if captured. They, too, were unable to communicate either with them or their IO – other than by word of mouth, hidden messages, or runner. Some patrols asked if the risks attendant upon their GC's presence underground were worth whatever co-ordination he was intending to supply. Although their patriotism was not in doubt, Auxiliers sometimes mistrusted GCs for other reasons. Taking too much drink was one of them. Indeed, so strongly did the men of the Stratford St Andrew Patrol in central Suffolk feel about the disadvantages of a GC's presence, that they unanimously agreed that he would be their first victim once the call to arms came. They even selected the executioner – Hector Wade, the biggest man. And he chose the garrotte to do the job!

In comfortable retrospect, it now seems inconceivable that the group attack system was ever seriously introduced as a tactic likely to be suitable for behind-the-lines irregular warfare.

Many of the problems were only sorted out by Lord Glanusk *after* the most serious danger of invasion had passed. Major Oxenden later explained that the third CO's greatest service was to throw doubt upon the wisdom of 'elaboration', both in essentials and detail. In other words, he abandoned the group attack system. This allowed Auxiliers, no longer required to work in concert with others and in blissful ignorance of a high-level hiatus, to return more or less to their intended role as independent units, following natural preferences and sensible instincts, rather than orders from above which restricted their discretionary action. They were again free to operate in their own, well-known localities until the end, whatever it was destined to be. They were again their own masters.

The meaning of Major Oxenden's comment that they would no longer be asked to think is now clearer. Patrol leaders would not have to think *in step with others*. They were permitted to move back to square one and do it all themselves.

Highlighting these problems, in what amounted to continuous experimental manoeuvres, was probably one of the greatest services provided by the operational Auxiliary Units, even if entirely unconsciously. Their empirical involvement in a brand new, untried form of warfare often revealed flaws in proposed undercover and irregular operations and some means at least of dealing with them. Some problems, however, were never cured until after WWII was over. Technical difficulties associated with close quarters communications in the field would, for example, never be overcome until sturdy, lightweight and secure radio transceivers became available. And they were still a very long way off.[†]

*

Much progress had been made before Colonel Major took over. The HQ was already operational at Coleshill, together with training courses, the content of which, though with modifications as experience was gained, remained mostly unchanged. For example, although Auxiliers knew the local patch where they were operating like the backs of their hands, map reading was still a priority subject. The *Few Typical Questions* pamphlet supplied to Willie Ingram, Patrol Leader of the Grange Patrol in Banffshire, remain valid to this day. They included:

† It will be read in a later chapter that one near-miss was a special radio transceiver issued to the Special Duties Section of the Auxiliary Units. Although not portable in the walkie-talkie sense, this was very nearly the real thing. Unfortunately for the men of the Operational Patrols, their chance to use this radio was vetoed in the cause of the secrecy which kept them operationally isolated from the SDS. The Army never had access to the design, it seems because the radio set was the product of foresighted genius in the SIS, which ensured that it remained within its own sphere of influence. Even today, details are not available and, as we shall see, the task of producing a copy is monumental.

What is a contour? What is True North? What does < mean on a road? What direction is 202.5 degrees? Show a road crossing under a railway. What scale is 1/15840? Give the number of degrees for SE, NNW, ESE, SE by E. What is compass error? Give the back bearing when the straight bearing is 158 degrees? Why can you not set a compass at the Base? How would you find True North at night without a compass? When contours are very close together what does it signify?

An advanced training manual disguised in an otherwise plain cover as the *Calendar 1937* had been put together by Wilkinson for MI(R) as war broke out; this was republished as *Calendar 1938*, and finally, probably in 1942, as *The Countryman's Diary 1939*. The ironic, and barely disguised threat implied in the careful wording on the nondescript cover, is significant for all to see now. It might have passed unnoticed by a harassed member of a German search patrol – if there ever was one:

Highworth's Fertilisers
Do Their Stuff Unseen
Until You See
Results!
With the Compliments Of
Highworth & Co
**You Will Find the Name Highworth
Wherever Quick Results
Are Required**

The pages within summarised the dirty tricks expected of Auxiliers and gave detailed instructions and diagrams for the use of explosives, booby traps, fuses and incendiary devices. With little doubt, these were mainly the work of MD1 under Millis Jefferis and they were, together with Gubbins's original booklets on irregular warfare, the basic instruction medium for Allied subversives through the whole of WWII. Thousands of similar booklets were translated and issued to Allied irregular forces in every theatre of war.

Intelligence assessments at GHQ, even with an improvement in the war situation, still generally agreed that the danger of invasion was far from over. With such top-level backing and the arrival of new and improved equipment – explosive devices, weapons, and uniforms – the Auxiliary Units under

Colonel Major were developing into a different force from that originally envisaged. They received, for example, belated acceptance even among many previously sceptical senior Army officers although, quite reasonably, they were still seen by them only as a last-ditch supplement to the regular forces. Increasingly, however, they could be fitted into a formal tactical framework if the balloon went up.

Field training also went energetically ahead, sometimes in conjunction with the Army and the local Home Guard. Don Handscombe recalled one aspect:

> We were never issued with poison pills but we did have morphine and orders on how to deal with members of the patrol if they were too badly injured to survive.
>
> One night I was chosen to be the linkman between our Group and the next, which was at Dengie. I was picked up by army truck and driven in the pitch black to a place I recognised as Rettendon and given a map reference to go to. It was Dengie, on the Essex marshes about 15 miles away. I had to make my way across country and the other patrols were out looking for me. I was able to travel by road for some of the way but nearly ran into patrols, so I had to resort to crossing fields and woods. It was quite a trip and I was just about all-in, soaking wet, black as ink and very pleased with myself at not getting caught – at about dawn.
>
> I got back in time to go to work for the day.

One evening when he was driving to shooting practice at Fambridge, Don – in denims and plimsolls and carrying his revolver in a holster – was stopped by the police. As instructed, he told them he was with the Home Guard:

> . . . a very sharp special constable said 'Get out of the car, you don't look like a Home Guard to me.' They were not satisfied and I was taken to Rochford police station and put in a cell. I was not disarmed and gave them Captain Ford's telephone number. He came along quickly and was arrested too and we were both taken to Southend and put in a cell there. Our Intelligence Officer had to come down from Whitehall and secure our release and from then on we were all issued with a piece of paper which said – 'You must ask no questions of the Bearer but phone this number.'

The Operational Bases, so critical to the success and survival of the small guerrilla bands of Auxiliers, also benefited from improved facilities. The arrival of 'elephant shelters' early in 1941 transformed OB construction and habitability and, at the same time, pioneers, engineers and, in Romney Marsh in Kent, civilian contractors, turned up to erect them. In Kent the contractors travelled in closed vans to camouflage just where they were digging and building. Their collective expertise replaced early Auxilier and Scout Section DIY. Instead of shallow, roughly rectangular, hastily dug hides, constructed with locally available timber and corrugated sheeting – but usually without any system of ventilation – Auxiliers could now look forward to certain comforts, although life below ground was only for the toughest. Above all, they could go to sleep without the risk of asphyxiation as all the candles went out and their canaries died.

While not all OBs were the same, many were connected by a standard, WD-issue field telephone to an Observer's Post – sometimes referred to as a 'one man OB' situated overlooking the more likely approaches to the cover in which the main OB was built. One man was left for the day in this well-concealed position to warn of approaching friends, or the enemy, delinquent schoolboys or courting couples. At times he was also a scout, responsible for identifying useful intelligence and reconnoitring a target for the main team at night. At Stratford St Andrew in Suffolk, the hide was entered through a hollow tree, close to the main A12 trunk road. Lookout was through old, carefully camouflaged 'bunny-holes'.

For the duration of the group attack system, the OP was also a rendezvous point for other patrols. Selected members of a group were made aware of the secret location of other patrols' OPs. Whether he was there or not, the observer's telephone could be used to contact the main chamber. Various experiments were carried out during this time to pinpoint nightly targets. Sometimes this was the observer's job; at others a scout – one of the six or seven members of the patrol – was left out to reconnoitre by day on foot, and return to brief the Patrol Leader in time for sabotage operations after nightfall. For a time, and if the full patrol consisted of seven men – leaving all too little space for those resting inside the main chamber – two men stayed out on reconnaissance. To get their sleep, they were then omitted from the team for the night's operations,

After some trial and error, the final inventory of stores issued from HQ for seven men for each patrol included:

Holsters, groundsheets, blankets, rubber boots (agricultural type), water bottles, carriers and slings – one for each man; a wire cutter, monocular and case, a Tilley lamp, two Primus stoves, and one Elsan chemical closet. One pair telephones, half a mile of cable, Type E. A first aid set (with morphia), water sterilisation sets, and three shell dressings. Composite ration packs, 10 gallons paraffin, 1 gallon rum.

The gallon jar of rum was only to be opened to relieve pain in the event of injury, or in the face of imminent capture – a tot or two might help to extend the time an Auxilier could be expected to resist interrogation and torture. The issue was plainly not for their pleasure.

In 1944 an ungrateful War Department demanded the return of every jar of rum, unopened and still with an official seal. Unfortunately, having recruited men with initiative in the first place, it failed to notice that many – while still apparently sealed – were filled only with a liquid like cold green tea. Or something looking remarkably similar!

Chapter Twelve

Operational Bases

'In order to stay behind, we needed somewhere to stay: and by sucking up to the Sappers we had already brought into being what might very loosely be called a network of subterranean hide-outs in which not only the striking force – Strix and about fifteen other idiots – but our far-flung, hand-picked collaborators in the Home Guard, would bide their time before emerging to wreak, in a variety of ill-defined ways, havoc among the invaders.'

'Strix', alias Peter Fleming, in The Spectator *8 July 1966*

If the operational patrols of the Auxiliary Units were to have any value as stay-behind bands of saboteurs, even in the short term of their life expectancy, a hideout for them and their stores was essential. The form and location of the early bases relied upon the ingenuity and local knowledge of the members of each patrol, and the encouragement of their Intelligence Officer.

In Kent, XII Corps had already set up a few hideouts for the Observation Unit, with the aid of the muscle power and know-how of the Royal Engineers and the Pioneer Corps. In Somerset two patrols adapted space in disused coal mines; two more used icehouses in the grounds of eighteenth-century houses at Prior Park and Kelston; and another was set up in the chambers of an old stone quarry. A patrol in Scotland modified a cavern whose entrance was behind a waterfall. In Essex, as we know, Captain Croft used his father's garden shed to store explosives. In Suffolk the Stratford St Andrew patrol simply took over, and made basically habitable, an old shepherd's hut dumped in a wood. Many patrols dug a rectangular hole in a wood, lined the walls and roof with timber-supported corrugated iron sheeting, arranged access through a tunnel or shaft of similar construction, and covered the lot with soil. Many of these were inadequate in every respect, but were tolerated by the hardy souls who were obliged to inhabit them until something better was put together by their IOs.

The best of the home-made OBs were constructed more substantially of brick or block or concrete, with soil camouflage overhead, supported by railway sleepers or – in one case at least – old railway lines. The specifications for an acceptable life underground were sufficient space for five, six or seven men to rest within, basic food preparation facilities, store space for food and water and, separately, for weaponry and explosives, and some sort of toilet arrangement. In November 1941 a drawing was produced which endeavoured to take these requirements into account, and to provide access through a camouflaged trapdoor and down shaft, and a form of escape tunnel. While this drawing had always to be adapted for local conditions and the availability of suitable materials, it remained the basic format for future Operational Bases, and a model was established at Coleshill to demonstrate to men under instruction. It was titled a Home Guard Shelter, but other titles proliferate in records. 'Hideaway' was abandoned as too negative and unadventurous. 'Hideout' was favoured instead, but OBs were also called 'funk holes' or 'bunkers'. Auxiliers themselves nearly always came to know their hideout as 'our OB'.

The key to the standard design was the provision of an 'elephant shelter' constructed from curved corrugated iron sheets to form a semi-circular tunnel about 21 feet long and over eight feet in diameter. When enclosed at each end with a supporting (often blast-preventing) wall and buried underground, this shelter solved a number of problems. It was time- and cost-saving, and no longer depended solely upon available (or acquired) materials. This construction could also be made reasonably watertight and – when fitted with hidden piping – capable of some sort of ventilation. With these new shelters, considerable local initiatives were still called for to provide a camouflaged entrance shaft and trapdoor, and a last-ditch escape tunnel. The better OBs also sported blast walls to help the defenders survive grenade bursts in the shaft or exit tunnel. Furnishings were sparse; wooden bunks covered with slats or wire netting, a table, one or two chairs and a chemical toilet were all that most contained.

In Essex, both Thundersley and Canvey Island Patrols – having a total of only four Auxiliers in each – were never up to strength. At first, both prepared their own OBs. This was a debilitating drain on stamina and morale as, night after night, they had to dig, mix cement and lay bricks. The group system did allow them to help one another with particularly difficult tasks but at Thundersley progress was slow, as the selected site remained stubbornly

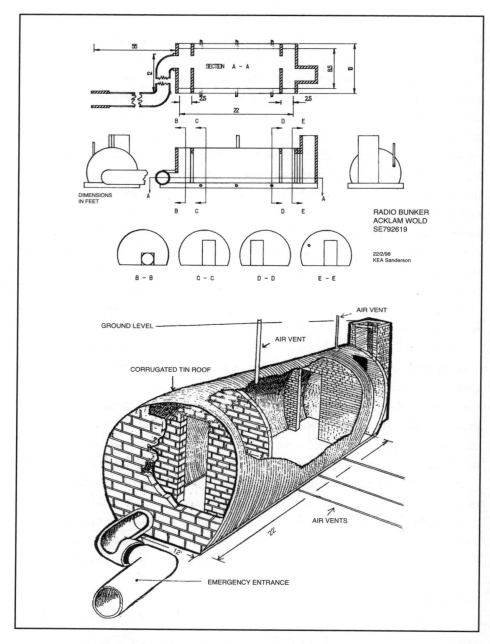

SECTION A - A

DIMENSIONS IN FEET

RADIO BUNKER
ACKLAM WOLD
SE792619

22/2/98
KEA Sanderson

B - B   C - C   D - D   E - E

AIR VENT

GROUND LEVEL

AIR VENT

CORRUGATED TIN ROOF

AIR VENTS

EMERGENCY ENTRANCE

Technical drawings of a classic Auxunits Operational Base
in the north-east of England. *(By kind permission of the North
Yorkshire and Cleveland 20th Century Defence Study Group)*

waterlogged, in spite of ingenious measures to keep it dry. After every effort, they still lived in continuous dampness, with water dripping from the roof and saturating the walls. This was obviously untenable and, eventually, the patrol was forced to abandon the site and give up on all their work. The problem quickly resolved itself with a move into an abandoned sandpit, where the shelter dug for them by a Royal Engineer unit stayed dry even during heavy rainfall. The new elephant shelter OBs could be stood with comparative ease on a concrete, railway sleeper, or brick (or block) base, entirely below ground level. Variations in construction were needed in proportion to the physical difficulties of the site chosen by the Intelligence Officer, his Group Commander or, sometimes more sensibly, the Patrol Leader himself.

Don Handscombe remembered the days of both the group system and the arrival of the Thundersley Patrol's elephant shelter OB:

> At the Group meetings we were given dummy exercises to carry out on approaching a target that was, perhaps, an old mill or a factory or a railway bridge or siding. We were instructed to attack it and to detail very carefully the method of attack and how it was carried out. Afterwards we analysed and kept a record of it and this was produced for Captain Ford, so we could discuss it.
>
> We always met once a week with other patrols in our Group and, in fact, helped one another out. We had to abandon our initial OB while the army dropped our 'Nissen' hut into the ground on a new site and the rest of the work, which was the entrance and escape tunnel, and the inside, had to be carried out by the members of the patrol. In our case, where we were often only four people, it was extremely hard work. At other times we helped out the men of the Canvey Island patrol.
>
> We kept our weapons and explosives at home, in our garages and places like that. The first OB was in a wood but the new site was in a well-drained sandpit drift, with just one or two sparse trees. There was a lot of cattle dung around which made a bit of a mess, but it did help to camouflage our entrance.

The escape tunnel was tackled with the help of other patrols in Captain Ford's group.

In some areas store space was sometimes created by digging out chambers in the sides of escape tunnels. Water was kept separately from food, explosives from detonators, and ammunition from weapons. Food was always basic hard tack and Army iron rations. Cooking was frowned upon after the discovery of one OB, during a Scout Patrol exercise, from the aroma of below-ground bacon and eggs. The longer the stay, the harder the life. Smoking was discouraged but not always forbidden. However, the West Norfolk Scout Section found its own answer. Jim Watson said: 'We had a rectangular hole in the floor of our OB, covered by duckboards. We kept our explosives there. It was no problem for us to stop smoking.' Other patrols wisely kept their cache of explosive in separate concrete-lined hideaways.

OBs usually had two exit/entrances. Entry was by a vertical brick shaft from floor level to a few inches below ground surface. Ladders – sometimes with built-in iron rungs – facilitated access and exit. The shaft was covered by a horizontal, counter-balanced trapdoor, supporting a tray about six inches deep and filled with earth. Weeds were encouraged to grow in this and it was regularly watered to ensure it was indistinguishable from the surrounding area – and the hatch, when gently lowered from within, was built to a sufficiently high specification to slip smoothly into place, camouflaging the entrance shaft. The trapdoor could, of course, be locked from within. Ingenious and well-hidden release-designs were devised to gain access from outside. Activation was by unlocking the retaining catch directly, or indirectly by finding a lever or push-pull mechanism, hidden some way from the hatch and attached to a buried cable. As the whole thing was often positioned under bushes and in a wood, watertight security was the intended result.

Hatches were one of a number of additional extras built on the spot – sometimes by Auxiliers, sometimes by Scout Sections, and sometimes under the direction of a Royal Engineer officer. Everything depended on the location. In mid-Suffolk, researchers found half a dozen concrete counter-balances, with gas piping pivots, originally the work of an RE corporal stationed with the Scout Section at Cransford. Over the years, the sheer deadweight of these had proved too much for the beaten-out corrugated iron trapdoors and trays to which they had been attached. Extracting these considerable objects from the bottom of collapsed shafts led to a high drop-out rate among the amateur archaeologist-diggers still expected to be at work the next day – in line with the demands once made upon Auxiliers themselves.

Another valuable extra was the escape tunnel. Once again they came in various modes. Many had simple timber and corrugated iron walls, and a roof just high enough to scramble through in a crouch, followed by an exit to another hidden balanced trapdoor. Others had brick or block walls, but probably the majority employed three-foot diameter concrete drainage pipes to crawl through on all fours. Where OBs were hidden in quarries, or old mines or in caves, these often dispensed with the elephant shelter and trapdoors, relying instead on bright ideas from Auxiliers or REs. The high water table on Romney Marsh called for a special, all-concrete design to avoid flooding, and these were probably the most comprehensively equipped OBs in the country. An overhead tank was included, to give a limited supply of gravity-fed running water; and there was even a toilet closet for privacy.

With six or seven men living in close proximity underground, potentially for long periods, and candles or paraffin-fired lighting and heating, condensation was always a great problem. This was dealt with as part of the ventilating system by installing three-inch diameter, glazed terracotta water pipes with hidden exterior vents, zigzagging down to the main chamber. Condensation was partly dealt with by the beige paint used to brighten the interior, amplifying to a degree the light from candles and hurricane or Tilley lamps. This paint, described to a layman as a mix of old-fashioned whitewash and early emulsion, with anti-rust properties, also contained small, lumpy granules of coke to absorb some of the moisture through the porous surface. Amazingly – even in 1940 – as the world's greatest-ever conflict developed – the War Office punctiliously lodged legal protection on this paint mix at the Patent Office in London.

Auxiliers themselves took on DIY responsibility for bunks and tables. Very few survive intact today, although debris may litter the floor. The best clues to Auxunits' provenance are the ventilating water pipes, impervious to rot and rust, and shreds of telephone cable.

The word 'comfort' was never relevant – not even to the issue of the Elsan chemical closet – unreasonably spurned by many patrols in favour of a standard WD entrenching tool and a patch of earth near the far end of the escape tunnel. As Auxiliers' life expectancy was notoriously short, they may have preferred the 'entrenching tool' expedient as a lesser hazard than trying to empty an Elsan in some sort of secrecy.

A decidedly experimental 'observer's role' was gradually developed in Colonel Major's time. Once out on his own to find the next night's target, the opportunity for the observer (or scout) to declare a unilateral intermission from battle and an unpleasant, hungry life underground, and sneak home for a refreshing bath and a good meal instead would have been a temptation difficult to resist. And, in working clothes – as Auxiliers originally were – and with intimate local knowledge and little danger of being spotted either by the enemy or his Patrol Leader, the scout might well have brought it off. When, later, Auxiliers were in more or less regular uniform as cover for their irregular intentions, they would have been unable to move anywhere in enemy-held territory in daylight except with the very greatest caution. Taking into account the human instinct for survival, it seems more likely that the observer might then have opted for the cramped but comparative safety of a prepared OP, well hidden and in field telephone communication with his comrades in the main chamber. Not all OPs were situated where sightings of enemy dispositions might be guaranteed – or even be likely – and it is well documented that some way or another the observer was expected to find, each day, an enemy target for the patrol to attack each night. For that he might need to be out and about.

Operational Bases were situated in the main within twenty miles of vulnerable coastlines. The best exception was around the city of Worcester, where the Auxiliary Units were part of the defences of the envisaged last-stand redoubt. OBs sited on the coast instead of slightly inland would have run the risk of being drenched in the poison gas which was prepared to annihilate the enemy as they landed. The War Office has never released a record of OB locations, and it probably never existed. Area IOs and local GCs knew where they were but the only way to map them now is piecemeal – from the memories of the comparatively few survivors and occasional paperwork in the archives. The Defence of Britain Project, with official back-up, substantial resources and volunteer manpower, did its best in the last decade of the twentieth century with – as its website discloses – valuable but admittedly imperfect results.

Perhaps 5,000–6,000 men were enrolled into the Auxiliary Unit Operational Patrols at one time or another and, if approximately 3,500 were in the field at any time, a total of 600 'working' OBs is a reasonable proposition. Many others had to be abandoned through structural failure, water penetration or dampness, or discovery by members of the public. A speculative best guess would be a further 400, bringing the number built during 1940–4 to approximately 1,000. Many were not destroyed after stand-down, but most were hastily sealed to keep out the inquisitive public. This stratagem worked well, but time and nature's erosive effect have now reduced the majority to mere shapes in the ground and telephone cable, timber, and water pipe detritus. But nothing will stop local exploration and, from time to time, another valuable discovery is made. Tracking down OBs is an enduring challenge for interested relatives and Auxunit researchers.

Chapter Thirteen

Arms and Ordnance[†]

'Any attempt to catalogue the first issue of firearms to the
Auxiliary Units is just a minefield of confusion. The Intelligence
Officer simply gave them whatever he could get his hands
on . . .'

*Graham Bines, former Curator, Museum of the British Resistance
Organisation*

Surviving personnel of the British Expeditionary Force returned from
France during May and early June of 1940, after the loss of virtually all
their supplies, transport, tanks, aircraft and weaponry. Some brave soul at the
top took a gamble and sent them on leave. On their return they were
hurriedly rearmed from the meagre stocks in reserve, and it soon became
clear that adequate weaponry for the guerrillas of the newly formed
Auxiliary Units – without which they were useless in a stay-behind role –
was simply not available.

The availability of dumps (or packs or Auxunits Mark I), many diverted
from the supplies of Section D and until then hidden almost indiscriminately
round the country, largely solved the immediate explosives' supply problem.
Auxiliers continued the production of home-made Molotov cocktails already
under way by the LDV/Home Guard in some places. Weapons' deficiency
was a different matter. So, with encouragement from individual Intelligence
Officers, Auxiliers exercised their ingenuity on a self-help basis. After all,
they were British and, with their backs to the wall, in not unfamiliar
circumstances. Lack of preparation for war was nothing new.

In the countryside, Auxiliers brought their own shotguns, and were
supplied with single-ball cartridges which 'would make a tidy hole in a sheet
of corrugated iron at a hundred yards' as Herman Kindred discovered with
his 12-bore down in Suffolk. Ivan Potter, at his workshop in Ipswich,
converted an elderly German .22-inch ratting rifle into a handgun. With the

---

† See Appendix One for additional detail.

barrel sawn off, it resembled an ancient duelling pistol. It may even have been safe to use.

XII Corps Observation Unit had already developed 'Operation Agincourt' tactics with the issue of crossbows down in Kent. Rather like for their brothers-in-arms in the Home Guard, such weaponry typified the extent of Auxiliers' initial response to any assault by battle-hardened soldiers of the Wehrmacht. With home-made close quarters weaponry, however, they came into their own.

Auxiliers dug into their own stocks of Boy Scout knives and over-the-counter, razor-sharp daggers and then, in their workshops, manufactured and armed themselves with garrottes and thrust (or 'punch') weapons. Garrottes, strong, thin wires with wooden toggles at either end, were for the silent and very permanent dispatch of lone sentries. Thrust weapons, T-shaped carpenter's bradawls with a wooden handle and sharpened steel spike protruding at right angles, were easy to make and carry, and formidably dangerous at close quarters. Some Auxiliers later adapted their revolver holsters to slip in a thrust weapon as well. Wooden clubs were home made, and rubber truncheons – almost forgotten in War Department warehouses since some riot control duty in a foreign land – were issued to every man. Knuckledusters and fearsome, metal-studded knobkerries soon followed.

Winston Churchill's minute that 'these men are to have revolvers' saw upgraded priorities for the Auxiliary Units, and weapons – including 400 Colt .32-inch automatics – started to arrive from America well before Colonel Gubbins left. In one early deal revolvers, ammunition, leather belts and holsters were sent from the stores of the New York Police Department. These survived the war as an individual issue to many Auxiliers. All of them soon had a handgun of one brand or another.

The subject of which weapon was issued to which man is complicated by other small-scale purchases abroad – from Spain and Argentina, for example, where British agents were urgently buying firearms from whichever source could be persuaded to sell – and the men were initially issued with any model that came the IO's way. These included not only the Smith & Wesson and Colt ranges, Webleys, but even random relics collected during local police firearms' amnesties.

Colonel Gubbins personally organised a delivery of Thompson sub-machine guns and automatic pistols from the anglophile son of a former American Ambassador, but was frustrated during a foray in the United

Kingdom, as reported from his private papers in the biography *Gubbins and SOE*:

> I knew that all weapons in private hands at the commencement of war had been called in by the police on orders, presumably, from the Home Office, and I naturally thought that this would provide a most useful source of supply. To our astonishment and suppressed rage, we discovered that everything that could have been of use to us had been disposed of irretrievably. I visited two county police stations myself to see if I could get hold of something; in Leeds I found that these weapons had been thrown into the lake in Roundhay Park, and at another station . . . that they had been dumped into the sea – presumably again on orders from the Home Office.

Most patrol leaders received one Browning Automatic Rifle (BAR) from US stocks. The BAR, manufactured by the Colt Firearms Company, was designed by the American John Browning during WWI, and fired standard ball, tracer or armour-piercing bullets at either automatic or semi-automatic rate. The BAR was unsuited to Auxunits work and it was replaced, generally during 1941, by the Tommy gun.

The drum-magazine version of the Thompson sub-machine gun with fifty rounds weighed in at nearly eleven pounds; in some cases possession was shared around and in others the weapon was given to the biggest man in the patrol because of its weight. Sharp-shooting was not a talent required to fire this automatic weapon, which, with formidable killing power from bursts of .45-inch calibre bullets, is a familiar sight to any aficionado of American gangster films.

Another distribution, two to a patrol, was the Enfield P.17 .30-06 calibre rifle. Both this and the BAR were heavy-duty enough to take the wear and tear of life underground. The P.17, dating from WWI when it was one of the US Army's standard rifles, was a development of a British design, built in America both by Remington and Winchester. Unfortunately, .30-06 bullets, although *nearly* the same calibre as the .303-inch in the British Lee-Enfield, were not interchangeable.

Secure storage caches of different designs were built or adapted for most patrols in due course, but a number of weapons, including the treasured Tommy gun – were sometimes simply boxed up in garages, or even indoors.

This was not ideally secure; and, although wives and mothers were rarely allowed to discover the contents, it would be unwise to assume that – war effort or not – their presence necessarily contributed to harmonious domestic compatibility in every case. Fortunately for him, perhaps, the mother of teenage Port Talbot Auxilier Roy Coleman never even asked him what he was keeping in the box under his bed.

In 1941, during Colonel Major's command, the list of stores and supplies allocated to each fully manned patrol included:

Arms
7 x .38-inch, American revolvers; 2 x .3-inch rifles; 7 fighting knives; 3 knobkerries; 48 No. 36 grenades, with 4-second fuses; 3 cases S.T. grenades [Sticky Bombs]; 2 cases A.W. bottles [Phosphorus grenades]; 1 x .22-inch rifle, with silencer; 1 Thompson sub-machine gun.

Ammunition
40 x .38-inch pistol rounds; 200 x .3-inch rifle rounds; 1,000 x .45-inch SMG rounds; 200 x .22-inch rounds.

Inclusion of the .22-inch rifle is important confirmation of the dangerous commitments expected from Auxiliers. In his August 1940 report to the Prime Minister, Duncan Sandys had acknowledged that sniping was included in their remit. This was followed by a similar task-allocation to Scout Sections. Sniping was not possible with comparatively inaccurate handguns, and a noisy P.17, with the associated impossibility of silent operations, was never a serious proposition either. But a marksman with a silenced .22 rifle with telescopic sight and long-range bullets would have a real chance of living to fight another day.

Winchesters, Remingtons and BSAs were among the sniping rifles issued. Don Handscombe was in no doubt about their intended use:

At home I had my revolver, of course, and dagger, truncheon, a cheese wire, face veil, some hand grenades and detonators, and some plastic explosive and rounds of ammunition. And we had one .22 rifle with a telescopic sight between the patrol and we shared the ammunition. So I had some .22 ammunition as well.

We knew of a list of people who might have collaborated with the enemy. But it was not produced to us. We were told that part of our duties may have been to deal with some of these people, but we didn't really know more than that. I would have felt justified in taking the lives of people we regarded as Quislings or collaborators. In the Stand-down orders Colonel Douglas wrote that he knew we would fight with orders or without. In my patrol we were all good shots. The .22 was passed round. We regarded it as an assassination weapon although it might have helped us to live off the land as well.

The best all-round weapon in the armoury was probably the Sten gun, which, after test firing early in 1941, gradually replaced the Thompson – until then the only sub-machine gun available to the British Army.

Folklore has it that the Sten was the inspiration of Colin Gubbins when, as head of operations in SOE, he recognised the urgent need for a cheap, easily assembled and maintained, lightweight machine carbine. However, the specifications were in fact written for RAF ground crew and the defence of airfields. A prototype, with box magazine based on that of the German 'Schmeisser', was designed at the end of 1940 'on a kitchen table', by Major Reginald Shepherd and Harold J. Turpin the chief design draughtsman of the Royal Small Arms Factory at Enfield, hence the name Sten. About 4 million were made during WWII at a cost in the region of £5 each. Being comparatively easy to conceal and assemble, the Sten was as nearly ideal as possible for work behind enemy lines and thousands were parachuted to partisans abroad, or ferried in by small boat teams – such as Andrew Croft's sorties to mainland France from Corsica. It is no coincidence that the calibre was 9 mm Parabellum – standard ammunition for the Germans and other continental armies since 1908. Exaggerated reports about unreliability were usually related to the quality of manufacture. Don Handscombe and his comrades in the Thundersley Patrol of the Auxiliary Units rated them more reliable than even the Thompson SMG.

Auxiliers were ordered to avoid firefights, especially if they were likely to be outgunned. Indeed a resort to noisy weaponry, irreconcilable with their training as silent, night saboteurs, was intended only as a last-ditch option. Major Nigel Oxenden expanded upon this farsighted guideline in his final report:

> *Personal Weapons.* There are strong arguments against the carrying of firearms on night operations. One shot could betray the presence of the patrol and turn the attack into a headlong rout.

The only weapon of this sort that could be used without wrecking the chances of the attackers is one that is silent and fitted with luminous sights. Such a pistol has been produced under the name of 'Welrod'.

With this damning conclusion, Oxenden recommended the disposal of all standard firearms for future clandestine operations. Nevertheless, his support for the Welrod was undoubtedly fully justified.

This 'rod', from a design initiated by the SIS for SOE executioners, was first put into production at Station IX, 'The Frythe' at Welwyn, in Hertfordshire (hence 'Welrod'). Production was later transferred to the Birmingham Small Arms factory. The weapon was not apparently withdrawn from active service by British special forces until well after the Gulf War. Technical drawings are still classified 'Secret'. It is an all-British, sound-suppressed pistol, designed for silent, close quarters assassination or the dispatch of sentries. It was later modified for US Special Forces by the removal of the handgrip, and re-named the 'sleeve gun'. It could be suspended up the sleeves of a jacket, it is claimed, before the furtive execution of a victim. This undoubtedly called for a degree of preparation and practice.

About 2,800 Welrods were made, some in .32-inch calibre but the majority in 9 mm. A magazine in the handgrip holds seven rounds and these are fed into the chamber by hand-rotating a knurled knob. Another knurled knob at the muzzle end allows access to the baffle assemblies. With an additional round already up the spout, the Welrod is therefore an eight round, single-shot, bolt-action handgun rather than an automatic or self-loader. The effective range is up to fifty metres. The sound suppressor makes the Welrod a cumbersome weapon. At only two pounds, it is usefully lightweight. The sights have a radium insert to help out in poor light.

*

Fighting knife issue – as opposed to those provided from the private means of Auxiliers themselves – was mainly the Fairbairn/Sykes design. Stilettos, nearly seven inches long – carefully measured to cause death by drowning in blood with a subclavian thrust – with sharpened edges in polished nickel and a serrated handle to reduce slippage, were made in batches by Wilkinson Sword. Originals are now collectors' items. The majority were similar in design but of darkened steel, more suitable for night fighting, with a custom-built scabbard and tags enabling the scabbard to be stitched to a trouser leg or sleeve for easier access. Some of the later models were contracted out.

Oxenden felt almost as strongly about knives and rubber clubs as he did about noisy firearms: 'The knife is perhaps the hardest and noisiest way of killing a conscious man, but is light to carry. The rubber club might be useful on occasions; but both are rendered superfluous by the Welrod.' Many of Fairbairn and Sykes's supporters passionately disagreed with the notion that killing with a knife had to be noisy and, when he wrote this, Oxenden himself could surely not have been fully aware just how advanced their killing techniques had become – in spite of his training role at Coleshill.

*

Explosives and Booby Traps
Featuring Winston Churchill's Toyshop and the Cloak-and-Dagger Boys

'Explosives, although very inflammable, are not dangerous to handle. They will not go off by being dropped or shaken. Small quantities burn quietly in the open; larger quantities may explode due to the heat generated by burning.

Do not smoke near explosives.'

How to Use Explosives, *attributed to Millis Jefferis*

In many Auxunit areas high explosive and the accessories necessary for sabotage and booby-trapping were available in abundance from mid-July 1940. These early *Dad's Army* days were soon replaced by professionally orchestrated training to standards of warlike aggression unique to civilian warriors. With intentional irony, Major Oxenden recorded his memories of those early times:

Auxiliary Units Mark I. The first dumps, afterwards called packs and finally Aux Units, were contained in cardboard boxes that disintegrated if buried or left out in the rain, and included, besides 10 lb of Plastic Explosive and a mass of feeble and uncertain incendiaries, a hollow bronze casting of a lump of coal that could hold about two ounces of H.E. and a detonator. This museum piece was a clue to our proposed activities in July 1940 – the crippling of our railway system, assumed to be in use by the enemy.

Containers for Auxunits Mk I were soon strengthened, made watertight, and declared fit for active service. This would entail long periods either buried underground or housed in uncared for hidey-holes of one sort or another – in wet weather or dry.

Oxenden's own impressive WWI military background tended toward the conventional and, although he enthusiastically embraced all the training and gadgetry necessary for irregular warfare and dirty tricks when he later became the chief instructor at Coleshill, he may well have been a touch cynical in 1940 about the devices produced by Section D, some of whose officers, more often than not co-opted from outside the War Office, could have impressed him as little more than mere playboys.

The volume and variety of explosives available to Auxiliers were soon vastly expanded. They originated from three main sources: the commercial world, Section D of MI6, and the War Office. Auxiliary Units HQ was the clearing-house. A carefully controlled market for commercial explosives, in more normal times for blasting in quarries, pits and mines, was always on tap and, with large-scale official contracts impending as war was declared, ever-ready for expansion. An absentee commercial provider was the Swedish chemist Alfred Nobel who, having invented dynamite, was one of the world's richest men when he died in 1896. His conscience persuaded him to leave a giant legacy for the creation of the various Nobel Prizes (including the Peace Prize) but his company continued to produce explosives in many parts of the world. One at Perranporth in Cornwall was relocated to Scotland after WWI. Local Auxiliers took advantage of the abandoned factory and established their OB in the ruins.

Nobel 808 had long been a dependable standard product for the tin mines. A light, buff-coloured jelly with a strong smell of almonds, it was a powerful cutting charge. Although well protected in wrappers and not vulnerable to damp, it caused bad headaches when carelessly handled. Nobel 808 was one of the first general issues to Auxiliers. Other well-known commercial trade names sometimes supplied included dynamite, the first and most widely known Nobel product; ammonal, a high explosive powder consisting of ammonium nitrate and aluminium; and gelignite (also known as blasting gelatine and another Nobel invention). In spite of handling and storage disadvantages, gelignite was finally the main explosive issued to the Auxiliary Units. Auxiliers also had access, through standard War Office suppliers, to guncotton, an explosive made by treating cotton or other cellulose fabrics with a mixture of nitric and sulphuric acids. Guncotton was produced in government factories.

According to imaginative TV producers who proclaim a serious interest in getting the *real* story, TNT was handed out to Auxiliers too. Their only reason for this claim is that workshops found it easier to stencil TNT on the top of a box than longer names such as dynamite, TNT was, in fact, never issued at all.

Supplies of Plastic Explosive (PE) were the preserve of the SIS. PE, an advanced, stable and highly effective material, had a putty-like consistency and could be moulded into the best shape for the job in hand (such as the side of a railway line or even a lump of coal). It had a dull yellow, or sometimes black colour and came in four-ounce sausages wrapped in cellophane or greaseproof paper. PE was frequently used as a primer for other explosives and could be handled without causing headaches. It was practically unaffected by storage conditions and did not deteriorate.

PE arrived at first in Auxunits Mark I. When activated by a detonator, it produced an easily controlled explosion; rolled into spaghetti-like strips, it was ideal for cutting metal. As such it was much preferred by Allied special forces and irregulars and, since the war, has been redeveloped commercially under a number of trade names. The record indicates that from June 1940, until output was sufficient to supply the Army too, PE was issued through Section D almost exclusively to the Auxiliary Units.

In *The Last Ditch*, David Lampe relates that no less than twenty years after the war, Reginald Sennet, the Dengie Group Commander, gave up waiting for the Army to come along to collect the stores which his patrols had left hidden in his milking shed after stand-down. Eventually he decided it was time to forget his commitment to the Official Secrets Act and tell the local police. They called the Army. The inventory included: 14,738 rounds of ammunition 1,205 lb of explosives, 3,742 ft of delayed action fuse, 930 ft of safety fuse, 144 time pencils, 1,207 L-Delay switches, 1,271 detonators, 719 booby-trap switches, 314 paraffin bombs, 131 fog signals, 121 smoke bombs, 36 slabs of guncotton, and 33 time pencils and booby-trap switches attached to made-up charges.

It is worth remembering that just a few pounds of explosive in the wrong hands are all that is needed to destroy major buildings or kill dozens of people. And the Dengie group of patrols handed in more than half a ton. It was about average for the Auxiliary Units!

*

Grenades were another core War Office supply for the Auxunits' inventory. The ubiquitous Mills Bomb – or No. 36 Grenade as officially styled by the Army – led the list. Every Auxunit patrol had a boxful and *nearly* every Auxilier tells the tale of the man in his patrol who stood mesmerised into stupefied inactivity, holding a live grenade with the safety pin out – or how someone was only saved by some bold initiative after a live bomb was dropped in the firing range. At such a moment the reliable Mills was likely to be hurled up to 35 yards, roughly the maximum range. It had a danger radius of up to 50 yards.

The No. 76 Grenade was another standard issue from War Office stores. It was also known as the 'A.W.' or 'S.I.P.' (Self Igniting Phosphorus) type. Contained in a strong glass bottle for safety, it was sealed with a crown stopper which, if coloured green, enabled it to be fired from the Home Guard's Northover Projector. *The Countryman's Diary* explains:

> The A.W. Bottles contain yellow phosphorus dissolved in benzol.
>
> When the bottle is broken the contents burst into flame and give off a dense cloud of foul smelling smoke. The smoke is not poisonous and the service respirator is effective against it. The fire caused can be put out with water but – as soon as the water dries up – the phosphorus will start burning again.
>
> Store the bottles on the floor of your dump, NOT on the shelf – as they might fall off . . .

Finally, Auxiliers were supplied with the No. 77 Smoke Grenade. Specific precautions were advised: 'Grenades should always be stored away from explosives' and 'Small particles of phosphorus will be thrown some distance when the Grenade bursts. Serious burns will be caused if these particles, which cannot be extinguished, fall on any part of the body.'

This presumably 'legitimate' weapon consisted of a tin with screw-down lid, containing white phosphorus and a detonator. Once in contact with air, the phosphorus ignited and gave off dense smoke for thirty seconds or so.

Major Oxenden also had strong words to say about the use of grenades, as we shall read later. Here is his final summary: 'In short, no arms are needed but the Welrod for attack and the 77 [Grenade] for defence.'

*

The Detonation of Explosives

'A suitable length of fuse had to be inserted into a detonator. These slim metal tubes containing fulminate of mercury were extremely sensitive and needed careful handling. The over enthusiastic insertion of a fuse could easily lead to the loss of one or more fingers.'

The late Geoffrey Bradford, Devon Auxilier

Explosives usually require a primer for maximum efficiency, a detonator to initiate the high explosive, and a fuse to connect them to a delay device.

A primer is a cap or cylinder containing a little gunpowder. Those supplied to the Auxiliary Units were either called 'C.E.' or 'G.C.' primers. As an expedient, one ounce of PE, or a 'big Cordtex knot' could be used instead. This was a three-coil slipknot of Cordtex Fuse, pulled tight and placed closely against the charge. A standard detonator was an aluminium tube two inches in length and approximately one-quarter of an inch in diameter. It was part-filled with a very sensitive high explosive, such as fulminate of mercury, reactive to heat. One end of the tube was open to insert either safety fuse, or Orange Line, which was then crimped into place with special pliers. The flash from either the fuse or a percussion cap then fired the detonator. The percussion cap of a delay switch or booby-trap mechanism could also fire the detonator. Detonators were supplied in tins of either 100 or 25. They were usually packed in sawdust to reduce the chance of spontaneous firing and to lessen any rattling noise. 'Dets' were so volatile that it was essential to avoid compressing the sensitive explosive within.

To prevent an uncalled-for explosion if the fuse was pushed home too far, the standard technique was to handle the detonator only by the open end and then to plumb the safe depth within, delicately, with a blade of grass. The fingerless veteran next to you in the supermarket queue, fiddling for change in his purse, may well have failed to master this critical technique in his younger days. After the fuse had been inserted into the detonator it was secured by compressing the tube end with crimping pliers.

Rather like the thigh bone connected to the knee-bone, the next stage – having selected the right explosive for the chosen target, and buried or attached the detonator and/or primer – was to link the best type of fuse to some form of activation. For Auxiliers, choosing the fuse was perhaps one of the easier parts of the operation. In those days fuses came broadly in two categories – burning or detonating fuse.

Burning fuse could be activated by a striker or match head, and came mainly from one of two types. Bickford (or safety fuse) was the safer, burning at the slow rate of two feet per minute. To light Bickford it was necessary to make a slanting cut to one end, exposing the core, and then to create ignition with a match or a copper igniter crimped on – or by one of various delay mechanisms or firing devices. As it allowed time to 'Walk away! Never run!' Bickford was favoured by Auxiliers.

Orange Line burning at the rate of ninety feet per second called for a more nimble departure from the scene or, more frequently, the introduction of a delay-firing device or self-activating mechanism. In this the orange outer cover of the line contained a powder core, the whole being wisely supplied in red tins. It was not, of course, ever lit directly, but was useful for the construction of booby traps, and especially to connect a number of charges, linked to explode simultaneously.

Detonating fuses were also of two types, either Cordtex or Primacord. With a silvery-white exterior case filled with explosive, Cordtex was virtually instantaneous. It could cut through the thin metal of petrol cans. Primacord had a wasp-like colouring and was similar to use. Whereas burning fuse could be ignited with a match or igniter-cap, explosive fuse needed a detonator. These instantaneous fuses could be used to activate a spaced row of Mills Bombs to attack a group of personnel using a known route, or to fire charges to the front and rear of vehicles in a convoy to facilitate an ambush.

*

It was now time for Auxiliers – having prepared the charge – to learn to survive each night's operation against the enemy, and for that they had to create time to get well away from the scene before the game was given away with a big bang. The sources of supply for delay devices and mechanisms were Winston Churchill's Toyshop and the SIS, via Section D. Both started dirty trick preparations before war broke out. Thanks to a larger budget and less accountability, Section D was first into the field.

Commander Arthur J. G. Langley was seconded from the Royal Navy in December 1938 and put in charge of research and supply. He had been introduced through a mutual college acquaintance and interviewed by Colonel Grand – wearing a red carnation in his buttonhole – in the lobby of St Ermin's Hotel. His new post entailed a loss of job security and largely unwritten terms of employment. Now paid in cash, he was no longer pensionable, taxable or the beneficiary of a health plan. On paper he effectively ceased to exist. His initial budget was the then enormous monthly sum of £50,000. Langley's first office was in Queen Anne's Gate, SW1, adjacent to the HQ of the SIS. His scientific expertise, energy and capacity for innovative ideas are reported to have matched those of Millis Jefferis, his opposite number in MI(R). Langley conducted early experiments in the (presumably) disused fireplace of his rooms.

In August 1939, as war was about to break out, the SIS commandeered Aston House, near Stevenage in Hertfordshire, and this became his new HQ, experimental test centre, workshop and production facility. By the time the HQ transfer was put into effect, experiments with time fuses and incendiaries had already gone a long way. Aston House was code-designated Station XII, although, as cover, successive COs dubbed it E.S.6 (W.D.) or Experimental Station 6 (War Department). This was a deliberate deception. Certainly the WD had no early part in Station XII, although all three armed services were involved later in the development of 'toys'. It was thanks to Langley's imaginative stewardship that Section D had early access to plastic explosive, developed as cyclonite at Woolwich Arsenal. He created the time pencil delay switch, and masterminded a secret system of radio-telephony, as well as many of the devices, explosives and incendiaries for the conduct of irregular warfare which were created or developed for special forces at Station XII.

Section D's incendiary devices seem to be either underplayed (by Oxenden) or overplayed by the media. Auxiliers themselves took them as they found them. Some igniters seem to have been too volatile for safe storage and were gradually withdrawn. Among these were the first home-assembled Molotov cocktails, and the Paraffin Incendiary, a small, cigar-shaped gelatine case containing a mixture of petrol and paraffin. One end was capped with a substance similar to a safety match, which caused prompt ignition when struck on strike-paper or a matchbox. In the instructions for use was this advice:

> If you place the tube where the petrol will run, i.e. on the lintel of
> a door or a sloping surface, or even in the crack between two boards,
> you will find that the petrol spreads more easily and you will get
> better results.

An ingenious additional extra came with the cardboard pack in which Paraffin Incendiaries were supplied. The carton was impregnated with an especially flammable substance. Active incineration could be delayed by the introduction of a PTI (Pocket Time Incendiary) or a time pencil.

Supplied two in a specially constructed tin, the PTI had a flammable celluloid case containing three slim tubes about five inches long. The two outer tubes were thermite incendiary candles and the centre a delay device of the time pencil variety, which activated an enlarged match head, igniting the incendiary from the base. In turn, the flame ignited the thermite – a mixture of powdered aluminium and a weak metal oxide that produced a burn at an extremely high temperature. The PTI was for use against stores of all kinds and, when combined with an explosive charge, for the destruction of petrol dumps.

It gets more difficult to see how Oxenden regarded all this as uncertain or feeble. The origin of another incendiary device, the Fire Pot – which was still in service with Auxiliers in 1944 – may also be attributed to Section D. It was certainly not a feeble affair either, as Suffolk Auxunit patrol leader, Herman Kindred demonstrated to departing American airmen at Parham Airfield at the end of the war. Their lively farewell party was interrupted in the early hours when four Fire Pots, which Herman had stealthily connected to time pencils, erupted dramatically at the top of a nearby water tower. 'How they old Yanks did cheer! For a few minutes they even stopped shooting up the Control Tower,' said Herman.

Station XII already had access to pastic explosive and it completed its part of the operation with the time pencil, a delay device produced in tens of thousands as the standard issue to British, and many Allied, special forces. (A similar claim is made for the L-Delay developed later at MD1.)

Gubbins is credited in some circles with bringing a prototype time pencil back to Britain from the Polish intelligence service during the summer of 1939. However, the facts now available tell a different story. The idea for this delay switch was that of Commander Langley, and the first tests were conducted in the fireplace of his Section D office in Westminster well before war started. The finished product was about the size and shape of a modern propelling pencil and was encased in a five-inch long tube. The firing mechanism within was a spring, striker, percussion cap and detonator. The system was activated by crushing, or crimping with special pliers, the thin copper body containing an ampoule of corrosive solution. With the glass broken, the liquid attacked a steel wire running alongside which, after failure, released the spring, activating striker and percussion cap.

Experiments were conducted on Langley's behalf at a university laboratory. The steel wire was modified at some time and replaced with piano wire, of more guaranteed consistency. As no clock-ticking mechanism was involved, one great merit of this device was its silent operation, obviously enough a great advantage to saboteurs trying to work in absolute silence.

With minor modifications, the time pencil remained a favoured Auxunits device for the duration. They were known to fail on occasion and later in the war advice was always to tape them in pairs to reduce this risk. Inadvertent activation was prevented by a safety pin. Coloured bands round the exterior indicated the expected delay time. Apart from the ten minutes expected with the black band, and used only for training, the shortest delay was thirty minutes (red) and the longest twenty hours (blue). Unfortunately, all this took longer in the cold weather of winter and a degree of approximation was inevitable.

MI(R)'s team of inventors declined to be impressed with the time pencil. Major Macrae, who headed the team which developed the later L-Delay, wrote:

> The Time Pencil did work to some extent. But it was a very dodgy device indeed and one had to be very brave to use it . . . The trouble was how long the [firing] process would take was almost anybody's guess.
>
> No attempt could be made to calculate these time fuses in hours. They could only be identified with coloured bands, which indicated that they should go off within a few hours, a fair number of hours, or a lot of hours. And the situation was complicated by the fact that they had a terrific temperature coefficient. In very hot weather a theoretically long delay fuse might go off in a few minutes. In cold weather it might not go off at all.

A safety pin was provided to interfere with the striker . . . The fact remained that this safety pin had to be removed sooner or later and this operation was not a popular one, particularly with me!

*

The War Office made a late start in the production of booby traps. Hampered at the outset by shortage of funds, and strict budget accountability, MI(R) nevertheless made rapid progress and – thanks to the assembly of a talented team and the personal interest of Winston Churchill – managed to manoeuvre an extraordinary escape from restrictive red tape. This seems to have largely been achieved by Stuart Macrae, the second-in-command who – coming into the army from university and the commercial world – introduced unorthodoxy to the set-up. This included a delicate balancing act playing off the War Office – by which this unit was funded and to which it was theoretically responsible – against Section D. Rather cleverly, he answered difficult questions from one with the explanation that he was working for the other. However, although both physically and managerially separated from Station XII, the two seem to have got along harmoniously enough and, indeed, where gaps had been left by Section D or later SOE, Jefferis and Macrae and their talented team sought to fill them.

These stratagems were undoubtedly made possible by Winston Churchill's personal interest both while at the Admiralty and after he became Prime Minister in May 1940. Not only did he have a youthful fascination with ingenious gadgetry, but he also provided the right climate for political shenanigans when he declared himself Minister of Defence, although a Ministry of Defence did not then exist.

In the beginning, most of the practical work was contracted out. The first workshop premises were requisitioned and rented by MI(R) from the London Broadcasting Corporation (Radio Normandie) at 35 Portland Place, W1, in 1940, and soon expanded – probably with Section D funding – to 'The Firs', Whitchurch, Princes Risborough, near Aylesbury, Buckinghamshire. Production went into immediate overdrive.

The formal designation for Winston Churchill's Toyshop – as Jefferis' development and production workshops were irreverently known by sceptics in the War Office – could then be changed from 'MIR(c)' to MD1 – or Ministry of Defence 1. With no accountable ministry, Macrae steered a clever path between bureaucratic Whitehall monoliths, knowing that the end products were vital to the war effort. Jefferis was tasked to run a more-or-less legitimate outfit producing unusual but 'respectable' weapons (as opposed to those of Section D), and normally reported directly to Colonel Holland and the Chiefs of Staff Committee. He was also in regular contact with the Prime Minister and his Chief Scientific Adviser, Lord Cherwell, both of whom attended practical demonstrations of gadgetry which was far from regular in any respect. The final tally was twenty-six new weapons.

Meanwhile, according to the perceptive Macrae: 'Grand and Co were getting double the money for running a cloak and dagger outfit.'

MD1 soon made up for lost time and was called upon for specialist design and production help by both the Air Ministry and the Admiralty. Even before the war, the Toyshop had developed cheap and effective booby-trap devices for land forces, including pressure and pull switches – both in full production before the end of 1940 – and then a release mechanism. Also perfected in a hurry was the design and production of the infamous 'Sticky Bomb', described by one Auxilier as 'clearly the product of a madman'. Although the purpose of the various switches was to give Auxiliers and, later, Allied soldiers, saboteurs and special forces abroad, some chance of escape after planting their explosives, the same could not be said for the Sticky Bomb.

This bomb was the brainchild of (then) Major Millis Jefferis, in his role designated as D/3, during the early days of MI(R) experiments with new weaponry. The name Sticky Bomb – or ST Grenade or later Grenade No. 74 – was doubly appropriate. The weapon looked rather like the famous German stick grenade (or, as someone said, a toffee apple). A special liquid explosive was developed by ICI at Ardeer in Scotland, sealed in a glass flask wrapped in a 'sock', and smothered with a fearsomely effective adhesive prepared by Kay Brothers of Stockport. The carrying and activating stick of the toffee apple contained a five-second delay mechanism based on that of the well tried Mills Bomb.

The 'madman' intended this contraption to be thrown at a tank on a good day or, on a bad one, *poulticed on by hand*. This had the promise of a suicide mission but the device was nevertheless approved as an anti-tank weapon, modified, and placed in mass production. The danger was not only from awesomely close proximity to the enemy. Should some not unlikely human error occur and the adhesive brush against clothing, such as a pair of trousers, it could not be unstuck. This was a bad time to let go of the stick and activate the fuse, of course. If a man was on his own, or under fire, a certain discipline was necessary to hang on to the stick with one hand while removing the trousers – plus boots and gaiters – with the other, before dumping the bomb and making a dash for it in double quick time to report to the quartermaster's stores in some disarray. After the QM had recorded on the loss of 'One pair, trousers, serge , khaki, WD property' in quadruplicate, our hero's next stop would be a parade for punishment by the adjutant.

The Pressure Switch was an early design. It cost 3/6d (call it 18p) and 2.25 million were produced. It required a pressure in excess of forty pounds to activate when trodden upon, or overrun by a vehicle, and was originally intended to blow up railway trains.

The Pull Switch was a device used in conjunction with a trip wire to activate an explosion or, as Royal Engineers prefer, to 'fire a mine'. Designed to operate after a pull of about four pounds, it was a particularly useful booby trap used, for example, with the trip wire anchored to a tree along his route, to polish off a patrolling sentry.

The Release Switch was activated once a weight was removed from it. Nearly 2 million were made and issued. It was a small, flat, hinged box about three inches at its longest and weighed only five ounces. This switch was undoubtedly responsible for a media obsession with lavatory seats. A regularly re-circulated story still insists that the Auxiliary Units planned to booby trap the toilet seat of every building likely to be used as a German HQ. This was robustly countered by a Devon Auxilier, the late Geoffrey Bradford, who was not only unaware of any such plan, but pointed out that a Pull Switch in the cistern would have been simpler, and both better disguised and capable of holding a larger explosive charge.

With these devices running off the assembly line, MD1 started work to improve the time pencil. From another brilliant idea of Millis Jefferis, experiments proved that the failure of a slim lead rod under tension – in turn firing a spring-operated striker – could be depended upon with more accuracy than acid working on a fine wire, and was free from the associated heat co-efficient disadvantage. Hence the L-Delay was born. Over 5 million were made during WWII. The Ordnance Board adopted the L-Delay as the only type to be used for future demolition work, and re-named it Switch No. 9. Like time pencils the L-Delay had the merit of total silence in operation. Although L-Delays were a widespread issue with the Auxiliary Units, they never held the same place in their affection as time pencils, although it does seem likely that Macrae's somewhat patronising reservations about time pencils' accuracy and safety were – technically at least – well justified.

As if to establish beyond doubt that MD1 had quietly moved well away from its remit to produce legitimate devices, the design team filled a missing link in the armoury of both regular and irregular forces with the design and development of the anti-personnel or AP switch. It was a device either for the protection of saboteurs in a hideout, or an Allied soldier in danger of pursuit, as it was designed to make a track or pathway unsafe to use. It consisted of a short gun barrel in an eight-inch tube, which could be driven vertically into the ground with a custom-built drift. A pointed steel .303-inch bullet, instead of the normal one, was slipped into the assembly with just the point protruding. When trodden upon the bullet fired vertically into the enemy soldier's foot, if he was lucky. Nearly 1.5 million were produced and, not surprisingly, were known descriptively to both soldiers and Auxiliers as 'The Castrator'.

The end product for Winston Churchill's Toyshop was a daring, simple, cheap collection of booby-trap devices to go with the explosives already available.

Gubbins remembered the co-operation received from Section D at the height of the invasion scare: 'They had apparently an unlimited stock of plastic, would make up and pack explosive charges for us to our specifications if we could find a couple of packers, and would help with Molotov Cocktails and sticky bombs for anti-tank work.' Moreover, the cloak-and-dagger boys of Section D stepped in to assist with their non-accountable funds provided through the reliable Joan Bright Astley.

By thus minimising red tape and maximising freewheeling innovation, the two units created an arsenal of explosives, delays, and booby-trap activators on an unprecedented scale, available – in spite of all the pre-war prevarication at political levels – for the Auxiliary Units as early as mid-summer 1940 – and for special forces for the rest of the war.

From her very special position in MI(R) as Colonel Holland's secretary, Joan Astley recorded that 'We became part of Section D.' Clearly any attempt to pretend that MI(R) and Section D were miles apart and antagonistic to one another – although responsible to different and not always harmonious departments – was ill-founded. And, as both were wound down in the autumn of 1940, and their best units and men absorbed into SOE, it seems fair to conclude that the British rush into irregular warfare had generally been well-orchestrated.

This hitherto undisclosed proximity of the Auxunit Operational Patrols to the Secret Intelligence Service proper, via Station XII and Winston Churchill's Toyshop, may be one of the reasons why they were intended to be cocooned in everlasting secrecy even after the war.

*

Major Oxenden, in his final report to the War Office, recommended the disposal of all noisy weaponry issued to the Auxiliary Units and proposed the Welrod as a replacement. With grenades, he went further, writing that the No. 77 should prove the most effective as there was no indication of the point from which it was thrown and there was no chance of an enemy patrol taking cover. In his opinion, the rest could be ditched. Simplicity should be the aim of guerrillas and the Welrod was all that was necessary for attack and the virtually silent No. 77 Grenade for defence. Finally, he proposed that custom-built explosive charges for each separate target were unnecessary. They should be replaced with a single, pre-prepared charge of about half a pound of explosive with a delay or activating device built in. By simplifying transport from the Operational Base to the target area, and reducing the time needed in the danger zone to place the explosive in position, the charge should be sufficient for most objectives. 'Oxo' thus summed up the more valuable lessons learned by Auxiliers as the result of their collective experience, and from trial and error. The results have been invaluable for special forces ever since.

However, not a single Auxilier mentions the bronze casting of a lump of coal and not a single such exhibit has ever been found early one morning on the doorstep of the Museum of the British Resistance Organisation, where anonymous donors – having displayed well-honed, silent nighttime skills – usually choose to leave their often highly volatile 'exhibits'.

Chapter Fourteen

Thuggery

'*Thug* – a ruffian or cutthroat. A member of a former religious organisation of robbers and murderers in India who strangled their victims.'

World Book Dictionary

The association between the word 'thuggery' and Major Beyts – veteran campaigner for the British raj in Burma before WWII – is obvious enough. He certainly used the term in the title of his lectures at Coleshill. It embraced close quarters combat and warlike dirty tricks of all kinds.

Beyts, with his own considerable experience of hand-to-hand fighting with the Indian Army against Burmese insurgents in the 1930s, was the man called upon by MI(R) to put into practical terms an irregular warfare philosophy which had been, until then, essentially hypothetical. His warriors, civilian and military alike, were left in no doubt about the ruthlessness expected of them. It was also made clear that they were authorised to do their scallywagging stuff in an entirely new and untried way and, once out there on their own, to do so without the need for referral upward to any of the powers-that-be. This unwritten authority was compounded by the desperate and immediate threat which Hitler and the Nazis presented. That authority was by word of mouth only, sometimes with nods and winks and, contrary to previous War Office practice, never in writing. In this respect, their position was well understood by most Auxiliers. As a result of their training, Auxiliers intended to stop at nothing.

It may properly be claimed that, in his teaching, Beyts formalised irregular, even illegal, warfare, for what was seen then as a totally worthy and justified cause – the national interest. At the same time, he created an example of terrorism as it has since developed worldwide – sometimes justified by the perpetrators from the very highest moral standpoint and, at others, with no justification at all. It all depends whose side you are on. With or without an ingredient of religious, political, criminal or nationalistic motivation, terrorism has now become ever more intense, sophisticated and fanatical.

Beyts's techniques had already been effective in combat in Burma, as he explained to researchers at the Museum of the British Resistance Organisation:

> You have got to be very quiet – you break a twig and it might have been your death. You've got to show originality in your approach to whatever work it is. When I was young, in the Burma show, I used to pretend, unless people in a village were to give us the truth, they would all be shot, or that sort of thing. I would string one of them over a tree and after about – there is a time recorded how long you do it before you lose consciousness when you are tied up under a tree – I would have him cut down straight away and the body removed and the hospital rum would be rammed down his throat, so that he would be perfectly well. Then the whole village would come forward hoping that they were going to save the boy's life whatever, and out came the truth.

Auxiliers were instructed that ruthless persuasion by the Nazis would be an everyday event, and left in no doubt that such strong-arm techniques were expected of them, too; and that they could assume that they would be absolutely justified. The bottom line was assassination and execution of collaborators or anyone representing a threat to security.

Beyts reduced thuggery, in its close quarters form, to formal lectures and practical instruction totalling no more than six or seven hours. But, through his enthusiasm and that of his instructors, the results left a lasting impression on Auxiliers.

They were all also motivated by the teaching and example of a remarkable pair of former policemen who, fortunately for them and British irregular forces, retired from the Shanghai Municipal Police Force just before war broke out – William ('Dan') Fairbairn and Eric ('Bill') Sykes. Following extensive personal training and research, as well as practical experience on their local battlefield – the waterfront of the world's most violent city – both were experts in hand-to-hand combat, armed and unarmed. Fairbairn, however, specialised in unarmed gutter fighting – after vast research and with finely honed technique – and Sykes with firearms. Dirty tricks were their speciality and from the end of 1940 they instructed Special Forces at Inverailort Castle in the Scottish Highlands. It was a memorable experience for all their students and, although Fairbairn is thought to have made only

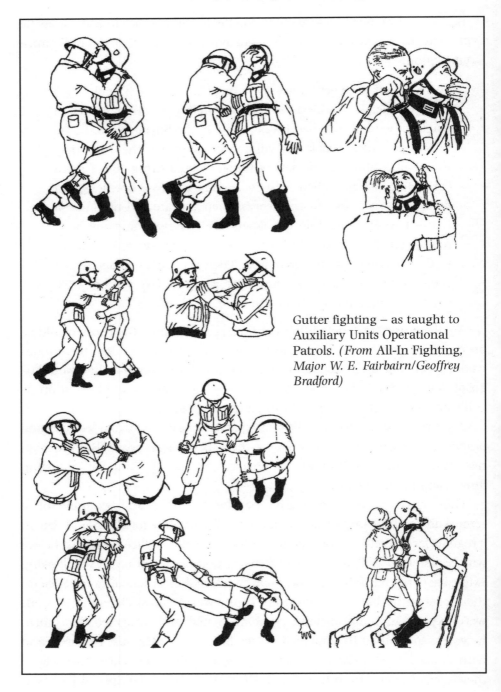

Gutter fighting – as taught to Auxiliary Units Operational Patrols. *(From* All-In Fighting, *Major W. E. Fairbairn/Geoffrey Bradford)*

one visit to Coleshill and the Auxiliary Units, his contribution to the training syllabus was recognised and confirmed by his biographer, the late Peter Robins.

Lieutenant Ronald F. ('Henry') Hall later Major R. F. Hall, MC, a pre-war Territorial soldier in the Artists' Rifles, led the Dorsetshire Regiment battle patrol from XII Corps to the Special Training Centre at Inverailort in the winter of 1940–1:

> We gathered at the foot of a large staircase in the house and two old gentlemen in their late fifties, dressed in battledress with the rank of Captain and wearing glasses, appeared at the top of the stairs. They proceeded to throw themselves down the stairs together, landing in a battle crouch position at the bottom, with a handgun in one hand and the Fairbairn-Sykes knife in the other . . .

In 1940, Fairbairn and Sykes proposed to the War Office that they should design a special commando fighting knife; the first pattern (of 1,250) was produced by Wilkinson Sword in polished steel. They remain collectors' items to this day (as well as being an effective hedge against inflation). A batch of 2,000 of the second pattern in darkened steel and more suitable for night fighting, was delivered before the end of 1941. Later models were mass-produced, with over 56,000 being made before the end of the war. The basic design had a chequered hilt, 'S' cross guard, and double-edged, seven-inch spear-point, stiletto blade, honed razor sharp. Modifications followed. This beautifully balanced weapon was the classic fighting knife for special forces during WWII and most Auxiliers had one. Some still do.

After a personal demonstration to, and request from, their president, United States Special Forces were later given instruction by Fairbairn at the top secret Camp 'X', just within the Canadian border near Oshawa, Lake Ontario. The Americans gave generous credit to the former Shanghai policeman – whereas detailed recognition of his contribution – with Sykes – to irregular warfare, only emerged in the United Kingdom more than fifty years later. For the Americans, their knife symbolised the very fighting spirit of Britain's elite raiding forces.

Fortunately copies of Beyts's lecture notes have survived. They follow closely the Fairbairn/Sykes guidelines, with 'Attacks, Defences and Releases; Frontal Holds; Wrist Releases; Arm Locks and Breaks; The Cross Buttock throw; Waist Holds; Strangleholds; Sentry Stalking; Ground Holds; Defence against Stranglehold and against Opponents armed with knives or revolvers, or rifle and bayonet; Parries and Trips.' The course went into detail on the value of the edge of a steel helmet, heel or toecaps – even just a matchbox – as aids to defence or attack. The objectives were limb breaks, dislocation and wounds, or complete disablement of an enemy soldier.

If Beyts's lectures were sanitised from the uncompromising example of Fairbairn and Sykes, the difference was only marginal. Later, when the War Office produced *Notes on Unarmed Combat for Soldiers and Home Guards*, their ideals were retained – but the sparkle was lost:

> *Object*
> It [unarmed combat] inculcates that spirit of self-confidence, initiative, and determination so necessary to the soldier. By these qualities, allied to a sound knowledge of the art, a man is enabled to acquit himself as a soldier even although he finds himself in the most desperate of situations.

These formal words contrast with Fairbairn's own blunt instruction 'Kick them in the testicles!'

As we have seen, in his final recommendations to the War Office Oxenden wrote: 'The knife is perhaps the hardest and noisiest way of killing a conscious man, but is light to carry.'

'Oxo' was admittedly an ex-Machine Gun Corps officer, but this extraordinarily uninformed statement entirely fails to take into account the vast experience of Fairbairn and Sykes, their custom-built fighting knife, their dedication to speed and technical repetition during practice, and the precise instructions they had disseminated through Inverailort on both the efficacy of killing with the knife, and also how to go about it all in almost complete silence. In *All-In Fighting*, Fairbairn describes the subclavian thrust below the collarbone, after which a victim will inevitably drown in his own blood within seconds. An alternative target is a neck thrust.

Major Ronald F. Hall confirms unequivocally that all this is not just theory. With his Dorset battle patrol he made night river crossings, after the failed Operation Market Garden at Arnhem, to rescue injured and abandoned paratroopers. His patrol's main weapon was the Fairbairn/Sykes knife which, combined with stealth, camouflage, and training, accounted for around a score of German soldiers during the rescue, and his award of the Military Cross for hands-on command. Noise was never an issue.

Moreover, the late Reginald F. J. ('Rex') Chaston, from the Carlton (Suffolk) Patrol of the Auxiliary Units, remembered in detail the technique he was taught to attack a sentry from behind. A right-handed attacker would first place his left hand over the face of the enemy, thumb upward round the nose, and the two lower fingers holding the mouth closed from under the chin. When dealing with a sentry, he expected to kill in almost total silence – and completely so if he kept strictly to his rules of training – during the few seconds he could expect a struggle from his victim. Rex did, of course, get Fairbairn's instruction at second hand, but directly from Oxenden's team at Coleshill. The only deduction is that Oxenden must have delegated this part of the instruction course to his subordinates. Nevertheless, he should not have been in doubt of the silent effectiveness of the Fairbairn/Sykes techniques.

*

Accomplished though he was in the skills of unarmed combat, Sykes's major contribution to CQC was with firearms. Winston Churchill, it will be recalled, had instructed that Auxiliers were all to have revolvers and, by November 1940, 2,500 had been issued, with a balance of 288 in the process of issue. If there were about six men to each patrol there were, by that time, nearly 500 patrols established or, on average, over twenty to each area. By any judgement, this was an amazing achievement under Gubbins's management – in just four months from a standing start.

As so few Auxiliers were previously trained in the use of a handgun, there was plenty to do – and it was Sykes's systematic agenda that saved the day. Accuracy with a handgun is notoriously difficult – the bigger the calibre and killing power the greater the kick – and he taught that, at close quarters, speed was everything. His method was called the double-tap, two bullets fired instinctively in rapid succession, without pause for thought, with the gun held single handed in the area of the firer's navel. Formal range methods were abandoned and replaced by practice with the left hand, from behind cover, in the prone position, and while moving. As several different, mainly American, firearms were on issue, general principles were vital, while the special features of each weapon could be explained in detail at Coleshill or by the local Scout Sections.

When the sums were done before stand-down in 1944, the quantities of firearms, ammunition, explosives and booby traps circulated to patrols was staggering. The champion area for packs of Auxunits Mark II was

Hampshire, with 780, followed by 630 in Norfolk. Every pack included 100 detonators and 20 lb of explosive. Each area averaged about half a ton and each patrol about 70 lb – by that time usually Nobel 808, Polar Gelignite or PE. With these quantities came various accessories, including pull and pressure switches, and L-Delays. Thanks to the qualities for which Auxiliers had often been selected in the first place, this Aladdin's cave gave scope for innovation.

By definition, patrols generally comprised like-minded comrades. The Bathampton Patrol in Somerset was no exception. Robert Millard writes:

> I suppose the patrol was not quite the same as the average; we were mostly teenagers – five had attended the same school – and were 'townies'. In 1939 I was due to go to Exeter College to train as a craft teacher but on the outbreak of war the course was closed and the workshops used to train munitions workers. I became a pupil teacher, training at the Bath Technical College, as did Mike Jones, another patrol member. This gave us access to the College's machine shops and Plumbing Department. Tony Hunt's father was a radio engineer and had a radio repair business, and Gordon James was an apprentice electrician, his father running an electrical business. As you can see this gave us a nucleus of practical facilities and technical know-how that was supported by our Sergeant's knowledge of explosives. He worked in a quarry.
>
> Put this together with the fact that the Devil finds work for idle hands and there you are!

The professional soldiers in Winston Churchill's Toyshop would have been proud of them. And, had the enemy arrived, the Nazis would have been wise to avoid hosing down their famous open-top Mercedes coupés. Here are some of the devices they would have been up against:

Tap booby traps were constructed from standard water pipe fittings, a wooden plug, a piece of wooden dowel, copper wire, and a modified time pencil connected to instantaneous fuse and a few ounces of explosive. The tap spindle was unscrewed and the washer holder replaced with a length of dowel, force-fitted, and with a hole drilled to take a length of copper wire. A wooden plug with a hole the diameter of a time pencil was forced into one end of a T-junction. The modified time pencil was pressed through the hole in the wooden plug. The spindle assembly was screwed carefully into the tap body, the various parts reassembled, and the fuse and explosive hidden out of sight. The expected gush of water when the tap was turned was replaced by a detonation commensurate with the volume of explosive attached.

Electrical detonators and switches. There is no record of these having been issued to Auxiliers from official sources but the Bathampton Patrol managed to liberate a few from their sergeant's quarry, and then developed a supply of their own by fixing a detonator in a tube containing a highly inflammable powder that could be ignited by an electric current.

Flammable powders. Black powder was available to farmers, and was purchased by the Bathampton Patrol at a local High Street shop; two pounds cost just 12/- (60p) in those unsuspicious days. A DIY substitute was made by carefully scraping the heads off matches, and then putting them through sieves. For safety, small quantities were prepared at a time and care taken to avoid igniting the powder during the process.

Igniters. The patrol made two types. The first was constructed from two pieces of insulated copper wire twisted together at one end, with the wires bared at the other and bent parallel about 3 mm apart. A piece of very fine resistance wire connected the bare ends and this glowed red – when attached to a suitable battery – and ignited the flammable powder. To complete the device, a pasted paper tube with a detonator glued into one end was then filled with a wire igniter and loose, flammable powder. Once the open end was sealed with wax, the whole contraption was waterproofed with a coating of shellac. The second device used the exposed filament of a torch bulb to ignite flammable powder.

The 'Bathampton bombers' next turned their inventive ideas to another accessory missing from their official inventory, an electrical pressure switch. They established by experiment that an ordinary domestic bell push was easily adapted. To design a home-made pull switch, they used a standard wooden clothes peg with two drawing pins – and wires secured with insulating tape – pushed into the open end as contacts. A piece of stiff plastic was inserted between the pins to keep the contacts safely apart. The peg was then nailed firmly to a tree or post, for example, through the central spring. When the plastic strip was displaced by a pull on a trip wire, the firing circuit was closed, and the explosion initiated. 'This switch was sensitive and needed caution when setting it up!' writes Bob Millard.

Another speciality of this ingenious team was a pendulum-operated electrical switch made from three lengths of copper wire, a sort of tilt or release switch. The pendulum itself was a straight piece of copper wire suspended within a copper wire circle, about 25 mm in diameter, with a small screw and nut securing it to a support. When this switch was assembled into a booby trap within a flat tin, with fuse, detonator and explosive in place, displacement swung the pendulum into contact with the circle, closing the circuit and firing the explosive.

Careful, but not difficult, assembly was called for. The first task was to make a home-made battery holder. Paper strips were wrapped round dowel of the same diameter as the battery, pasted and, when dry, coated with shellac to stiffen the tube. The dowel was then extracted. Three suitably sized and bored circular plywood discs were fitted inside the tin to take the battery holder, and supported in position with dowel rods. The explosive charge was fitted between the two lower discs and assembled with a pendulum switch. Uncalled for activation was prevented by an arming switch on the top disc. Any container in everyday use, such as a tobacco or cocoa tin, was suitable and should have been virtually undetectable during routine searches.

Fine replicas of some of these devices have been prepared by Bob Millard and are now exhibited at the Museum of the British Resistance Organisation. Others, such as the incendiary device they created to replace the 'feeble' official supplies identified by Nigel Oxenden, are more difficult to exhibit. Bob Millard assures us that: 'Electrical igniters having no detonator but a generous black powder charge can ignite a condom or balloon filled with a petrol/petroleum jelly mixture.'

> Put a vee notch in a Bickford fuse; insert a non-safety match stalk into the fuse so that the head is in contact with the fuse core. If a glass-paper tube is made to fit over the fuse, pulling the abrasive tube firmly across it will ignite the match head. This enables the fuse to be lit in windy conditions and avoids the flare from a match being observed by the enemy.
>
> The match and tube can be protected from damp by covering them with a condom.

A charge prepared in that way could be taped to a vehicle's exhaust system, with the match then being lit by generated heat. It was not just at Bath that such a technique for destroying enemy vehicles was developed. A Norfolk Regiment soldier, Tom Colquitt, posted with an Auxiliary Unit Scout

Section at Wroxham, on the Broads, had similar ideas, using official issue – rather than home-prepared – stores.

Tom taped two sticks of Nobel 808 with a detonator under the driver's seat of a truck. These were connected by instantaneous fuse to another detonator taped out of sight under the exhaust manifold. Generated heat soon set off this device. His patrol carried prepared explosives around on exercises in modified car inner tubes – one end tied with rope and a noose round the other acting as a sling. Bicycle inner tubes were adapted to carry 'sausages' of prepared charges to lay along the wing or, preferably, the tail section of an aircraft.

His Scout Section put together a test-firing rig to blow up passing cars. A wire strung across the road from trees was intended, when hit by a vehicle, to set off grenades suspended – with safety pins removed – in cocoa tins alongside. Unfortunately, overkill marred this otherwise promising experiment. Their subaltern – observing the test from nearby in the comfort of his private, under-insured car – was struck by debris when the windscreen blew in.

In neighbouring Suffolk, Rex Chaston and the Carlton Patrol found the most difficult part of an early warning system in the vicinity of their Operational Base was to knock the bottom cleanly off a beer bottle. Once this was achieved, it was simple enough carefully to fit a Mills grenade with safety pin removed inside, to stand the bottle upright in a place where enemy troops were likely to assemble, and offer temptation in the form of a risqué magazine partly underneath. As soon as the bottle was lifted or tipped, the grenade would fall out – giving an enemy search party just five seconds to live. Or die.

His patrol was issued with anti-personnel grenades of plastic appearance with a length of ribbon attached to the firing pin (these were probably No. 69 grenades). These were smaller than tennis balls and could be thrown easily. The weight of the grenades was enough to pull out the pin if the ribbon was secured, causing an instantaneous explosion. They also used these grenades to booby-trap a door which, once opened, allowed the grenade simply to drop. The weight falling on the secured ribbon would do the rest.

Chaston's patrol planned defence against all comers once the enemy arrived and the patrol was stood-to in the OB. They intended to use phosphorus grenades hung, camouflaged, in trees and attached to trip wires – with pull switches, instantaneous fuse and detonators – covering approach tracks. Anyone approaching would be in danger of incineration. These traps could not discriminate between friend and foe, of course, but by then his patrol had been trained that dirty tricks were just another part of the total war in which they were involved.

In nearby Ipswich, Ivan Potter's conversion of a .22 rifle into a handgun has already been noted. As an engineer, he had his eyes on bigger targets as well, and he too has kindly supplied replicas to the Museum of the British Resistance Organisation. He used everyday materials, cocoa tins for anti-personnel devices and larger biscuit tins for mines. The cocoa tin, hidden with trip wire attached, could be tied to the side of a tree or staked down into soft ground. A detonator was attached to instantaneous fuse, which fired guncotton, blasting six-inch nails in all directions. Since then, in other hands, this type of weapon has become the staple of terrorists worldwide.

The biscuit tin mine was also filled with guncotton and nails and had to be buried in soft ground about an inch below the surface of a track. The lid of a ten-inch diameter tin is slightly flexible, and when over-run by a man or vehicle, this slight movement was used to fire a .22-inch bullet. This exploded the guncotton and nails. Although not expected to take out a tank, it would immobilise vehicles fitted with pneumatic tyres, or kill a man.

It is no surprise that Auxiliers found all this thuggery, both official and self-developed, considerably more absorbing than patrols and watch-keeping with the Home Guard.

However, by 1943, with the Germans now seriously bogged down on the Russian Front, their homeland under ever increasing aerial attack, and the Second Front looking imminent, it was less and less likely that Auxiliers would be called upon in their stay-behind role. It was a waste of specially trained men and some of them were targeted by Allied special forces, including the Chindits in the Far East, SOE, 'Jedburgh' teams, and the reforming Special Air Service Regiment under Colonel 'Paddy' Mayne. For a couple of hundred Auxiliers, war was soon no longer some sort of prank.

On active service, some would give their lives for their country.

Chapter Fifteen

On Active Service, 1943–1945

The life that I have is all that I have,
The life that I have is yours,
The love that I have of the life that I have
Is yours and yours and yours.
A sleep I shall have, a rest I shall have,
Yet death will be but a pause,
For the peace of my years in the long green grass
Will be yours and yours and yours.

Leo Marks

This poem was read at the Service of Thanksgiving for the life of John Lewis Fielding, JP, FRICS, WWII Auxilier and SAS trooper,[†] held at the Church of Saint Peter Mancroft in Norwich town centre, on Saturday, 7 August 2004. The organist played the one-time popular French song '*Sur le Pont d'Avignon*' and Leo Marks's poem was the reading by John's godson, Andrew Colman. It had been written affectionately for Violette Szabo, the SOE agent briefed by Marks before she was parachuted into German-occupied territory, and the significance of the music was not lost on the representatives of the Special Air Service Regimental Association who were there, as well as John's family and friends – and a few Auxiliers.

*

† It is acknowledged with gratitude that much of the information in this chapter came from the late John Fielding and papers supplied by his family. John continued his SAS service, usually with Captain John Tonkin, for the rest of the war in Europe, finishing up in Norway, on a mopping-up operation. Former Auxiliers John Fielding and Peter Weaver – both county cricketers in civilian life – took part in a match between two SAS squadrons on a makeshift pitch at Bergen before a crowd of hugely bewildered Norwegian spectators. Peter Weaver was out for a duck but, rather like Ian Fenwick before him, he was voted 'demon' bowler for the day, taking five wickets for just seventeen runs.

General Claude Auchinleck, C-in-C Middle East, approved the formation of a new irregular unit of the British Army in North Africa in the summer of 1941. In the beginning the detachment often worked alongside soldiers of the experienced Long Range Desert Group (LRDG), mainly Rhodesians and New Zealanders. The insignia of 'L' Detachment was the flaming sword Excalibur. David Stirling was appointed to command, promoted to the rank of captain, and given the go-ahead to recruit six officers and sixty NCOs and other ranks. On the orders of Brigadier Dudley Clarke the new unit was called 'L' Detachment, Special Air Service Brigade.

The SAS might have been stood down after the North African campaign, in spite of its remarkable achievements in action. Irregular fighters – including Commando units and the foreign armies created by SOE – were thought by some officers to be little more than diversions from the main effort before the Allies – namely, to liberate German-occupied countries using conventional forces. Their case was not helped by the SIS which notoriously differed with SOE and the SAS on how clandestine warfare should be conducted – the SIS remaining convinced that overt, short-term action would simply draw down a rat-hunt of enemy retaliation endangering the security of its own agents, already in position, and collecting and communicating intelligence with long-term, softly-softly methods.

A further problem was the fact that British special forces recruited the finest soldiers, sailors and airmen they could find. The argument by reactionaries at staff level was that this reduced the quality of men available for conventional units and any peripheral benefits achieved by irregular action would be outweighed by commensurate manpower disadvantages for the units expected to carry the main burden of liberation, particularly county infantry regiments. It was further argued that the arms and munitions supplied to SOE partisans in enemy-occupied countries, were never likely to repay the manpower and expense involved.

The crux came in 1943/4 as planning for the Second Front advanced. SHAEF (Supreme Headquarters Allied Expeditionary Force) plans for conventional operations were being co-ordinated with the activities of Special Forces, SOE and the so far untried and untested indigenous resistance forces poised for action in German-occupied territories. The Auxiliary Units were not by definition a large part of these strategic disputes but their existence was not forgotten. As manpower problems loomed, some Auxiliers, previously exempt from conscription, had that exemption withdrawn. All ranks from the Scout Sections returned to regimental duties and the best Intelligence Officers were transferred into sharp-end units The result was that many Auxiliers found themselves in khaki and being invited to volunteer for Special Forces service of one sort or another.

Jedburgh teams were one such special force. The Jedburgh programme was laden with deliberately confusing code words. Despite some historians' imaginative speculation, 'Jedburgh' itself was simply the next choice on a meaningless pre-prepared list. Each man had a code-name and so did each operation. The Jedburghs were an example of what Gubbins, during his pre-war years with MI(R) preparing *The Art of Guerrilla Warfare*, had forecast and described as the 'third type', embodying 'operations of large guerrilla forces, whose strength necessitates a certain degree of military organisation in order to secure their cohesion and to make and carry out effectively a plan of campaign.' He went on to propose that:

> In cases where guerrillas are a nation in arms, or part thereof, fighting for their freedom in alliance with or assisted and instigated by a third power which is willing and anxious to render all assistance to them, it will usually be advisable for that third power to be represented by a mission at the headquarters of the guerrilla movement. The duties of such a mission would be to provide expert advice, to ensure liaison, to arrange the supply of arms, ammunition, money, etc., and to provide leaders and assistants to leaders, if such were found to be necessary.

This prescient summary fairly clearly defined the Jedburgh teams' function. The product of SOE planning for paramilitary action behind enemy lines after D-Day, Jedburghs eventually matured into teams of three men, sometimes in uniform and in civilian clothing at others. One was a 'Jedset' radio operator and usually an NCO. With SOE retaining primacy, the leader was usually a British officer, preferably with a knowledge of France and the French language; the third was an American or French officer.

The general objective was to parachute Jedburgh teams into prepared drop zones (DZs), with supplies of sabotage material and arms, to contact French *résistants*, establish radio contact with the UK and then – as already envisaged by Gubbins and Peter Wilkinson – to arm and prepare indigenous partisans for action when SHAEF decided they could lend useful weight to the advance of regular forces. Two of these teams were led by former Auxiliers.

One such team leader, in Operation Felix, was Captain John Marchant (code-name 'Somerset') of the Wiltshire Regiment (and until recently – according to research by Roger Ford published in *Steel from the Sky* – an Auxunits Intelligence Officer). Felix was an unqualified success. The team parachuted into Brittany on 9 July 1944 and kept on the move for their own security, stopping overnight in remote farmhouses. After contacting local partisans, more than forty aircraft loads of stores were dropped onto marked DZs, sufficient to equip the thirty companies of armed partisans who were called into action after a BBC broadcast on 2 August 1944. Among their numerous battle successes, they killed 300 or so German troops and captured twice that number. Contact was made with advancing American soldiers – whose task the partisan forces must have greatly assisted – on 6 August, after which the area was soon cleared of the enemy. Team Felix returned safely to England three weeks later.

Lieutenant Victor Gough of the Somerset Light Infantry is on record as a Scout Section subaltern in Somerset and, like his comrade Lieutenant Roy Bradford in Devon, was probably reshuffled and promoted as an Intelligence Officer within the Auxiliary Units in 1942. Again, like Bradford with the SAS, Gough responded to an invitation to join special forces and, code-named 'Arran', was selected to head Jedburgh team 'Jacob'. After several postponements, his team was inserted on 12 August 1944 into the area of the Vosges mountains in eastern France, together with advance elements of the ill-fated SAS Operation Loyton.

Working with French partisans in the same area, the Jacob team first lost their radio operator, Sergeant Ken Seymour ('Skye') – apparently with his Jedset. Seymour was captured and interrogated but, uniquely and surprisingly, survived as a prisoner of war. Gough's French comrade, Captain Maurice Boisserie ('Connaught') was then killed in action. Keeping apart from the local SAS operation as far as possible, while retaining working contact, Gough survived with the help of French *résistants*, while staying in touch with Special Forces HQ in London through the SAS radio network. Gough himself was captured toward the end of September 1944 and brutally interrogated; during his incarceration he drew a number of cartoons – later recovered by Major Eric Barkworth and a team of SAS investigators known as 'Secret Hunters'. Gough was executed by firing squad at Gaggenau on 25 November 1944.

His murder and that of his SAS comrades was, for the Germans, entirely in accordance with Hitler's orders. This excuse failed as a post-war legal defence, and a number of appropriate convictions were obtained at war crimes' tribunals. However, sentences imposed on the perpetrators were considerably ameliorated as the imminence of the Cold War was recognised and new political, military and diplomatic imperatives became paramount.

Other volunteers for Special Forces were Captains Joshua ('Stuart') Edmundson, Royal Engineers, and Donald ('Ham') Hamilton-Hill, of the Seaforth Highlanders. They had been the first Auxiliary Units' IOs in Devon and Lincolnshire respectively and joined SOE under Gubbins – Edmundson in 1943 and Hamilton-Hill at the end of 1941. As already noted Edmundson went as SOE liaison officer to Earl Mountbatten in Ceylon, where he spent the rest of the war.

Donald Hamilton-Hill, born in 1906, was educated at Dulwich College in London. He was a dashing character, a good cricketer, and a top-class polo player. He was commissioned on 25 November 1939 and after his service with the Auxunits in Lincolnshire, his next job was second-in-command of SOE training schools. After promotion as chief training officer, 'Ham' was frequently on active service behind enemy lines in the Middle East and Greece until the conclusion of hostilities. He died in 1985.

In his book *SOE Assignment* Hamilton-Hill explained SOE as:

> An amalgamation of organisations which directly or indirectly, and subject to British Cabinet control, operated eventually in virtually any enemy occupied and many unoccupied territories throughout the world . . .
>
> Assassination, sabotage, prisoner of war escape routes, female seduction, sophisticated blackmail, resistance armies build-up, gun running by parachute drops, by land, by sea, forgery, currency deals and the making – and sometimes breaking – of foreign leaders and even governments. Such were some of the headings on files marked Most Secret in the various Country Sections within SOE Head-quarters.

This was no exaggeration. In 1943, an American observer, Major John Tyson, spent three weeks touring SOE training establishments. His findings were summarised in a report to his Chief of Special Operations:

> It should be definitely understood that the training any prospective SO [Special Operations] agent has received in our Washington

Schools prior to his arrival in this [the European] theater is entirely inadequate and no trainee should be considered for field operations until they have had further training in this theater . . .

The quality of the training given, the manner of handling the men and caliber of instructors in the SOE schools is far superior in every detail to anything we have to offer in our training centers in the U.S.A. This superiority is the direct result of three hard and confusing years of trial and error.

Within this sphere of preparation for D-Day at least, the Americans wisely conceded *de facto* superiority to the British.

Sergeants Cyril Hall and Jack Steward, of the Suffolk Regiment and Auxunit Scout Section at Cransford, near Framlingham in Suffolk, although not full-scale volunteers, found themselves in Special Forces in the Far East. Jack remained in the Suffolks and served with airborne supply forces. Cyril Hall (later a company sergeant-major) was first posted to the Nigeria Regiment in West Africa and, after jungle warfare training, was sent to India. His new regiment prepared to enter the Burmese jungle with Major General Orde Wingate's second Chindit long-range penetration force – latterly under the command of acting Brigadier 'Mad Mike' Calvert, Peter Fleming's former Auxunit colleague with the XII Corps OU in Kent.

Cyril was not to enjoy a 'good war'. None of the Africans had been in an aircraft before. Neither had the mules they were to accompany. Neither had Cyril Hall, their NCO. They were to be flown in an American Dakota 150 miles behind Japanese lines. Cyril described the start:

The pilot gave his instructions. 'Get those mules in first and make 'em happy. The rest of you get behind their crates, equal numbers each side to balance the ship.'

Two hours later with No 1 Air Commando, USAAF, we were over 'Aberdeen' [a landing strip and base]. Small lights were shining below like Piccadilly Circus. We bumped down on the rough strip, disembarked in one piece, and soon disappeared into the night to bivouac. The Japs were around somewhere. The next morning, a reconnaissance patrol returned with orders to move to the 'White City' which should have been called 'Red City' from the amount of blood that flowed there. It was a fortified roadblock straddling the Japs' main line of communication.

To get there we had to cross a mile of open paddy covered by Jap machine guns. As we approached we heard the drone of approaching aircraft. It was our fighting boys of the RAF, six heavy bombers and nine fighters. They came in low on smoke markers laid by our mortars. The fighters let go 50 lb eggs and the bombers dropped parachute-retarded bunker-busters. It was a gift from heaven and kept Johnny Jap's head down as our column arrived.

This campaign was nothing less than terrible. We were fighting two enemies, the Japanese and the natural elements of the jungle, especially the dreadful monsoon rain.

Fighting was continuous and Cyril was injured when a jagged hole was ripped in his thigh by a sharpened panji stick booby-trap hidden at the side of a jungle trail. In the first Chindit operation wounded British soldiers were shot by their own officers rather than be abandoned to a cruel enemy and, to avoid a repetition now, American pilots were trained to fly L.5, single-engine aircraft into a short airstrip hacked from the jungle. After several days, the area of Cyril's wound was badly infected. To survive he had to keep walking.

At this time everyone was suffering from some sort of fever or illness because of the terrible monsoon conditions. I not only had my leg wound, which now looked like a piece of raw, stinking meat, but was full of fever, had sores on my feet, and a very painful right ear where several abscesses had formed.

A skilful US Air Commando pilot 'just dropped in' and flew him to a larger nearby airstrip. He was next taken by Dakota to a base hospital in India.

Cyril Hall never doubted that his training in the Auxiliary Units was a material factor in his survival in Burma. He died in Lincoln in 2006.

*

The strong possibility exists that former Auxiliers were deliberately recruited into other special forces, such as the Commandos but, if so, this was unsystematic and the details remain unconfirmed. The Special Air Service, however, seized the opportunity to absorb the offered gift of hardened, fit young men, carefully selected and already partly trained and to employ those who responded to the call for volunteers to participate in the sharp end action being planned as back-up for the Normandy landings.

After informal personal approaches to Auxiliary Unit commissioned officers, Lieutenant-Colonel Robert Blair Mayne ('Colonel Paddy'), the legendary Ulsterman destined to win four DSOs (but not the VC), extended his urgent search for suitable new troopers for the reborn 1st SAS Regiment to men from the dispersed Scout Sections and volunteers from Operational Patrols whose exemption from military service was withdrawn as D-Day approached. The process by which he brought this about is unclear but it could hardly have taken place without compliance from the Auxiliary Unit HQ at Coleshill.

A number of subalterns, NCOs and other ranks from Scout Sections whose personnel had been returned to regimental duty from the end of 1942 and through 1943, were assembled – officers at the Curzon Cinema in Mayfair and other ranks at the requisitioned Grosvenor House Hotel in Park Lane – and called upon to volunteer. As 'Tiny' Kidner of the West Dorset Scout Section said later 'It would have taken real guts to remain seated!' Again, apparently with identifications supplied from Auxunits' HQ, a number of men formerly from Operational Patrols were approached at regimental level; it is known that at one time more than a hundred were collected for assessment in a holding camp at Northampton.

Subsequently, Monmouthshire Auxilier Private Fred Rowe and eight volunteers from the Dorset and Wiltshire Scout Section, including Private Jack Blandford, joined B Troop, B Squadron, 1 SAS, and were employed in Operation Haggard, the main party parachuting behind the front line in France, near Bourges, from 14 August 1944. Haggard operated for five weeks with great success and light casualties until relieved by advancing American ground forces.

At Intelligence Officer level, Captains Roy Bradford (Sussex Auxunits, and former Scout Section subaltern in Devon), Ian Fenwick (Somerset) and 'Dick' Bond (who preceded Bradford as IO in Sussex), were approached individually by Colonel Mayne. After proving themselves as leaders, all were destined to be killed in action.

Bradford, who originally served with the Devon Regiment and was an architect in civilian life, is buried in the village cemetery at Crain, in the Nièvre department near the Massif de Morvan wilderness 150 miles south-east of Paris where, just a fortnight after D-Day, he led a section of Operation Houndsworth for A Squadron, 1 SAS Regiment. Houndsworth was active for a month without casualties but, on 20 July 1944, Roy Bradford with his

SAS driver, two sergeants and a *maquisard*, travelled by Jeep to rendezvous with a neighbouring *reseau* (resistance group) outside the village of Lucy-sur-Yonne. While taking every care to avoid 'friendly' fire from the Allied aircraft strafing anything resembling an enemy unit, they shot a pair of German soldiers who had mistakenly tried to flag them down. The Jeep then unexpectedly ran into a convoy of troops and lorries parked just out of sight on a narrow country lane.

With no options, they roared alongside and opened up with the Jeep's twin Vickers machine guns, but came under return Spandau fire from the very last lorry. Captain Bradford and his rear gunner, Craftsman 'Andy' Devine were killed instantly, and their *maquisard* guide and Sergeant White injured. Husbanded by the only uninjured survivor, Sergeant 'Maggie' McGinn, the wounded men got away through a forest and two adventurous days later made good their escape – to be cared for by friends in the *maquis*. McGinn was later awarded the Military Medal. Fifty years later, the local villagers – who help to maintain the SAS graves in pristine condition – erected a memorial at the spot where the SAS men were killed and re-named the road 'Rue du 20 Juillet 1944'.

Captain Ian Fenwick of the Auxiliary Units and the elite 60th Rifles, King's Royal Rifle Corps, was an all-round sportsman and demon bowler at Cambridge University before the war. Having been soundly beaten by him at tennis, his friend, the film actor David Niven, gave up the game for ever. In a preface to a book of Fenwick cartoons, *Enter Trubshawe*, published after his death, Niven wrote:

> Later we became good friends and many summer holidays were spent by the seaside taking the corks out of people's rowing boats and smoking blotting paper up trees.
>
> I remember we laughed a good deal at most things; but even in those days, Ian was especially fascinated by big moustaches.

Fenwick had in fact been a successful pre-war cartoonist for, among other magazines, *The Tatler*, *Men Only*, *London Opinion* and *The Strand*. He seems to have maintained links with the SIS, too. It was Niven who introduced him to the man who became his favourite character – the hirsute Trubshawe: 'In real life he is six foot, six inches tall and has a moustache which you can see from the back at a range of a hundred yards on a clear day.' *Enter Trubshawe* was Fenwick's final book. He concluded the acknowledgments with:

> This book has been got together during a difficult and busy time, and only just before I embark with one or two others on my liberating mission to other lands, so that if anything should seem hurried or wrong, or lacking, I would ask for your indulgence.
>
> There's a war on!

The war really started for Fenwick in mid-June 1944 when he parachuted into the Forêt de Fontainbleau as commander of D Squadron, 1 SAS, to take part in Operation Gain. His unit was ordered to attack and disrupt German communication and rail networks in the Orleans area. On one occasion, having successfully strafed a troop and ammunition train at night, chasing alongside in Jeeps and firing until it was burnt out, he ended his radio report 'We are happy in our work!'

However, on 7 August, while on a mission away from his base, Fenwick heard that his men had been attacked and captured. Although reports differ, this was not the whole story. He was not to know that, although surrounded by hundreds of the enemy for seven hours, most troopers had dispersed and fought their way clear. He immediately set off in his Jeep on a rescue mission but – with all weapons blazing – was himself ambushed and killed in the village of Chambon-la-Forêt, where the Germans had already executed seven French hostages in reprisal for local resistance activities together with the SAS. He is buried in the nearby village of Nancray. Two French *résistants* and his SAS sergeant died with him; a dozen of his troopers were captured in the main action. All except one escaper were later murdered.

One of the cartoons in *Enter Trubshawe* features Iris Edmundson and her two-year-old son, Will. This dated from a holiday which the two Auxiliary Unit Intelligence Officers from Devon and Somerset and their families took on the North Devon Coast in 1942. When he bought a copy of the book for 5 rupees at Bhawani and Son, Stationers and Booksellers, Connaught Street, New Delhi, while on leave in 1945, it was the first time that Stuart Edmundson had seen the cartoon. It was also the first he knew that Ian Fenwick, his comrade and friend, was dead.[†] Thanks to David Niven's influence, however, the real Michael Trubshawe went on to appear in films such as *The Guns of Navarone* and *The Pink Panther*.

[†] In August 1997, Lieutenant-Colonel J. W. Stuart Edmundson formally opened the Museum of the British Resistance Organisation at Parham in Suffolk, and his family has kindly loaned his copy of *Enter Trubshawe*.

In a now-famous photograph of the Auxiliary Units' staff and Intelligence Officers taken on the steps of Coleshill House, Captain Charles Frederick Gordon ('Dick') Bond of the Wiltshire Regiment, aged thirty but looking younger, stands alongside Ian Fenwick. Later a temporary major, he was probably promoted after a transfer to the Auxunits' Special Duties Section.

Bond, too, volunteered for the SAS and commanded B Squadron, 1 SAS, in Operation Howard, one of the final SAS episodes in the North-West Europe campaign. According to the SAS Regimental Association, after crossing the German border just one month before the end of European hostilities, his squadron came under heavy enemy fire from nearby houses and went to ground. As they tried to reconnoitre forward ahead of the advancing Canadian 4th Armoured Division, 'Dick' Bond and his driver were killed by snipers. He is buried in the large war cemetery at Sage, near Oldenburg, Germany, and was probably one of the last SAS casualties before VE-Day.

The deaths were soon avenged. Colonel Mayne, virtually single-handed, wiped out the enemy defenders and rescued wounded SAS troopers. He was recommended for the award of a Victoria Cross by Field Marshal Montgomery but, at the level at which decisions are made, 'VC' was crossed out and '3rd Bar DSO' substituted.

*

Captain (later Major) Geoffrey Brain, former subaltern to a Scout Section, volunteered for Phantom, the 'Most Secret' GHQ forward observation and signals unit. As such, he served with Polish, Canadian and US troops throughout the campaign to deliver Western Europe from German occupation, being Mentioned in Dispatches and awarded the prized Polish Cross of Valour.

Norwich Auxilier John Fielding was another successful volunteer. He was accepted into the SAS for re-training at Darvel in Scotland, followed by parachute instruction at Ringway, near Manchester. Together with ten other former Auxiliers, and about thirty other troopers, John Fielding was then confined to 'the cage' near Fairford airfield, Gloucester, used mainly by the SAS as a departure point for airborne operations. Secrecy was their guarantee of safety, and once in they were not allowed out. Some troopers grew tense and bored as departure was delayed on several occasions – changes of plan being necessitated by continuing amendments to the operational schedule for D-Day. A final postponement on 4/5 June was due to the adverse weather which delayed the whole invasion programme.

Two members of the advance party of Operation Bulbasket, for which Fielding and his comrades were standing by, were, however, released on 1 June, and driven in great secrecy to SOE HQ at Baker Street for re-briefing. The CO, Captain John Tonkin, a 23-year-old SAS veteran, and Lieutenant Richard Crisp, formerly of the Royal Armoured Corps, were given full details of their mission, including targets coded as LOT 1–4, railway lines likely to be used by the *Das Reich* Armoured Division of the SS, now refitting near Toulouse after suffering heavy casualties and loss of equipment on the Russian Front. Bulbasket was one of a number of operations by SOE and the RAF – which included extensive co-operation from suitably located French partisans – to delay the transfer of *Das Reich* to the invasion beaches of Normandy.

Tonkin and Crisp passed the hours remaining before embarking at the SOE airfield at Tempsford, in the considerable comfort provided at Hassel's Hall, near Sandy in Bedfordshire. Moreover, they spent some time in the agreeable company of two attractive female SOE agents. One was the courageous Violette Szabo, about to embark on her second and final mission before being captured and cruelly executed at Ravensbruck concentration camp. Vera Atkins, personal assistant to the head of SOE's French Section, found her calm, even as pre-take-off tension mounted.

As the D-Day invasion fleet at last headed for Normandy on the night of 5 June 1944, Tonkin and Crisp parachuted into the Vienne region of France. John Fielding and the main party followed in two RAF Short Stirlings from 190 Squadron, RAF Fairford, on 11 June. They arrived at the selected DZ near Poitiers on schedule. It was not, however, an uneventful arrival.

Indeed, in retrospect, it was a mixture of drama and comedy. At the very moment Fielding's stick left the aircraft, advance elements of *Das Reich*, with headlights ablaze, were grinding along a trunk road close to the DZ. It was impossible for two four-engined Stirling bombers to transit the Channel and the northern half of France at low level in the hope of avoiding radar interception, to identify small marker lights and coded flash-lamp signals on the ground, and then to circle at drop height of a few hundred feet, without making the very devil of a racket. The DZ was only just out of sight of the trunk road but, in charge of the reception party on the ground, Tonkin decided to take a chance. Marker fires were lit and recognised and the Stirlings circled noisily into position for the drop.

The SS soldiers of *Das Reich*, it seems, with the noise of their heavily armoured transport, were unaware of this, but were alerted by the sight of a cascade of coloured lights falling from the sky dangerously near them. Fearing an assault by some new British secret weapon, the convoy pulled off the road and established a complete black-out. Much of this was briefly witnessed by the descending parachutists and the thoroughly alarmed reception party. The lights were the latest SOE modification to parachute-supply containers and were intended simply to help the ground party find them more easily. They were, however, intended to activate at ground level and not 500 feet!

SAS troopers were encouraged to work in pairs and John Fielding's experienced partner, Sam Smith, followed from the Stirling so immediately that he snagged John's parachute canopy. John's kitbag of explosives also failed to detach as planned and he landed heavily, thinking at first that he had broken a leg. Fortunately he had not and was soon able to 'march off into the night'. It was his first trip abroad and his first taste of action.

'It was exciting!' he remembered many years later, with typical understatement – and the spectacle of much of the feared armoured division driven to passive defence by an unplanned airborne display of pyrotechnics was not easily forgotten. At the DZ, the stand-off with *Das Reich*, blacked out and immobilised less than two miles away, created an incentive for furious activity by both SAS troopers and French partisans to collect and hide the parachutes, to load bullock carts with containers of urgently needed supplies, and melt away into the night before *Das Reich* came looking for them.

Three other sticks of troopers – each with a LOT target – were dropped separately and in the face of considerable operational difficulties. It seems that no blame could properly be attached to anyone, but all landed well off target. Trooper George Biffin, formerly a Dorset Scout Section Auxilier, was inadvertently dropped into the town square at Airvault, heavily garrisoned by the enemy, and captured. In the light of later events, it was nothing short of miraculous that, after brutal interrogation, George Biffin was handed over to a Luftwaffe anti-aircraft unit, acquired PoW status, was badly injured by 'friendly' fire from Allied aircraft while being convoyed to Germany, survived further privations as a PoW – and yet eventually returned to England and civilian life in good form.

Another small group of four former Dorset Scout Section Auxiliers, commanded by their subaltern, Lieutenant Peter Weaver, was dropped well away from its LOT 4 target. Without food supplies, or a single French speaker among them, they nevertheless found and destroyed their allocated target and were then faced with a sixty-mile cross-country march to find and rejoin the main group. They were helped by French partisans, and a couple of American soldiers they came across in a wood one night, surrounded with abundant supplies of food, explosives and weaponry. The Americans had failed to find the French *résistants* for whom this bounty was intended and the SAS men were invited to help themselves. Weaver and his group eventually found Tonkin's main party in woodland near Poitiers, where their CO gave them a waspish reception for being later than expected.

For three weeks, Bulbasket was at full stretch – receiving supply drops, liaising with and training French partisans, attacking trains and communications targets on most nights, and regularly moving camp to avoid detection by the enemy. Lieutenant Tomos ('Twm') Stephens, convincingly disguised as a French peasant, bicycled forty miles each way to identify a dozen or so tanker loads of fuel, essential for further progress by *Das Reich*, in marshalling yards at Châtellerault. A prompt RAF response to an urgent radio message saw the total destruction of the whole supply. It helped greatly to delay the relocation of this feared armoured division to the Normandy battlefront. In his book on that infamous division, Max Hastings agreed that this was 'Bulbasket's most significant success'.

Morale generally was good. BBC radio messages for Bulbasket were preceded by identifying music, for them the French tune '*Sur le pont d'Avignon*' and this usually brought the troopers into action, jiving and finger-wagging in the popular dance style of the day. At the same time, with Tonkin taking more on his own shoulders, and those of his officers and experienced NCOs, than perhaps he should, some troopers were under-employed and security was carelessly prejudiced. With two of his NCOs – Bateman and Eccles – missing after a night raid near Poitiers, there was a serious danger that the whereabouts of the encampment, now in a forest near the small village of Verrières, south and east of Poitiers, had been forced from them. Tonkin also had complaints from the commander of *résistants* working with him – all too rarely security-conscious themselves – that troopers had openly fraternised with local girls and taken them for drinks at the nearest bar. On top of all this, rumours persisted that agents of the SD, the SS security service, were in the area.

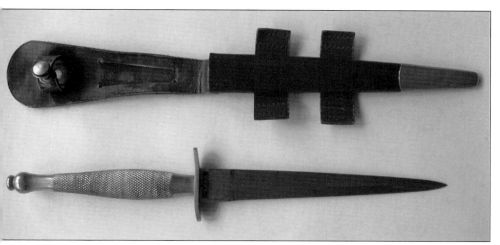

The classic Fairbairn/Sykes fighting knife was issued to each man in an Auxunits Operational Patrol. *(Ann Warwicker/Graham Bines)*

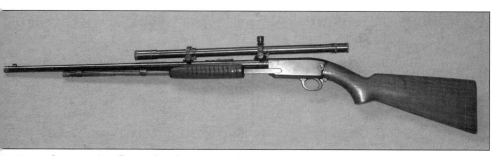

A .22-inch sniper's rifle, with telescopic sight, was issued to Auxiliers, usual one to each Patrol, for 'shooting bunnies' (or assassination of collaborators, or enemy sentries or officers). This pump-action Winchester was a typical example. *(Colin Wroth)*

A close image of an Auxiliary Units' sniping rifle. Although various types of telescopic sight came with them, it was not until 1942 that silencers were available too. *(Colin Wroth)*

A Thompson sub-machine gun – imported from the United States – was in the hands of each Patrol until the later distribution of Sten carbines. *(Ann Warwicker)*

The Welrod – a sound-suppressed handgun – was developed for SOE and Special Forces and issued to a few Auxiliary Units, usually for field testing. Although still on the 'Classified' list, it is believed to have been only recently withdrawn from active service. Although accurate to fifty yards, its prime purpose was close-range silent assassination. *(Ann Warwicker)*

Geoffrey Bradford at the graves of his brother, Captain Roy Bradford, and Trooper 'Andy' Devine in the village cemetery at Crain, Morvan, France. Both had been killed in action during SAS Operation Houndsworth on 20 July 1944. *(Geoffrey Bradford)*

Formerly a Scout Section subaltern in Devon and, after promotion to captain, Intelligence Officer in Sussex, Roy Bradford was killed in action behind the lines in France on 20 July 1944, fighting in SAS Operation Houndsworth. *(Geoffrey Bradford)*

Former Norwich Auxilier Trooper John Fielding was on a sabotage mission away from the Bulbasket encampment and survived the German assault. He was later safely exfiltrated from France by the RAF and continued on active service with the SAS abroad until the end of European hostilities. *(Ann Fielding)*

Company Sergeant-Major Cyril Hall who, after serving in the Cransford, Suffolk, Scout Section, was transferred to the Far East, where he campaigned and was injured during the Chindit long-range penetration into the Burmese jungle, behind enemy lines. *(Jean Hall)*

An experienced SAS campaigner, Liverpool Trooper Sam Smith had picked John Fielding, on his first active service abroad, as his comrade for Operation Bulbasket. He too, survived the war. *(Ann Fielding)*

This snapshot taken during the ill-fated Operation Bulbasket shows Lieutenants Richard Crisp (second from the left) and Twm Stephens (seated), together with French partisans. Both officers were killed during or after the well-coordinated German attack on the SAS encampment on 3 July 1944. *(Ann Fielding)*

Trooper John Fielding (right), armed with an M1 carbine, and transport 'acquired locally' behind the lines in France. *(Ann Fielding)*

This underground Auxiliary Units radio Out-Station near Axminster in Devon was entered by a shaft concealed under the outdoor privy. The small radio room for transceiving was cleverly hidden behind the railway sleeper end wall and the aerials buried under the bark of nearby Scots pine trees. *(Andrew Mothersole)*

The entrance to the outdoor toilet radio station near Axminster. The wooden, twin-seat non-flush toilet within could be lifted to reveal a downshaft to the radio room below. *(Andrew Mothersole)*

Special Duties Section Out-Stations were fitted with secret R/T sets, well hidden from inadvertent discovery. *(Ann Warwicker)*

All the original radio sets were 'put beyond further use' at the end of the war and this is the only replica – carefully constructed and assembled by members of the Vintage and Military Amateur Radio Society in concert with the Museum of the British Resistance Organisation at Parham in Suffolk, where it can be seen by visitors. *(Ann Warwicker)*

Teenager Jill Monk on 'Merry Monarch' during her years as a runner collecting agents' messages from secret dead letter drops by night for her father's SDS spy network. *(Jill Monk)*

Yolande Alston, née Bromley, was an early recruit into the Control Station personnel. Here she is pictured in her cover as an ATS subaltern assigned to the Royal Corps of Signals. *(Gill and Timothy Alston)*

Subaltern Thea Ward was the wife of Captain Ken Ward, Royal Corps of Signals, one of the design team that, pre-war, developed the secret TRD transceiver used by the Auxiliary Units (Signals). Thea and her colleagues were known by male officers as 'secret sweeties' – a sobriquet which these ladies deplored. *(Captain Ken Ward)*

RIGHT: Junior Commander ATS Captain Barbara Culleton was known as the 'Battling Bantam' at Auxunits' HQ, Coleshill House. *(Barbara Culleton)*

BELOW: Rudolf Hess, the Nazi Deputy Führer, parachuted into Scotland during the night of 10/11 May 1941 with peace proposals, just prior to the German onslaught into Soviet Russia. The Auxiliary Units Special Duties Section monitored his 'unexpected arrival'. *(BRO Museum collection)*

BELOW RIGHT: The memorial tablet commemorating the arrival of Rudolf Hess near the estate of the Duke of Hamilton. *(BRO Museum collection)*

THIS STONE MARKS THE SPOT WHERE BRAVE, HEROIC RUDOLF HESS LANDED BY PARACHUTE ON THE NIGHT OF 10th MAY 1941 SEEKING TO END THE WAR BETWEEN BRITAIN AND GERMANY

The Castle Rising Patrol, Norfolk, at stand-down. NCOs are distinguished by the General Service cap. Deryck Neville stands third from right. *(Deryck Neville)*

South Essex patrols at stand-down. Captain C. G. Ford (in beret), the Group Commander, is seated centre and behind him stands the sturdy Donald Handscombe. *(Donald Handscombe)*

This stand-down photograph of Northumberland Auxiliers, taken in the Black Swan at Morpeth, shows an unusually smart turn-out and Group Commanders identifiable with neckties. Their first commander was (Sir) Anthony Quayle, later to become famous as a star of stage and screen. *(W. A. 'Willy' Ricalton)*

The Leiston, Suffolk, Patrol headed by Group Commander T. H. Denny (seated, centre), at stand-down in 1944. Looking purposeful, the standing Auxiliers were armed with Mark III Sten carbines. *(Pamela Denny)*

A post-war reunion of Monmouth Auxiliers. Lord Glanusk (with prominent moustache, seated centre), was the third Auxiliary Units Commanding Officer. *(BRO Museum collection)*

A 1990s reunion at Tottington Manor, Sussex. Captain Barbara Culleton stands at the left of the front row; in the back row local Patrol Leader William Webber is second from the left and third from the left is visiting Devon Auxilier Geoffrey Bradford. *(BRO Museum collection)*

A reunion of East Anglian Auxiliers held at Colchester Barracks in the mid-1990s. Donald Handscombe is seated centre, and on his right are David Antill and Raymond Cottis of the South Essex Patrols. Albert Cocks, standing second from the left, was author of 'Churchill's Secret Army'. Next to Bert Cocks is John Fielding, Norwich Auxilier and survivor of SAS Operation Bulbasket. Standing second from the right is Stratford St Andrew Auxilier, and the first Suffolk man bold enough to defy the Official Secrets Acts, Herman Kindred. *(C. Jack Grice)*

Roy Coleman, then a sixteen-year-old coal miner in South Wales, was recruited into the Cymmer, Port Talbot, Patrol, by his Scoutmaster, Wally Thomas – a former regular soldier, who was the leader of the local patrol. *(Andrew Miners)*

Trevor Miners – Perranporth, Cornwall, Patrol (top left); Geoff Bowery – Suffolk Scout Section (bottom left); Robert Millard – Bathampton Patrol (centre); Alfred Cable – Stratford St Andrew, Suffolk, Patrol (top right); Ralph Clarke (left); and Ivan Mower, Stradbroke, Suffolk, Patrol (bottom right). *(Author's collection)*

Arthur Gabbitas, left, and Albert Cocks, veterans of the Auxiliary Units, organised the first reunions in East Anglia. *(C. Jack Grice)*

Veterans at a Parham Open Day in 2007. Left to right, seated: George Gibbs, Alfred Cable, Barbara Culleton, Jill Monk, David Antill; standing: Roy Coleman, Trevor Miners, Ivan Potter. *(Andrew Miners)*

WWII Auxunits Special Duties Section personnel included women. Jill Monk (left), a 'runner' for the north Norfolk network – usually on horseback at night – is pictured here during a 2007 reunion at Parham, together with Captain Barbara Culleton, ATS Junior Commander at HQ with special responsibility for testing two-way R/T installations at Control Stations. *(C. Jack Grice)*

David Weeley, leader of the Weeley Patrol in Essex. This post-war picture was taken inside his former Operational Base. *(BRO Museum collection)*

This image indicates the determination with which Carlton Auxilier, Reginald ('Rex') Chaston, tackled the Ministry of Defence head-on after the Medals Office refused his 1996 application for the Defence Medal. It arrived just before he died – eight years later. *(C. Jack Grice)*

While acknowledging the need to move camp, Tonkin urgently wanted a supply drop, scheduled on an excellent nearby DZ, and was also finding it difficult to establish a new camp with an adequate water supply. The crisis began on the afternoon of 1 July. Fielding was on guard overlooking one of the approaches to Verrières forest. He saw two Frenchmen on a motorcycle and sidecar, with a punctured tyre. He watched for a while before showing himself, and then escorted them for interview with partisans resting in the SAS encampment near the north side of the forest. They were satisfied that the motorcyclists were genuine *résistants* from a distant *reseau*. Assistance was given to repair the puncture and they were allowed to go. In retrospect however, it seems certain that they were Milice – French traitors working for the SD. They had certainly discovered the exact whereabouts of the SAS camp. Fielding later said 'Of course I should have shot them.'

Several events of significance occurred during the nights of 1 and 2 July. After nightfall on the 1st, Sam Smith headed a small party, including John Fielding, on a sabotage operation intended to take about four days. The following night, Tonkin left in one of four Jeeps, armed with Vickers K .303-inch machine guns and long-range fuel tanks – the Jeeps had successfully been parachuted into a DZ by RAF Halifax aircraft. He scouted the area for a safer campsite and returned in the early hours. Neither of these parties noticed anything suspicious near the forest. There is no record of any trooper being placed on overnight guard duty.

At around 7.00 a.m. on Monday, 3 July, 500 enemy soldiers attacked. Well-deployed units from a reconnaissance squadron and an SS Panzergrenadier division opened fire. Mortar and heavy small-arms fire erupted into the main camp. Provisional contingencies for such an attack were largely disregarded by both the SAS and half-a-dozen partisans who were with them. In the panic which followed, Tonkin was quick to see the immediate imperatives – to destroy their radio and codes, to make the best use of the armoured Jeeps, and for small groups to disperse into the numerous defensive positions provided by the forest itself. Orders passed along by his officers were, for whatever reason, unfortunately ignored by a large contingent of both troopers and partisans, who made unsuccessful attempts to leave cover as one group and escape through surrounding cornfields. After being injured by gunfire, Lieutenant Twm Stephens was beaten to death with the butt of his own carbine. Three troopers, including Auxiliers Joe Ogg and 'Sam' Pascoe, were also wounded.

Realising that escape was impossible, the main party surrendered. All the French partisans were massacred on the spot. After being cared for by French medical staff in Poitiers hospital, the injured troopers were removed by the SD; their bodies have never been found. It is probable that they were murdered by lethal injection. The other prisoners were harshly but not, it seems, brutally treated while the German authorities agonised over Hitler's 'Commando Order' of 18 October 1942 – of which the SAS is reported to have been unaware – that captured Allied special forces' troops should be executed. (The origins of this order are more fully described in Chapter Twenty-One.)

Although this order was in obvious contravention of all the accepted laws of warfare, it was a clear directive for the execution of the troopers of Bulbasket but not one for which the average German soldier wished to be held responsible. It was realised that their own record, as parachute troops behind the lines in Holland, Greece and Crete, for example, had also created new rules for similar operations by Allied forces. Indeed, many German Army commanders considered that SAS operations were similar to those expected of their own soldiers.

After delays and attempts to shelve responsibility, and in spite of their clear entitlement to prisoner of war status, the SAS men were taken – after being re-joined by the two missing NCOs – to woods at St Sauvant, south of Poitiers, in the early morning of 6 or 7 July, lined up and executed by a firing squad. Official, and obviously specious, German reports claimed that they were allowed to smoke a final cigarette, to say farewell to one another and that they then died bravely and with dignity. However, when their bodies were discovered by Allied troops in November 1944, they were found to have had their hands and arms bound behind their backs. Lieutenant Lincoln Bundy, the unfortunate American pilot of a Thunderbolt of 486th Fighter Squadron, 352nd Fighter Group of the USAAF, who, on a sortie from Bodney in Suffolk, had been shot down over France and then passed along through *maquis* groups to the Bulbasket team, was captured with them and suffered the same fate. The carefully tended SAS graves are in the village cemetery at Rom, south of Poitiers; there is a separate gravestone for Lieutenant Bundy. Among the dead were former Auxiliers Alan George Ashley, George Cogger, Sidney Ryland and Henry James ('Sam') Pascoe, all of the Dorset Scout Section, and Les Long and Victor ('Chalky') White from the Norfolk Scout Section. Joe Ogg had been with a Morayshire Auxiliary Unit patrol before volunteering for the SAS. Memorial trees in memory of Alan Ashley and 'Sam' Pascoe are planted in the grounds of Coleshill House.

After successfully going to ground in the forest, Captain Tonkin, Lieutenant Weaver, and six NCOs and troopers survived and, although shattered by the devastation wreaked on Operation Bulbasket, re-grouped for offensive action. After the safe return of the sabotage parties headed by Sam Smith and Lieutenant Morris, and amalgamation with a Phantom unit under Captain Sadoine, Tonkin went back into action with just eighteen men from the original complement of fifty-four.

Exfiltration of the survivors was a high priority at SAS HQ and with the RAF. SAS Captain Surrey Dane parachuted in to select a suitable landing site and, with the compliance of a patriotic farmer and after the removal of just one tree, he established a rough-and-ready airstrip of 1,600 yards, just about enough for a Lockheed Hudson – the aircraft selected for the operation – to land and take off. The airstrip was code-named Bon-Bon. On the night of 6/7 August 1944, in a remarkable display of co-ordinated airmanship, Flight Lieutenant A. H. C. Boxer (later Sir Alan) landed and took off safely with the Bulbasket survivors.

Following radio messages to the SAS Brigade at Moor Park in Middlesex, and Special Forces HQ at Montagu Street in London, from Captain Tonkin, and the 'Hugh' Jedburgh team operating nearby, the barracks of most of the German 'repression column' SS troops was identified at Bonneuil-Matours, north-east of Poitiers. Easily seen from the air, it was the target for a retaliation raid by fourteen de Havilland Mosquito FB VI fighter-bombers of 140 Wing, 2 Group RAF. Armed both with high explosive bombs and incendiaries, they attacked from low level at dusk on 14 July. Total surprise, coupled with precision bombing, virtually eliminated the barracks and many of the SS within. All the Mossies returned safely to Thorney Island. Estimates of the German dead varied from forty or so to several hundred. In any event, the barracks was abandoned by the survivors.

A second target soon presented itself for further retaliation by the RAF. The Caserne des Dunes, a pre-war French Army barracks on the eastern outskirts of Poitiers, was now occupied by enemy soldiers and agents of the Milice, who were massing for a sweep against French partisans. On 1 August the barracks was attacked – again from low level at dusk – by twenty-three Mosquitoes from 140 Wing. The result was the total devastation of the barracks and, thanks to pinpoint accuracy, a minimum of civilian casualties.

One aircraft crash-landed after engine failure – but the crew evaded capture and were back in action with the wing before the end of September.

Less satisfactory were the post-war trials. Following investigation by an SAS team known as the 'Secret Hunters', two Germans of senior rank were sentenced to be hanged for their part in the Bulbasket massacre, and a number of heavy prison sentences were imposed on others. In the event, after appeals, no hangings took place and the longest sentence finally imposed on these war criminals was five years' imprisonment. As John Tonkin later recorded: 'I have always felt that the Geneva Convention is a dangerous piece of stupidity as it leads people to believe war can be civilised. It can't!'

Chapter Sixteen

The Special Duties Section

'The simple fallacy behind the argument that total disclosure is the only alternative to total secrecy ... escaped serious challenge for so long because the intelligence community acquired the status of an unmentionable taboo, exempt from any process of rational public or parliamentary debate. Since 1924 successive governments have done their best to keep the taboo intact.'

Christopher Andrew in Secret Service

'On one occasion in July [1940], they [Intelligence Officers] found themselves with an equal number of strangers, officers and civilians and even a woman. "You may as well get to know each other, gentlemen; you are all in the same game." This was the first contact between Ops and Special Duties and was the last they were to see of one another for some time.'

Nigel Oxenden in Auxiliary Units – History and Achievement

With the entry of the Soviet Union and United States into the war, the danger of invasion had realistically passed by the end of 1941, and this was well recognised by GHQ. Half-hearted propositions to disband the Auxiliary Units completely were successfully countered by Coleshill and instead GHQ surprisingly authorised a programme of expansion. New areas were one result. The number of training courses was stepped up, a nominal roll collated;, 'phantom' so-called GHQ Battalions were created for administrative simplicity – 201 (north of Britain); 202 (centre); and 203 (south). Competitions were organised between patrols locally, and at Coleshill. Although these innovations were intended to maintain morale and a high state of readiness, Auxiliers sometimes complained that too much emphasis was placed on speed – in contradiction of all they had previously been taught. Arms and foot drill became an often-unpopular new norm.

It was a very long way indeed from the secret army envisaged at the outset, and many of the changes brought about during Colonel Major's command survived even the arrival in February 1942 of the third CO, Lord Glanusk, a TA colonel. Now that the War Office had its administrative sights on the Auxiliary Units, there was no going back. Paperwork and red tape proliferated. However, Glanusk did quickly order the abandonment of the group system, and kicked Group Commanders out of Operational Bases and upward as office managers for IOs. Glanusk's arrival at Coleshill in a Rolls Royce, accompanied by a young wife and a staff of Guards' officers with public school accents and double-barrelled names, with his complete wine cellar on sale in the officers' mess, and a stable of thoroughbred horses, can hardly have inspired the existing officer-instructors and men into renewed enthusiasm for total war.

Indeed, in spite of trappings of activity, the Operational Patrols stagnated. As we have seen already, many of the best young men were conscripted. A letter of 4 February 1943 notes a decision that fifty-one assistant patrol leaders and 181 Auxiliers should be made available for recall. 'Recall' simply meant 'conscription'. It went on to explain:

> When called up these men should, if possible, be kept together and posted to units, such as R.E. field companies, that will be employed in an assault role, where their previous special training can be made use of.

Scout Section regulars were also on the War Office hit-list:

> A large number of men from Scout Sections of Auxiliary Units are being made available for re-posting to field force units. These men also have had specialised training in explosives and it might be appropriate when they are re-posted, to make a note to that effect for the information of their units.

In spite of impressively worded protests from Glanusk, and the final CO, Colonel Frank Douglas, they were inevitably presiding over the decline of the Operational Patrols, which were formally stood down, together with the Home Guard, on 30 November 1944. A skeleton staff of physically low-grade officers and men were sent out to seal or destroy the Auxunits' Operational Bases and recover all the explosives. This process was hurried and piecemeal.

The Special Duties Section of the Auxiliary Units, however, continued to survive from 1941 to 1944 with its *modus operandi* more or less intact. Then, with an important deception role added as Operation Overlord was mounted, the Section flourished until a month after D-Day. But, in July 1944, the SDS disappeared forever. Or so it was intended.

*

There have been few disclosures by SDS personnel, no books written and – apart from insignificant, immediately post-war leaks to the press, featuring secret spy networks and lurid headlines – no authentic memoirs or serious investigative media cover. The pattern that is now clearly discernible, however, has come from a very few brave souls who – like Christopher Andrew – could see no point in everlasting secrecy.

But the first source material is to be found in public records, where there are internal reports from both MI6 and MI5. Avoidance of truth is the natural preference of both and, without further confirmation the contents necessarily call for carefully considered analysis. Fortunately, statements from veteran survivors provide useful corroboration on essentials, as well as details of recruitment and training. Not surprisingly it is impossible to discern much of a standard pattern of SDS activity; very much depended upon the experience of the Intelligence Officer involved.

The stand-down report from Section D in August 1940 was for internal inspection only and so was a summary from MI5 prepared some time in 1943 or 1944. This was also classified. With no outside scrutiny then envisaged, Section D assumed a certain freedom with the truth, and MI5 sniped at its sister service. MI6 first went into a sulk over the disbandment of its Home Defence Organisation, but then consoled itself with an over-blown list of achievements before most of Section D was relocated into SOE. MI5 lapsed into a lengthy grumble about MI6, which, although never named directly, is obliquely referred to either as 'the predecessors of the Auxiliary Units' or 'the previous organisation'.

MI5 recorded how Regional Security Liaison Officers (RSLOs) were placed throughout Britain in advance of the outbreak of war. They developed contacts at all levels, including businesses and commercial communities, factory managers, local government officials, aristocrats and prominent land-owners. Their principal conduit for information, and in many cases direct action, was the local chief constable. As these were usually appointed in the first place with backing from the Director of MI5, their Special Branch units could also be counted upon as useful cover for counter-espionage operations masterminded by the Security Service proper.

Once it was aware of the activity of Section D – after it had disappeared into SOE and the Auxiliary Units, it may be assumed – MI5 concluded, in a petulant sort of way, that the Home Defence Organisation had been liquidated without taking steps 'to clean things up'. It found that the HDO had left 'dumps of explosives all over East Anglia and the southern counties, some of which were known to the police and all of which gave them cause for considerable anxiety'. Things improved, the report agreed, with the arrival of the Auxiliary Units, who took over most of the explosives and whose IOs were generally co-operative 'over the explosives they had inherited, but who were unaware of the hidden location of others'.

MI5 reported specifically on the use of hidden wireless sets and, as we can be certain that the Operational Patrols had no access to this form of communication, it is confirmation – if it were needed – that the Special Duties Section did. In the first case, an RAF officer, found a 'member of the Auxiliary Units' transmitting from a wireless hidden in a wood. Soldiers were called and only at the last minute resisted the temptation to shoot the Auxilier as an enemy agent on the spot. In another example, 'a gamekeeper' found a wireless buried in a wood. In both cases the persuasive intervention of MI5's RSLO 'disposed of the incident'.

The Security Service also stumbled across the previously less-than-perfect – at best localised – Auxiliers' security vetting procedure and introduced an unofficial check through its regional controllers, who did a name search and gave the necessary advice. The date is not given but the beginning of 1942 seems the best guess as this was when, for the first and only time, a national nominal roll of the men in Operational Patrols began to be compiled from IOs' personal records. That MI5 was given access to the names of the personnel in the SDS, still watched over by MI6 without doubt, seems highly improbable.

This gives some idea of what to expect from the Special Duties Section of the Auxiliary Units. It was a network, absorbed in July 1940 from personnel originally recruited by officers of Section D as saboteurs. These were civilians to be left behind in their normal jobs, trained to collect and communicate intelligence. In a nutshell they were to be spies. The intelligence was then to be passed onward by a voice radio system. The range expected from the radios very much depended upon line-of-sight. Networks generally worked in small 'cells'. As a general rule – but not always – the key man at the centre was the only person who knew the identity of the others in any one cell. Secrecy intruded at every level. This was both for the safety of the men and women in the field and to conform with the MI6 golden rule that its activities had to be entirely secret from top to bottom.

On just one occasion in the otherwise typewritten Section D closing report, the name 'Bearsted' is added in pen and ink. This appears to identify Walter Horace Samuel, second Viscount Bearsted. Educated at Eton and Oxford, he won a Military Cross with the West Kent Yeomanry in WWI and is on public record as a colonel in the 'intelligence corps' in WWII. It is understood – and it will be no surprise if true – that intelligence corps may simply be cover for his role for the Secret Intelligence Service as overlord of the SDS. His son, the third Viscount, is similarly reported as a Section D officer.

Whatever the influence of the Samuel family behind the scenes, the principal SDS personality at Auxunits' HQ, Major Maurice Petherick, is a shadowy figure if ever there was one. He had fine establishment credentials. Born in 1894, he was educated at Marlborough and Trinity College, Cambridge, and had addresses both in London and Cornwall. His clubs were Buffs and the United University. His First World War service was originally in the Royal Devon Yeomanry but, significantly, he is recorded at 'the War Office' during 1916–17, when he was a mere twenty-two years of age. A National Conservative, he served as MP for Penryn and Falmouth from 1931 to 1945. As we shall confirm later, this was a typical background, with plenty of cover for a full or part-time association with MI6. In 1939 he was commissioned from the TA with the rank of major on the usefully nondescript War Office General List.

In due course 'Bill' Beyts described Petherick as the 'genius behind Special Duties'. Petherick was a superb manager – selecting personnel, re-writing objectives and terms of reference, collecting experts, delegating his authority, raising finance, and topping it all with personal dedication and example. Petherick was nominally directly responsible to the Commander Auxunits, and his initial SDS HQ was at Hannington Hall, conveniently near Coleshill. Indeed, the distance between the two country mansions was described as a pleasant walk on a good day.

The SDS system was intended to be activated as the enemy invaded. In some circles field agents were known deceptively as observers or coast watchers – but their intended role was further-reaching. The command structure fitted well into that developing within the Auxiliary Units proper. SDS Intelligence Officers, including some former Section D Regional Officers, were allocated to Areas which, conveniently, were roughly comparable with those of the Operational Patrols. The SDS IO had a number of key men and women already secretly enrolled by Section D for the Home Defence Organisation and recruited others on an opportunistic basis. Key men were equivalent to Operational Group Commanders. Security dictated the rules – IOs knew the key men and both knew the coast watchers and neighbouring cell leaders. But the agents were not to know one another and, as the most likely to be captured in the act of espionage, could not therefore give away their comrades under torture or even inadvertently throughout prolonged interrogation.

It did not always work in the way intended. From the summer of 1940 in Auxiliary Units' Area 19, for example – covering Wales, Herefordshire and Worcestershire – the maverick IO, Captain John Todd, alias Tommy Atkins, seems to have set up the whole network himself (including, uniquely, the Operational Patrols), swearing-in new recruits under the Official Secrets Acts, on the spot with his own pocket Bible. Todd did not depend upon cellular secrecy. He trained his key men *together* with their agents. Instead of the protracted but more usual one-to-one instruction given elsewhere he held meetings of his band of agents. As well as saving time, this enabled each member to know just what was expected of another. They assembled in a suitably discreet barn, difficult to approach other than on foot, and with a number of escape exits if discovered. Although this otherwise efficient system got a whole lot done in one go, it was also seriously insecure. However, it does highlight the authority delegated from HQ to IOs in the field.

Originals of the instruction material employed by one key man at Bewley Down in Devon are now exhibits in the Museum of the British Resistance Organisation. It seems that the set-up in Devon fell somewhere between the collectivism of John Todd and the absolute isolationism favoured by other IOs. For some reason Cornwall, although densely populated with operational Auxiliary Units, was never covered by the SDS, and Bewley Down radio out-station was the furthest in the South-west.

Douglas Ingrams, a farmer and pre-war special constable, was the key man at Bewley Down. For some reason he knew all his agents as *runners*, although elsewhere, runners were distinctly different and had separate roles from agents or coast watchers. It was more normal, in areas where cellular secrecy was paramount, for agents to obtain intelligence, and pass it along one stage further by notes left in dead letter drops (DLDs), secret hides from which the messages would later be removed by runners and posted in some sort of hidden letter box for the radio operator to transmit at scheduled times. The coded messages were received directly, or through relay stations, at in-stations situated at local Army HQ, assessed by an intelligence officer and passed upward to the CO if necessary.

The Ingrams family was not unconnected with the secret services. Indeed Douglas Ingrams's brother was a member of MI6. Douglas himself later moved from Bewley Down and, with the cover rank of major, for he was not a professional soldier, became SDS Intelligence Officer in Norfolk. Information about the Bewley Down cell came from his son, the late David Ingrams. The reliability is undoubted because, amazingly enough, Douglas decided that, rather than try to hide everything going on from a curious twelve-year old son, he would actually involve him, at least at a peripheral level. This included witnessing the unique construction of the underground radio-station and, as homework in the evenings, crayoning-in outline insignia of British and German soldiers.

DLDs varied; some were behind loose bricks of a wall or the plank of a garage door. Culverts, birds' nests and hollows in trees were adapted too. Those demonstrated and installed under Douglas Ingrams's direction included hollowed-out and sleeved doorknocker studs and the hinges of otherwise derelict five-bar gates.

His favourite DLD was the identifying number plate pinned into a telegraph pole. Once the plate was first removed it was straightforward to hollow out the core of the pole and fit a sleeve to take the rolled-up message. Once the DLD had been set up, the runner knew it held a message from the agent if the number plate was upside down. The runner for the Bewley Down group would then go to a garden refuse dump in which children's toys were discarded. Among them was a tennis ball with a cut in the cover in which the message was to be inserted. The runner then continued a few yards further, to the stump of a beech tree. This had been carefully sawn horizontally and fitted with an off-centre pivot. When rotated by someone in the know, a hollow section was disclosed and this married with a terracotta water pipe passing downward into the ground. The tennis ball and message were dropped into the hollow, then rolled along the pipe and down to a container in the hidden underground radio bunker. The operator would take the tennis ball, encode the contents and transmit to his control station.

Victor N. Hogben, of Foulmead Farm, Sholden, Deal in Kent seems to have been an SDS agent too. According to notes which his son found after Victor's death, his occasional secret service career started during WWI when, with special skills in horsemanship and sharp-shooting, followed by a course in Arabic, he lived with a guide and a local interpreter as a native behind Turkish lines in the Middle East conflict – even meeting Lawrence of Arabia. The SIS must have kept him on its lists and in WWII, now aged forty-one and too old for conscription, he volunteered 'to help if needed'.

After a few weeks, a man in civilian clothes came to his farm, identified himself as 'from the War Office', and invited Victor to join Civil Defence 'with a roving role to move around, keeping my eyes open for anything unusual'. With many local areas declared 'Restricted', travel was limited but he had a dual opportunity to scout within a radius of five miles or so of his home on 'farming business' with petrol coupons supplied, and – with a special sugar ration – to visit beehives as the secretary of the local beekeepers' association. With a travel pass for his car and his ostensible role in Civil Defence, he was in an ideal position to scout around without creating suspicion.

He claimed to have justified his selection by identifying two German agents, posing as a disabled man in a bath chair and his nurse, who were regularly transmitting from a radio hidden under the seat to a German vessel waiting in the English Channel. Both were 'interned'! With an unusual remit, Victor not only passed on his own discoveries, from a radio station hidden in woodland inland, near Nonington, but also others he collected from the local Operational Patrols which were left for him in a DLD. He was thus both spy and runner and, unlike the bulk of the country where patrols and SDS were not to know one another at all (to the surprise of Major Peter Forbes in Scotland, who had realised the value of the local knowledge of his Auxiliers), their daily observations were all fed into the spy network, with a safety cut-out in position through the use of the DLD. Nevertheless, in a close-knit farming community, there was some overlap of security. Even so, it was not until after the war that Victor was fully aware of the number of colleagues and friends near him who had been involved in either the Operational Patrols or the SDS of the Kent Auxiliary Units.

However, with security working well, as far as Victor knew the station was a 'radio room run by the army' and, he believed, his messages were relayed to another station near Caversham in Berkshire – a distance that would have required Morse transmission, never part of the SDS network. The inference is that he was, advertently or not, using a transmitting station run by MI6, possibly even the very unit shown to Captain Norman Field by the C-in-C Home Forces, General Alan Brooke in August 1941. This is further evidence that the connection between the SDS and the Secret Intelligence Service was an ongoing thing and not totally discarded when Section D stood down in July 1940. It is worth adding that Victor Hogben's records for both WWI and WWII are missing from the National Archives. The only official excuse offered is the possibility that 'they may have been destroyed in the Blitz in 1940'.

Victor Hogben's son Stephen writes: 'But was it just co-incidence that both father and Norman Steed [Manston Auxunits' Operational Patrol Leader] were appointed magistrates in the early 1950s? Or was it reward for their wartime service, as father believed?'

In their book *The Mercian Maquis*, the highly respected WWII researchers Bernard Lowry and Mick Wilks describe the 1941 SDS recruitment of a retired Monmouthshire farmer, the late George Vater. From his recorded account, he was first known as a runner and later as a cut-out. John Todd was his IO and George's job was to collect messages from DLDs and deliver them by hand to the address of a local vicar, who had a radio hidden behind the altar of his church. The aerial was disguised behind a lightning conductor running up the church tower. Once he had proved himself, George was given the names of the others in his cell – three vicars, a doctor, an engineer, a carpenter, a gardener and a farm worker. The spy network was certainly democratic. Edible paper, tasting like chewing gum, was issued for writing messages.

In 1942 at Aylsham in Norfolk, sixteen-year-old Jill Holman was recruited as a runner by her father, the local SDS key man. Whereas George Vater was never too sure how he had been picked out in the first place, Dr Alex Holman was perhaps a more obvious candidate. A WWI naval officer and a local GP, he was a pillar of the Aylsham community and well known. Jill was a keen equestrian and had already met the Norfolk SDS Intelligence Officer, Major John Collings of the elite 5th Royal Inniskilling Dragoon Guards, after his numerous visits to their house – usually timed as lunch was about to be served – both on SDS matters and to ride one of her stable of horses. At the time she was unaware that he had been injured during the Dunkirk evacuation in May 1940. He was bilingual and temporarily diverted from Norfolk and dropped behind the lines into France before D-Day on a spying mission, probably with a 'Sussex' team. During his exfiltration he was injured again. To account for his absence, Jill was led to believe that he was incapacitated with lumbago. It was at this stage that he was replaced as Norfolk SDS IO by Douglas Ingrams from Devon.

Jill Monk, as she became, used her horse Merry Monarch for secret night cross-country rides to her allocated DLDs. Messages were brought back to her home, where the underground coal cellar had been converted – ostensibly as an air raid shelter for her family – into an 'out-station', with the radio hidden behind an electric heater fitted into the former coal chute. Only when an invisible catch was released with a thin knife could the stove be eased forward to reveal the small transceiver. Again, the aerial was disguised as a lightning conductor running upward on a chimney breast.

This type of secret service was replicated elsewhere according to the preferences and experience of individual IOs. Allotted tasks did not stop at observation, however. David Ingrams maintained that an organisation so well developed would also have undertaken intelligence-gathering by apparently collaborating directly with the enemy. This would have mainly been the task of selected German-speakers among SDS personnel, and would have called for considerable skills. A special opportunity presented itself for women, who might find it easier than men to open contact with occupying troops. The downside was that anyone seen collaborating with the enemy was likely to be added to the Operational Patrols' hit list. At the same time they would promptly have been executed by the enemy if their role as double agents was discovered. The work of this 'other side' has not of course been confirmed.

Neither has that of assassination, either of collaborators or enemy officers. The dangers of ruthless retaliation were clear-cut, but here we are near to the bottom line of total war. George Vater acquired a .22 sniper's rifle with assassination in mind; when he was told, Todd showed disfavour but did not order the weapon to be abandoned. In any event, operational Auxiliers were equipped and trained to do this job when ordered.

Elsewhere, convincing evidence has been recorded that assassins were deliberately recruited and trained for a special task. In one locality, for example, four teenage sharp-shooters were picked out from a school cadet corps by men in Army officers' uniform, and put through sophisticated training in marksmanship, disguise and deception. Each boy used a false name. The prepared cover story was that they were receiving special training as Home Guard messengers. They were provided with firearms, including a silenced .22 rifle and telescopic sight, as well as other weaponry, explosives, and a one-room, underground OB – all similar to those issued to the Auxiliary Units. Their task was specified as finding and killing enemy soldiers. Rigorous training was conducted by two hard, mature men dressed as Army NCOs in battledress without insignia. When the danger of invasion passed in 1942, the cadets were suddenly told by the sergeant 'That's it lads; it's finished.'

A final burst of SDS activity was initiated at the end of 1943, and lasted until D-Day. With the compliance of the SIS, an imaginative campaign was orchestrated by the London Controlling Section under Colonel 'Johnny' Bevan. His principal task was to deceive Hitler about the location selected for Operation Overlord, the Allied invasion of Europe. The Germans had to be persuaded that the Allied attack would be in the Pas de Calais instead of along the Normandy beaches.

The LCS created an entirely fictitious First US Army Group (FUSAG) under the (temporarily unemployed) American General Patton. False troop camps, tank and lorry parks, and dummy installations of all kinds were concentrated in the South-east and East Anglia. The SDS contribution was to accept the issue of 200 standard War Department No. 17 radio sets and work them night and day in the same areas, transmitting any old rubbish that came to mind in open language. It was known that transmissions by No. 17 sets were easily intercepted by the enemy and it was the calculated intention to convince German listeners that this abundance of low-level talk, normal enough for any army group, was a sure indication of the presence of an Allied invasion force massing for a cross-Channel attack – and preparing to take the short sea crossing to Calais. It is impossible to say just how worthy this SDS contribution was. However, the deception scheme did lead to a temporary increase in womanpower, and kept the SDS alive and comparatively well long after a German invasion was impossible.

Public records show that on D-Day itself, 6 June 1944, the SDS comprised 240 male officers, 57 ATS subalterns, and 92 other ranks. On 29 June, when the stand-down was finally settled, the War Office summed it all up:

The SDS consists of a regular cadre and approximately 3,250 civilians, who man R/T Stations and are trained to transmit information about the enemy in the event of raids or invasion.

The axe finally fell on 4 July 1944. Here is part of the farewell message, dated 7 July, from the Commander, Auxiliary Units, to members of the SDS. (Colonel Douglas enclosed a copy of the letter he had received from the Commander-in-Chief, too):

In this letter paying tribute to your splendid services he gives the reasons for the War Office decision.

The war is undoubtedly going well on all fronts . . .

To find the manpower to maintain the pressure and follow up our successes, thus tipping scales definitely in our favour, will strain to the utmost our already over-taxed resources, hence the necessity for making available the handpicked and highly trained regular specialist personnel of Special Duties.

Now that we have come to the parting of the ways, I must tell you how proud we all are to have been associated with the unique organisation and for which, latterly, I personally have had the additional privilege of being responsible.

On behalf of all my officers and myself, I would also like to tell you how much we have admired your disinterested loyalty which has made constant demands on your time, energy and initiative, all of which you have so generously and selflessly given.

Finally, for your keenness and enthusiasm which has been an inspiration to us one and all. Thank you.

George Vater was shown the letters by Captain Todd. They were then burned on the spot. No *original* copy has been donated to the Museum of the British Resistance. No group photographs were taken – neither groups nor photographs would have complied with the SIS need for everlasting secrecy. The Special Duties Section of the GHQ Auxiliary Units was intended to disappear.

Did any of them get paid for their secret service? 'Good God, no!' said Jill Monk.

We just did whatever came to hand to get rid of Hitler and the war. Nothing high flown or romantic but just determination, like so many others, to avenge all the deaths – including my own brother.

In those days, life was a serious business.

A number of SDS civilian personnel did subsequently benefit from indirect rewards. Several, for example, were mildly surprised to find themselves appointed as justices of the peace, or in receipt of civil honours. And who would bet that no SDS agent was ever scooped up later, for counter-espionage or counter-subversive operations on the home front, as memories of WWII faded and a brand new Cold War was declared?

Chapter Seventeen

The Signals Network

Research into the Special Duties Section of the Auxiliary Units has to be approached ultra-cautiously. Sidetracks of deception and secrecy were left to cover their activities. We are indebted to the few bold personnel who, in the mid-1990s, started to recall just what had happened to them. For the first time they assembled the SDS solution to the serious problem of communication across the front line. It was not easy to unravel. The answer was a unique radio transceiver network, operated by the agents, ATS subalterns and soldiers of Auxunits (Signals) – and with technology which few of them fully understood. Details are in Chapter Nineteen.

With the SDS under pressure, there was understandable paperwork muddle and disorder from the beginning. Then came the change of role for the HDO/SDS agents from 'obstruction' or 'destruction' to espionage. Add to all this the seeds of deliberate deception planted by the SIS for the confusion of outsiders with no need to know. Research into the British secret services is further perpetuated by the Official Secrets minefield.

The Royal Corps of Signals (RCS) – by definition, well equipped to handle new, secret electronic technicalities – was generally assumed to have led research and development for the SDS communications network. 'Royal Signals' appears regularly in SDS paperwork and in returns to GHQ. To wrap it all up neatly, even the best veteran eyewitness of all, Arthur Gabbitas, fell into the 'Royal Signals' trap when writing his personal reminiscences.

However, although a number of RCS officers were posted to the Auxiliary Units, the corps itself had no direct participation in the SDS communications network. Major John Hills, who re-designed their first transceiver, was the founding CO but not on the Auxiliary Units' payroll. His successors were also from the RCS but it would be wrong to deduce that the major technical advance in radio communication upon which so much of the stay-behind set-up would have depended came from RCS expertise. Indeed, enquiries at the Royal Signals Museum about connections with the Auxiliary Units have always drawn a complete blank.

It seems that, when invited to participate in the emerging SDS espionage network, the RCS was unable to provide either the manpower or the radio itself. The soldiers who developed and improved the first transceiver and who serviced and helped to man the SDS network under Coleshill command, were officially – according to the stamps in their pay books 'Auxiliary Units (Signals)'. Moreover, the women involved, nominally ATS subalterns, were merely using their uniform as cover. It is better to forget most of what can be found in previous books and the National Archives about the importance of the Royal Signals within the Auxiliary Units' SDS.

In *The Secret Wireless War*, Geoffrey Pidgeon explains how RCS uniform was used as cover for secret activities in one instance at least – in this case, civilian specialists working for Section VIII at Whaddon Hall, the SIS communications' base seven miles from Bletchley Park itself:

> After an approach to Military Intelligence at the War Office, it was agreed that Section VIII civilians should ostensibly be enrolled as members of the Royal Corps of Signals, although they were not paid from Army Funds.

With the Special Duties Section emerging from the Home Defence Organisation and Section D, and with the RCS marginalised, the only conclusion is that the SIS created both the SDS radio network and supplied the transceivers, either directly or indirectly. As we shall see, the SIS had help on the final furlong from some other technical experts who were never to know how skilfully their talents were being exploited.

The genius behind the collective SDS network was Major Maurice Petherick. His experience and contacts within MI6 were critical to progress. Here is the only occasion on which he appears in the relevant extract from the National Archives – in a handwritten and signed note at the end of an otherwise undated memorandum from an unnamed member of his staff to Colonel Grand himself, and filed under D Section:

> Captain Westbrook rang up, and left the following message:
> 'Saw Copper this morning. He stated that he had heard nothing of any new form of organisation, and if he did he has promised to

advise me, as he will under no circumstances agree to anything which would conflict or jeopardise existing arrangements.'

Fortunately, to give some help with the coded inferences, the following is appended in handwriting:

Dear Grand,

I hate to worry you but isn't it time a halt was called before the organisation which you conceived is jettisoned to national disadvantage.

Sincerely

Maurice Petherick 15.7.40

These comparatively few words can be interpreted with some likelihood of accuracy or – shall we say – de-coded?

'Copper' sounds very much like the Director of the SIS, Sir Stewart Menzies himself. As the date of Petherick's addendum is 15 July 1940, this correspondence was after the conclusion of the War Cabinet session in which Section D was dissolved, part of the Home Defence Organisation absorbed into the Auxiliary Units, and the remainder moved *outside* the SIS to Special Operations Executive. It is on record that Stewart Menzies was not notified that this part of his empire was to be removed and he was mightily displeased when he finally found out.

Petherick was not in the know either but was, it seems, serving somewhere within MI6. Although technically junior in rank to Colonel Grand, Petherick wrote to him in terms which assume at least equality of status. In other words, they were experienced SIS personnel and well known to one another as equals. The one question remaining is this. Did Petherick perhaps already know not only that Section D was being broken up, but also that the HDO would go to the Auxiliary Units, and that he was to take charge of the new SDS? If so he may have wanted to keep on the right side of Grand, and appear – disingenuously perhaps – to distance himself from all the intrigue involved.

Whatever internal complexity was involved, Petherick's ability to draw from the technically advanced expertise of the SIS was unimpaired and therefore a more than adequate substitute for anything the RCS might have been able to offer. It also accounts for the one time he broke from his cover – leaving just this one clue of his SIS credentials for posterity.

Although it is not known whether he had electronic know-how, Petherick was without doubt the SDS mastermind. His HQ, established at Hannington Hall, was owned by the Fry's chocolate and cocoa family, who were, initially, hosts to three or four male and two ATS officers, including – in 1941 – Junior Commander Barbara Culleton, who had enlisted in the pre-war Territorial Army. Her role in the field was to test the radios installed at 'In' (or 'Control' or 'Zero') Stations and, back in the office, to supervise ATS administration. From the volume of records on view, this included a vast amount of time pounding a Royal typewriter. At little over five feet, she was respected by other officers as 'The Battling Bantam'.

Subaltern Culleton (later Captain Culleton, TD) benefited from a clear and distinctive speaking voice. This was also one of the criteria for the rest of the (nominally) ATS officers, numbering more than a hundred at one stage. Most of these women were recruited on an old-girl network from public and girls' finishing schools – whose clear and rather up-market accents were then regarded as essential qualifications both for radio work and also, in those naïve days before communist infiltration became the fashion, for security clearance on secret work as well.

The head of Auxunits' ATS was Senior Commander Beatrice Temple, the niece of the Archbishop of Canterbury. Many of the young ladies on her interview shortlist were first directed to the ATS Officers' Club at Hyde Park Corner in London, or the teashop in Harrods of Knightsbridge where, if they could conduct themselves with proper decorum, and speak nicely too, they were more likely to be recruited into Britain's ninth secret service than not. After a short and often painful OCTU course at Craigmillar in Scotland, they were nominally commissioned as second-subalterns, although their sole connection with the ATS proper was a pay chit. One benefit from their new rank was protection from unwanted attention by male other ranks with whom, according to King's Regulations, fraternisation was a serious offence. They were also allowed to work in groups of three or four; ORs in the ATS were never allowed near soldiers in groups of less than ten. The wildly mistaken presumption was that middle- or upper-class ladies were more worldly wise than the hoi polloi.

Whenever the Auxunits future was reviewed in the light of the declining likelihood of a German invasion, the number of 'Secret Sweeties' as these often formidable ladies were disparagingly known by some officers, was whittled down and one attempt, in 1942/3, to replace them with male other ranks was robustly resisted by Colonel Lord Glanusk. He not only out-manoeuvred the War Office by confusing it with its own rules, but lived long enough to see a renaissance of numbers, as the SDS took on an additional front-line deception role for the London Controlling Section in advance of D-Day. At the same time the ATS subalterns maintained communications with Out-station operators and endlessly twiddled their dials – for they never gave up the search for other radio traffic on their frequencies, whether friendly or not.

In 1942, Hannington Hall was taken over as an 'Attery' – a billet for ATS other ranks. There is some doubt about the location of the SDS HQ from then. However, as there were sophisticated land-line communications both with Control Stations and Station X, the communications HQ of MI6, it seems likely that Maurice Petherick may well have stayed where he was – using the Attery as useful cover.

An early act of Petherick's genius was to co-opt the first CO of Auxiliary Units (Signals) in 1940.

*

This timely demonstration of Maurice Petherick's judgement came with the acquisition of Captain (later Major) John Hills, supposedly on secondment from the Royal Corps of Signals. Until then he was leading an interception team, listening to radio transmissions from German E-boats in the English Channel. Hills was then assigned to the Y Service.

With a university radio-technological education, pre-war employment with Fairey Aviation, cover from the RCS, and connections with the intelligence community through the Y Service, John Hills was a valuable capture for the SDS. His worth was manifested well before the end of 1940. Just a few months after the creation of the SDS, he set up, or adapted, an existing pilot radio network in Kent – manned by the first half dozen of what were later the Auxiliary Units (ATS). Hills also provided their unique radio transceivers. All this was seriously secret and hidden covertly from the public, the rest of the armed forces and, of course, the enemy if they decided to look in.

Hills was also instrumental in setting up a training establishment at Tunbridge Wells in Kent, and it was there that Yolande Bromley arrived with a small case of belongings at the end of 1940, having travelled down from Yorkshire as an ATS secretarial grade other rank, protected only with a War Office rail warrant. She met Kitty Hills, John Hills's wife, and Thea Ward, 'Mickey' Brown and the other ladies of the pilot scheme.

Yolande had been told to join XII Corps but never at any stage saw a soldier. Instead, in the greatest secrecy, she was tested for clarity of diction, working from a hut about a mile from her ATS billet. The course required no intensive study of the Morse code. Indeed, the operation was simple enough with the set provided. The only dials were for volume and wavelength search. Yolande was never sure how she had been selected for this secret service but assumed it may have been because she had volunteered for service overseas. However, it seems far more likely that someone who knew of both her family background and education used the right connections to put her name forward.

Considerable time was spent practising the spoken code, which simply involved the replacement of key words – such as tanks, aircraft, numbers and map references – with other words. This made plain speech possible, if considerably scrambled. The use of this system continued for the rest of her service, the code sheet being replaced daily once she was in the field. This was never intended to fool a skilful enemy for good but perhaps just long enough to enable commanders to digest the contents and take tactical action before the Germans worked it out too. However, as far as Yolande was aware, their communications with the unique, 6-volt, battery-powered transceiver, known simply as the 'TRD', were never picked up by the enemy at all.

After training in Kent, and practical participation in the pilot scheme there, she went on an abridged two-week OCTU, before returning south, first to Hatfield Peverel in Essex, and finally to her main Control Station at Thornham Magna, on the Suffolk/Norfolk border, where a Scottish division was stationed in the grounds of Lord Henniker's estate. One of Major Hills's final instructions was to explain that – although not in the Royal Corps of Signals – it was in order to wear its badge in her headgear and sport the two 'pips' of a full subaltern as cover.

Yolande and her team, which varied from three to five ATS officers, worked with TRDs positioned in a 'Met hut' in the grounds of divisional HQ, out-of-bounds both to officers with no need-to-know, and all other ranks. Barometric charts and other weather data on the walls supported their disguise as meteorological staff. Their tasks were to 'twiddle the knobs', and maintain communication with Out-stations in the vicinity, mostly responding to the 'Bowling' network call-sign. The talk sounded like gibberish once messages were encoded. The hut was equipped with toilet, cooking and rest facilities and mains battery chargers. The radios themselves always depended on battery power and were never hooked up to the mains.

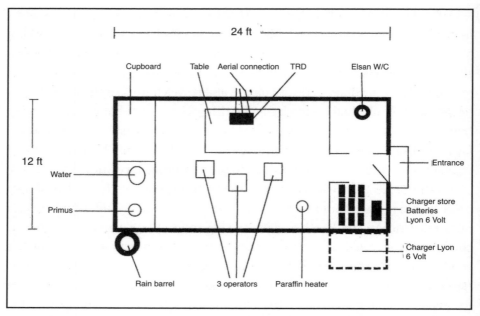

Above and right: An Auxunits' Signals Control (or In-) Station, typically given cover as a Meteorological (or 'Met') Hut. These huts were sited in the grounds of Army Area HQ, but were strictly out-of-bounds to other ranks.
(Captain Ken Ward/BROM collection)

There was a downside. The ATS operators understood they were to continue operating until the very last minute, even *after* British forces retreated and the enemy took over. At Thornham Magna there was no last-ditch 'Zero station' but at other Control Stations, such as Ousden, near Bury St Edmunds where she was later posted, she and her team were instructed to destroy their radios at the very last minute, to leave the hut door swinging as though hurriedly abandoned, and retire to a secret underground position nearby, with a hidden trapdoor entrance, and there to continue receiving and transmitting until either captured – and most likely executed – or relieved by counter-attack. For this do-or-die mission, their secret base was sparsely equipped for a subterranean existence, perhaps lasting a fortnight; and also with a revolver and a poison pill with which to take their own lives as a last ditch option.[†]

*

† Yolande Alston, née Bromley, died on Saturday 16 September 2006. She was one of a small group of very brave ladies.

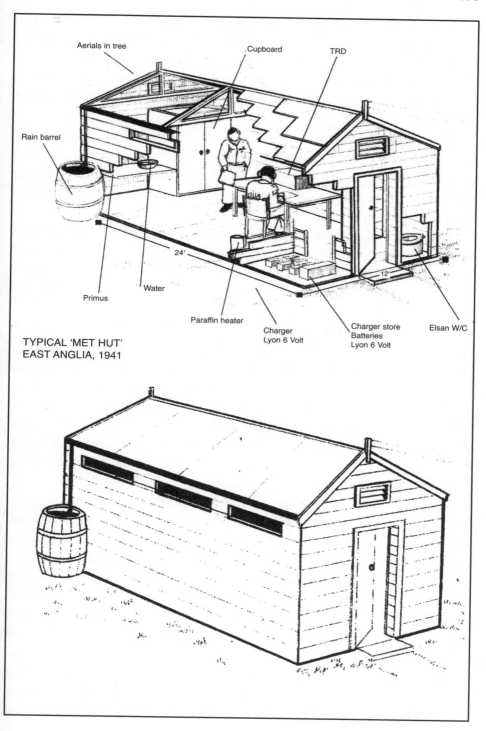

Aerials in tree · Cupboard · TRD

Rain barrel

Primus · Water

Paraffin heater

Charger
Lyon 6 Volt

Charger store
Batteries
Lyon 6 Volt

Elsan W/C

24'

12'

TYPICAL 'MET HUT'
EAST ANGLIA, 1941

Another link in the chain was forged at the end of 1940, when Captain Ken Ward, who had worked alongside Hills in the Y Service, was invited to start up a workshop, manufacturing, testing and developing the TRD sets and providing essential servicing back-up. He, too, was covered by the uniform of the Royal Corps of Signals. He may once even have been in it, but that is doubtful.

The official War Establishment for Auxiliary Units (Signals) included a number of officers appointed as part of the SDS set-up, a Royal Engineer or two to plan and supervise the purpose-built construction of both In-stations – for incoming messages – and Out-stations for the agents. A large transport (MT) section was positioned at HQ.

A brilliantly conceived addition to the personnel was the brainchild of Major John Hills, himself a pre-war radio ham, with the call-sign G2AW. When the Royal Corps of Signals was unable to provide the manpower required he turned to the Radio Society of Great Britain (RSGB), the focal point for the expanding body of radio amateurs.

Their president had already provided MI5 with the names of enough members with a command of Morse code to create another of Britain's WWII secret services, the Radio Security Service (RSS). As a result, a highly dedicated, skilled group of men, added to those on tap from professional institutions such as the Marconi Wireless Telegraph Company, were soon listening and noting any enemy transmission that could be traced on their dials. They picked up both low-level messages and those transmitted after being encoded by the Enigma machine, all of which were fed to the codebreakers at Bletchley Park.

An approach on behalf of the Auxiliary Units SDS was now made to John Clarricoats, secretary of the RSGB, for the names of radio hams who had already been conscripted into the Army. After identifying those with the technical skills needed, they were poached from their respective regiments, one by one. In this way some of the most qualified radio technicians were assembled for the SDS. They included (with their call-signs): G8CK Bill Bartholomew, GM89MO Jack Millie, GM2COI Jimmy McNab, G8PP Les Parnell, G2KI George Spencer, G2FWX Bill Ayre, G8JI Tom Higgins and G2RD Ron Dabbs

These soldiers served as NCOs with Auxiliary Units (Signals). Their technical contribution to the development of the TRD sets and their interactive communications network was decisive. Perhaps Bill Bartholomew and Ron Dabbs were the most influential – but none of them ever received the slightest hint of recognition, promotion or reward. On the contrary, as soon as no longer needed for the Auxiliary Units, they were dispersed. Only after the war did they manage to resume contact again, through the RSGB.

All this took time but, within six months of the creation of the SDS, a country house had been commandeered – Bachelor's Hall, Hundon, Suffolk, where several of the former hams were posted under the command of Captain Ken Ward. The task at Hundon was to upgrade a lightweight, short-range, radio transceiver, the prototype of which had been built in the mid-1930s and now brought from some SIS store for testing, improvement, and strengthening adequately to work in a harsh environment. A barn in the grounds of Bachelor's Hall was converted into a workshop. There was no mains electricity. Light was provided by Tilley lamps and reflectors; soldering irons were heated by portable gas units. Nevertheless, progress into previously uncharted areas of technology was rapid.

It all sounds very British.

*

With their administrative HQ at Coleshill, and a workshop in Suffolk, the Auxiliary Units (Signals) were nearly ready to play their full part in the SDS network.

Units of two or three other ranks were posted away under an NCO to service radio Out-stations. In addition to technical proficiency for minor repairs and battery changing at least once a fortnight, this required a good head for heights to fix or adjust aerials often near the tops of high trees.

In some areas, they also had a multi-purpose role at In-stations where they not only made service visits, and were sometimes responsible for the distribution of new code sheets too, but also provided a radio watch at otherwise unmanned Zero stations. As usual, no co-ordinated picture can be discerned about their likely course of action (as for the ATS operators) if the enemy appeared on the doorstep. Indeed, a final decision seems largely to have been left to the local military CO. The late Arthur Gabbitas, one of the best-informed sources, understood that they were to use their own initiative if over-run; Stan Judson, a non-specialist NCO, thought it likely they were expendable and would be ordered to take over from ATS officers at the last moment. As the danger of invasion diminished, it seems probable that the powers-that-be avoided this contentious issue.

Mobile signals team members were provided either with a motorcycle and sidecar, or what they called a scout car, often a tiny Austin Seven coupé. They had considerable freedom, often living in lodgings with allowances to eat out when away from base. It was a good war; just one man was killed, when a rope failed as he climbed to reach an aerial high in a tree at Thornham Magna in Suffolk. Skilful subterfuge was called for to avoid being seen by civilians near Out-stations, some of which were concealed in well-frequented places such as factories, offices, toilets or churches.

Out-stations came in many shapes and sizes. They were in general, designed to accommodate just one civilian man or woman radio-operator. Hiding places for radios had originally been simple, semi-watertight boxes, buried in holes in the ground. But these were abandoned once signals teams, often an officer and one of the ham NCOs – perhaps with a sapper and the local SDS IO – had been able to search for ideal locations. Adequate clearance above surrounding obstructions was essential to ensure enough transmission distance, and so was good security on approach paths, proximity to an SDS post-box, and adequate disguise, or cover, to enable transceiving to take place without being overheard.

One set was installed in an office, using the back of a roll-top desk. Others were in cellars or behind lavatory cisterns. Attics were also a favoured hiding place. At Aylsham in Norfolk, the set used by Jill Monk and her father, Dr Alex Holman, was at the bottom of a former coal-chute, as we already know, but first prize went to the radio hide of Douglas Ingrams at Bewley Down. Modification by a section of sappers to the outdoor privy, resulted in an underground chamber almost certainly made from the materials of a civilian Anderson air raid shelter, with standing headroom and enough space for a table and camp bed.

The secret approach from ground level started with a turn and tug on a wall-mounted cup hook inside the door. This released a catch under the twin toilet seats, allowing counter-weights into play. The whole assembly was then easily moved upward a couple of feet, to reveal a down-shaft and built-in ladder. On his way down, the operator encouraged the counter-weight to ease the toilet seats, complete with bucket-and-chuck-it, back into position, and then secured the catch. A crouch along a short tunnel led to the main chamber where another hidden catch could be activated to bring further counter-weights into play. With these, a section of the railway-sleeper far wall rolled away on a monorail to reveal a small radio room, together with

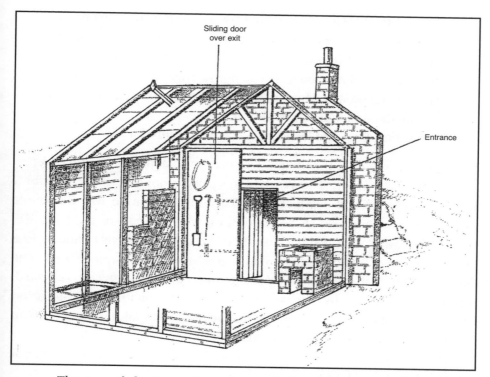

Sliding door over exit

Entrance

The concealed entrance to an Operational Base in the North-east;
probably into an SDS Radio Out-Station. *(By kind permission of the
North Yorkshire and Cleveland 20th Century Defence Study Group)*

the saucer-shaped dish on the floor in which a message-carrying tennis ball
might rest.

Perhaps the most popular hides were protected by the presence of nearby
animals. A disproportionate number of Out-stations were in chicken huts, or
surrounded by geese or free-ranging Rhode Island Reds. When servicing a
radio set hidden by a trapdoor under a chicken roost, Stan Judson
complained 'and they were not toilet trained either!'

Someone in high places had decreed that as well as chickens, dogs were
a natural deterrent to nosey-parkers and, it may be assumed, the enemy
alike. However, Stan Judson was not all that happy with the decision:

We put the set under the floor of his dog's kennel with the dog's
bed resting on top of the trapdoor. We couldn't get in without his
Red Setter escaping and rampaging round the garden, alerting the
gardener and everyone else . . .

> The aerial was in a tree behind the garage but the army put an Ack-Ack unit nearby and their cook used our tree to chop his firewood and severed our wire. We chose another tree but there was an armed guard marching up and down. Then the guttering broke over our station and when it rained the set got wet. We decided to relocate the station inside the house.
>
> It worked fine until Jerry came over and bombed it flat.

Stan also suffered with the longest legs ever tucked into an Austin Seven.

Thanks to researcher Tim Wray, Stan's story is not only confirmed but it is now possible to add detail. The GP running his station was Dr George Armour, and his partner, Dr Leonard Boys, was also part of the local SDS group. They were recruited because they had a vehicle to visit patients in a fairly large area, a petrol supply and a good reason to travel around. The doctor's children discovered the set at one stage, and it was (again) relocated, this time to the attic. His wife never did know of his planned, after-invasion role. Sally the gun dog – one of two Red Setters – was later trained to swim the River Witham to deliver secret messages.

Tim Wray reports that pieces of the aerial were still in the tree when it was felled in the mid-1990s.

The erection of these aerials at the top of steeples or factory chimneys, or high in large trees, called for certain qualities of derring-do. Sometimes the up-lead could be disguised as a lightning conductor, but, wherever possible, it was literally buried in the tree after a strip of bark had painstakingly been removed, a runnel dug for the lead, and the bark then replaced and secured by panel pins or adhesive. The horizontal top section of the aerial had to be precisely aligned for maximum efficiency and security. All this required a delicate touch and a cool head for heights. It is hardly a surprise that one of the team much in demand was said to have been a professional cat burglar before the war.

Zero stations, where they were linked to Control or In-stations as last-ditch transceiving units, seem to have followed a more regular design. Each required similar specifications for the accommodation of a small team of three to five personnel and two (or sometimes three) TRDs: storage and cooking space and a separate and well sealed off room for a battery-charging, petrol-driven generator. This usually called for three chambers, and a separate cubby-hole for an Elsan chemical toilet. The generator also doubled as power for very basic air conditioning, usually ducted along earthenware piping. This was not for long-term comfort, but to try to ensure adequate ventilation. With a number of people living in close proximity underground, heating and lighting from portable paraffin stoves and Tilley Lamps, toxic fumes from the batteries, and insidious carbon monoxide exhaust from the generator, ventilation was always a problem. Fumes were generally ducted through the escape tunnel and out to hidden ventilators.

These tunnels varied according to the terrain. Generally, they consisted of water culvert pipes, with sufficient diameter to permit a hands-and-knees escape to a camouflaged hatchway, often drawn to specifications similar to those in everyday use by Operational Patrols. At the end of the war, orders came to block or destroy each Zero station and officers-in-charge – relying upon the hunch that the War Office would be preoccupied with greater things and happy with a piece of paper – faithfully reported that this had been done. Fortunately, a few survived and stand as confirmation of eyewitness memories. It is no exaggeration to say that life for the men or women left underground would have been nothing less than grim, a horrible amalgam of discomfort and danger.

It is now time to describe some of the life of one man deeply involved with the radio network in Kent during 1942 and 1943. It is representative of the national set-up.

Chapter Eighteen

An Inside Story

'There was one ex-'Y' Service chap who told his wife that he was
going to a meeting and his wife said that was fine because she
had an appointment too. And they met up at Bletchley Park for
a reunion! It was only then that they realised that they had both
served in the war in a secret role without ever telling each
other.'

Lieutenant Roy Russell

Sixty years after the war, Roy Russell visited the museum at Bletchley Park.
Bletchley Park had been the HQ of Britain's brilliantly conducted
programme to decrypt intercepted enemy radio traffic. In the museum, he got
the surprise of his life.

During a conducted tour of the exhibits, he inadvertently showed an
insiders' hand by identifying to the guide an American Hallicrafter radio
unit. This was fitted with a spin-wheel for rapid frequency scanning and
interception and was, in 1940 at least, technically, well ahead of anything
built in Britain. After an interval – to confirm his identity, no doubt – the
directors of the museum unexpectedly offered him the Freedom of Bletchley
Park on the spot. With the award of this rare distinction, he realised for the
first time that security wraps had finally been removed from his own WWII
career in the Y Service with the Royal Signals.

Roy Russell is still convinced that the Y Service was a very secret branch
of the Royal Signals and also overlord of the Auxiliary Units (Signals)
network, in which he served later. As both Major John Hills the first CO,
and Captain Ken Ward, who headed the Auxunit workshop at Hundon,
wore the Signals uniform and served with Y Service, too, his opinion has
obvious merit. However, nothing to do with secret services is as
straightforward as it seems at first sight. The Y Service was staffed by
members of all three armed services, but was also in the domain of the
Secret Intelligence Service. The Y Service itself was dedicated to the
interception of enemy radio communications and the advance of

associated technology. While the RCS was responsible to the War Office for its administrative support, the nature of the work inevitably involved intelligence interests and the technical expertise of MI5 and MI6 as well. Intercepted enemy traffic was assembled and the complexities unravelled by boffins at Bletchley Park, but the whole product was distributed through a single centre, an SIS clearing house seven miles to the south-west of BP known as Section VIII at Whaddon Hall. Overall security was masterminded by the SIS.

In view of the undoubted fact that most of the invaluable radio ham NCOs recruited into the Auxiliary Units (Signals) were withdrawn from regiments other than the Royal Signals, Roy Russell's otherwise logical conviction that Y Service controlled Auxunits (Signals) therefore needs some examination. The two principal Auxunits (Signals) officers had admittedly been drawn from 'Y', but 'Y' itself was masterminded by the SIS – and was not averse, with War Office knowledge and acquiescence, to using RCS uniform and insignia as cover. Overall control and responsibility for both funding and security was always retained by MI6.

Moreover, it seems inconceivable from what is now known, that the first commitment of Major Maurice Petherick, CO of the SDS, was to any other service than MI6. This would dovetail with the progressive SIS development of Section D, followed by its Home Defence Organisation, and then the Special Duties Section of the Auxiliary Units. As part corroboration at least, it is known that Auxunits (Signals) Control Stations could report directly by discrete telephone line to a department other than their local Army HQ and the assumption has always been that the link was to Bletchley Park itself. This was simply because it was BP that came first to public attention. Only comparatively recently has Whaddon Hall been disclosed as the focus of SIS radio activities and it seems far more likely that Control Stations had this telephone contact directly with Section VIII of the SIS.

Against this background it seems fair to conclude that – while the SDS was nominally under the command of the Auxunits' CO at Coleshill – its overall commitment was to the Secret Intelligence Service. This included the Auxunits' communications network, even though it was nominally set up and controlled by men and women with overt or covert attachments to the Royal Corps of Signals. It must be remembered that those vital radio ham NCOs all had 'Auxiliary Units (Signals)' stamped in their pay books – *irrespective of the regiment from which they were drawn*. Most if not all of them were never from the RCS itself. This arcane set-up may be of particular significance before long.

*

However, it was all way out yonder for Mr Roy Russell, aged twenty-one, when he left his City job in 1940, to present himself for conscription into the Army. The technique for task-selection in the armed forces had long been established along the lines: 'Do you play the piano, soldier?' 'Yes, sergeant-major, I do!' 'Right lad! Double march down to the NAAFI and scrub the floor.' It was not that much different for Russell:

> The enlisting officer asked me all the routine questions; then, what my interests were other than sports? I told him 'music'. He asked what sort? I said symphonies – Brahms, Beethoven and Mozart.
>
> He said – 'Why enemy stuff?' I said that didn't matter, I just loved the music.
>
> 'You should do well in the Royal Signals!' – the officer decided.

This decision changed the direction of Roy Russell's life forever.

The Army first decided to harden him up. As soon as they were fighting fit, he and a dozen other Royal Signals recruits were sent to the Merchant Navy Wireless Telegraphy School in Hull, learning to key Morse code from script in the mornings and deciphering five-letter groups in the afternoon. Within six weeks he achieved the target of twenty words a minute, receive-and-send. Only a few new men did so.

As military campaigns loomed early in 1940, he was on a draft for Norway. However, the transition from old-fashioned, brass-buttoned uniform into the new battledress treated with an anti-gas chemical had a devastating effect on his skin and he was taken off the draft and hospitalised. From then he was graded Category B, fit for service only in the UK.

It was another significant landmark in his life. While unfit for service abroad he had, nevertheless, shown particular aptitude for Morse. Thanks to an improvement in the War Office selection process, he was posted to No. 1 Special Wireless Group at Rothamsted House, Harpenden, Hertfordshire. This was his introduction into the very secret world of radio interception. He now had to master the skills of direction-finding as well as learn what was known about German radio procedures and their transmitters, both static and mobile. Knowingly or not, Signalman Russell was now working with the Y Service.

With the first mass bombing of London in the autumn of 1940, Signalman Roy Russell, fully trained but still without experience, was posted to 105 Special Wireless Section at Cardfields Farm, near Hatfield Peverel in Essex, under a former GPO executive, Captain Greening. He and several other ORs were joined by a group of experienced regular signallers withdrawn from India. They erected an experimental complex of aerials to intercept communications to and from enemy planes flying overhead.

The task was to pick-up enemy Morse signals and make sense of them. According to Russell, they found that Luftwaffe wireless operators transmitted a three-letter code which indicated 'Bombs gone. Request permission to return to base.' Once the Luftwaffe started blanket bombing London the section successfully identified these signals but was initially baffled by the seeming absence of any further transmissions. The assumption had to be that, after 'bombs gone', enemy aircraft adopted radio silence. Fortunately, the Special Wireless Section soon cracked open the true sequence of transmissions. It was here that the advanced design of the Hallicrafter set was invaluable.

Russell believed German procedure was in fact more complex. It involved closing down their bombing raid frequencies, and opening sealed orders. These gave a new call-sign and the radio frequency of a different controlling station. Once contact was established, this new station passed along instructions to return to a *different* airbase. By being split up in this way, the crew of each surviving aircraft were not initially aware how many of their squadron had been shot down; no doubt this rather clever procedure was intended to maintain morale as British air defences improved and German losses increased.

By rearranging their radio room, the Y Service men were able to intercept both incoming and outgoing signals from enemy aircraft. As they grew more adept, they even identified both the new airfield and the runway in use there. Hallicrafter radios – specially imported for search operations – were critical for the rapid interception of that second frequency. Each day's loggings were collected regularly by a dispatch rider who, when asked where they were delivered, would go no further than to reply 'The War Office'. However, Roy Russell's post-war conclusion was that they all went directly to Bletchley Park.

With the reduction in the bombing campaign against London in mid-1941, 105 Wireless Section closed down. Roy was promoted to sergeant, got married, and then went for further technical training. Recommended for a commission, he spent a tough six months on an OCTU course at Catterick, after which he was selected – with the Army resorting to its old kick-and-rush selection technique – for 'Beach Landing (Signals)'. He boldly pointed out that this was likely to conflict with his 'UK only' service restriction – and gave some details of his previous postings. The CO had never heard of 'Y' and curtly dismissed him when Roy explained that it was too secret to explain further.

He was by now conversant with both German and Italian radio techniques – which, he found, 'were totally different from ours' – and a posting appropriate to these skills might have been expected. However, a movement order, accompanied by a rail warrant for Highworth in Wiltshire, soon arrived, with an unusual instruction to report to the postmistress. It was unreal and singularly unmilitary:

> She was expecting me and rang for a car. She said she didn't know where it was to take me. It turned out to be Coleshill House, which I found occupied by officers, from all levels of the Army, Navy, Air Force, Fleet Air Arm – French Forces and civilians. I was given a room of my own and found myself next to different diners on both sides at meals.

Roy's conclusion was that he was being assessed for a job in Special Operations Executive He was unaware that he had been posted back to a secret force similar to that in which he had served in the ranks. After finding out what was planned for him he was not to speak of it again for fifty years. In the event, his 'UK-only' health grade may have influenced the decision and he was posted to an Auxunits (Signals) unit at Carmarthen in Wales. There he discovered that his Morse skills were superfluous, the radio sets in use being 'R/Toc', Signals jargon for plain speech.

> Speech was now invented, workable one-to-one, or in a group, by line or radio. I was lucky in my new sergeant – Jack Millie was a boffin in army uniform. He knew more about electronics than I could dream of.

Jack Millie, who had already played a significant part in the modification and improvement of the Auxunits' unique radio set, was of course GM8MQ, one of the linchpins of the network, indirectly recruited through the RSGB list of pre-war hams and having no association whatever – at that stage at least – with the Royal Corps of Signals proper. The two of them travelled most days high into the Brecon Beacons to test and calibrate the sets, with which anyone even totally unskilled could safely hold a conversation via a telephone-like handset.

Some time in 1943, Lieutenant Russell and Sergeant Millie were posted to another Auxunits' Operational Station at Sevenoaks in Kent, where they worked from a previously derelict building behind the Odeon Cinema. They were responsible for service and maintenance of two Control Stations and linked Out-stations from the Isle of Sheppey clockwise round the Kent and Sussex coastline to Arundel. Control Stations were manned by ATS subalterns and Out-stations by civilians, many with reserved occupations.

> Our front-line civilian informers were rarely seen by me or my staff. Their received information would be passed on to the radio people without them knowing each other, so that if either was captured, neither could be made to give the other away.

The 'right or wrong way up' telegraph pole number system was favoured for their dead letter drops. After many exercises, the system worked smoothly. With nine ATS to each Control Station, they covered the network – three to each watch – for twenty-four hours a day, receiving messages from Out-stations, each of which was equipped with just one radio. The ATS subalterns were regularly supervised during visits by two senior officers, Ann Gunter and Sally Waterhouse-Brown. Roy Russell remembers Ann Gunter as an accomplished artist; one evening she told him that he had an interesting head, and sat down and moulded his bust. He still has this souvenir in his home.

Royal Engineers built the stations, and devised secret entrances to the In-stations. The unseen hatchway design was brilliant:

> You had to know exactly where to look, usually on the fringe of a copse of tall trees, where the camouflaged aerials were strung high. There would be a small stone, which hid the square top of a metal rod. I carried a crank-handle, which fitted over it and, by turning it, raised a manhole-like circle of the ground revealing a vertical entrance; you stepped down a fixed ladder, wound down the grassy manhole behind you, and found yourself in a small chamber with

shelving all round, and just one empty ammunition-box. Clearly it was an abandoned small-arms dump if seen by an invading force.

Not if you were one of us! On one shelf there was a stiff piece of wire. Push this through a small hole and the whole wall of shelves cantilevered to let you into the set-room, where three ATS staff were at work, talking to, or logging messages from the OUT-stations. If an exercise was in progress you would have to wait for a lull to be greeted, and to learn what problems needed to be addressed.

In Out-stations, manned by civilians, the radio sets were always well hidden. Small and robust, with metal cases, some were cached in strange places:

For instance, a schoolmistress had ripped the treble hammers out of her upright piano to create a hidden space. A chicken farmer dug chalk out of his land to make an underground room in which to use his set; and a vicar told me no one would find his radio. It was hidden in his pulpit. 'Who else but me goes up there?'

Apart from radio set failures, which could be handled *in situ* as a rule, the main faults were usually with aerials. Out-stations in Lieutenant Russell's area had inbuilt antennae, but Control Stations, needing more range and therefore height, called for the erection of high dipoles, usually in trees. They also needed precise alignment and were vulnerable to displacement after strong winds.

One of my lads would volunteer to be hauled up, standing in a noose of rope thrown over a high branch. The other end was attached to the front axle of my Humber car and, by slowly backing, he was drawn up the tree. He sometimes had to climb the last few feet carrying specific tools and spares on his back – a task we shared in view of the risk of falling.

We hid the co-axial cable running up the trees by removing the bark in the line of travel, gouging out a trough to house the cable and replacing the removed bark. The aerials were copper wires stretched by insulating pots into exact positions and virtually unidentifiable from the ground.

All this was so effective that when RAF engineers built a landing field nearby, they laid some netting on the ground, which covered the hidden entrance to a Control Station. The ATS staff within radioed to say that for some reason they were unable to get out through the manhole disc. Roy Russell had to see the RAF commander:

> . . . who took some convincing of the problem. He had the netting cut back, probably to convince himself that I was telling the truth. I swore him to secrecy without explaining anything. He wasn't too pleased, being so much senior in rank to me!

As D-Day approached, and the deception programme orchestrated by the London Controlling Section moved into overdrive, Auxunits (Signals) in the south-east of England played their small part by stepping up the volume of on-air traffic. Some operators just read their favourite poems aloud; others prepared carelessly coded five-letter messages, and transmitted them to Out-stations − receiving meaningless replies in turn − twenty-four hours each day. While it was unlikely that much could be intercepted from TRD transmissions, less sophisticated War Department No. 17 sets were also issued to selected SDS networks; their traffic was deliberately intended to be detectable by the enemy.

During local travel in the south-east of England, Russell also saw a poorly camouflaged build-up of landing craft, tanks and military vehicles − easily visible to Luftwaffe reconnaissance. Part of the LCS deception master-plan too, these inflatable dummies were sometimes difficult to distinguish from the real invasion force massing nearly a hundred miles to the west around Portsmouth for the real cross-Channel invasion.

Sevenoaks was in 'Doodle-bug Alley', as the approaches to London were dubbed during the flying bomb assault in 1944. One summer evening, Roy Russell walked into Knowle Park, near Sevenoaks, with his camera to watch these V1s droning low overhead. His idea was to take clear photographs of the deadly missiles, to help the boffins who were trying to devise counter-measures. Instead, he found himself arrested by military policemen as a suspected enemy agent. The Whitehall telephone number he produced to establish his identity went unanswered; as far as the military police were concerned, the War Office had closed. He was released only after an uncomfortable night in the cells.

The Special Duties Section was dissolved in mid-July 1944 and Roy Russell's direct contribution to the war effort went with it. He was, however, denied early demobilisation. Instead he was posted to a holding company near Shrewsbury. It was there that the final change to his future life-style took place, when he was encouraged by his CO to start a concert party for both his troops and the locals. Equipped with many talents, the soldiers themselves provided the cast as well as an enthusiastic audience for topical tomfoolery.

Roy discovered a latent aptitude for scriptwriting. After his return to civvy street, and a few failures, he gave up the City career, which had been held open for him for six years, and entered the emerging world of television production as a professional playwright. By the time he retired, Roy had written scripts for around a hundred productions – series, plays, dramatisations, documentaries and animations – for TV, radio and theatre. He also wrote a novel, *A Family at War*. He holds the Laurel Award of the Writers' Guild of Great Britain.

When, in 1940, the enlisting officer found Private Russell a job with the Royal Corps of Signals instead of sending him off to scrub the NAAFI, the direction of his life was certainly changed. It also led to his unique, clearly remembered and well-informed account of one man's experience in the – rather special – Special Duties Section of the GHQ Auxiliary Units.

Chapter Nineteen

The Final Link

'A good deal of other useful work was done on explosives and incendiaries, and the output of devices from production was considerable, for other users as well as "D" Section. Colonel Grand mentions £50,000 a month. Research also diverged into other paths, such as the use of free balloons and the development of "secure" R/T, which had no future in SOE.'

The Secret History of SOE, *William Mackenzie*

This extract comes from a book, commissioned by the Cabinet Office soon after WWII, and finally cleared for sale to the public more than fifty years later. It comes from a chapter entitled 'The Work of Section D' and follows shortly after an insert: 'PASSAGE DELETED ON GROUNDS OF NATIONAL SECURITY'. Although not dated, the relevant paragraph includes a summary of work in hand at Aston House, Station XII.

This paragraph contains a vital clue to the path which led researchers – far from inevitably – to today's comprehensive knowledge of the communications system eventually developed for the Auxiliary Units Special Duties Section. With its secret service connections it is hardly surprising that knowledge of the scheme was suppressed then – and still is. The search for clarity was long and confusing. With virtually no other official facts sourced directly from Whitehall, research first concentrated on a few eyewitnesses, followed by – possibly inadvertent and overlooked – corroborative leaks into the National Archives.

The hunt for the TRD was on.

*

The first help came from just a few witnesses, survivors from Auxiliary Units (Signals) and (ATS). After so many years, memories often differed, both over the appearance of the sets and the technology involved. The sets also obviously included pre-war component parts, virtually unrecognisable to today's enthusiasts. Even the colour of the sets seems to have varied. Much of the confusion was gradually resolved once it was realised that modifications and improvements from trial and error had called for several changes to the TRD as the scheme developed.

Progress also followed finds in the National Archives where precise dimensions of the sets were discovered, together with the designation TRD but no explanation for the use of these particular initial letters. Clarification was not immediately helped by discovery of the number of sets manufactured: TRDs 250, TRMs 28, and TRFs 36. It seemed likely that as the TRD was modified, new identifying letters were allocated.

An associated discovery was a 1944 map of the radio network, signed by Major R. M. A. Jones, then CO of Auxunits (Signals). The next item was a closing-down report, dated 17 August 1944, c/o GPO Highworth, Nr Swindon, Wilts, to Chief Signals Officer, Home Forces, signed by the last CO, Major H. M. Green:

> *Wireless Sets*
> No. 17 Sets and No. 36 Sets have been returned to Woolwich. All special sets have been handed over to No. 1 S.C.U. Whaddon
>
> All batteries 2V 16AH, 6v 16AH and 6V 85AH, have been disposed of either to C.S.O.s of the various commands or to Woolwich.

Here was official corroboration of the existence of a useful number of Auxunits radios, not officially acknowledged elsewhere. Note that the 'special sets' were not sent with other standard War Office stores to Woolwich. Neither, it became known from a reliable inside source, did they stay for long, if at all, at Whaddon, the Signals Communication Unit in Berkshire. They were instead kept until after the war in SOE's Central Stores at Knebworth, Hertfordshire.

Obviously, the next call went to the Museum of the Royal Corps of Signals at Blandford; either they knew nothing, or had been told to know nothing. Indeed a spokesman for the Vintage and Military Amateur Radio Society (VMARS) is satisfied that any connection between Auxiliary Units SDS and the TRD, on one hand, and Royal Signals on the other, was 'tenuous'. This helps to confirm the strongly held opinion of researchers at the Museum of the British Resistance Organisation.

A worthwhile addition to knowledge came with the release of the 'final' SOE papers in 2002. These included the closing report, and associated documents, from Section D in the summer of 1940. Several useful, if unspecific, clues were found. For example, after acknowledging that the section had benefited from the facilities of the SIS, it outlined new Section D devices:

> ... three very remarkable inventions ... one of them probably a most startling advance in telephony. These are:
>
> (a) The 'D-Phone'. A telephone which leaves 'scrambling' far behind and encodes and decodes the human voice in any code which the Olympian gentleman using the 'D-Phone' may care to devise and insert in the mechanism.
> (b) The 'Duplex Transceiver'. A wireless telephone using a wave too short to be picked up by any other known receiver. This instrument has been designed for communications between agents operating in foreign countries. Its range is strictly limited.
> (c) A high powered loudspeaker ...

The 'D-Phone', if we are to give Section D the credit it clearly sought, albeit with limited circulation potential, might well have been installed on the network used for SDS land-line communications between Control Stations and Hannington Hall or Whaddon.

Initial reaction to (b) was that this exactly fitted the TRD job-description, apart from the intended use in 'foreign countries'. We shall never know for sure, but our source has asserted that the Duplex Transceiver was not the TRD. He is satisfied that the Section D technology differed, was over-weight, depended upon the import of rare foreign components, and ended up being sent to guerrillas in Yugoslavia. Moreover, of seven sets produced, only one ever worked! This certainly did not fit the TRD. Nevertheless, it was an encouraging near miss.

It was time to return to survivors.

Thanks to the late Sergeant Arthur Gabbitas, some of his Auxunits (Signals) colleagues and veteran ATS subalterns, this produced a steady stream of clues for assembly into what was now becoming more clearly understood as an enormously complicated puzzle. Arthur Gabbitas had asked for an invitation to the first Auxunits national reunion at a hotel near Coleshill in 1994, but his inclusion was initially refused because the organisers, including Devon Auxilier Geoff Bradford, had never heard of Auxunits (Signals). This spoke volumes for cellular secrecy. Fortunately,

Arthur produced an ace – his pay book – clearly and indisputably stamped Auxiliary Units (Signals).

Arthur dedicated much of the rest of his life to tracing his former comrades. Not only did he manage to find most of the survivors but, at the same time, roped in many ATS subalterns as well. With their help, he painstakingly assembled all the know-how they had in their various spheres – the origins of the first working design, experiments, improvements, and finally production, distribution and use. His own knowledge as a pre-war radio ham was invaluable, helping him to collate all that his colleagues remembered and of which there seemed to be no official records.

That could have been as far as research ever went. However, one development was the discovery that all the TRDs had been collected at the end of the war and 'put beyond further use'. In other words, not unlike the 'Most Secret' decoding technology developed at Bletchley Park, the TRD was far too clever for posterity to hear about. This had more fingerprints left by the Secret Intelligence Service. Not that, by now, anyone had much doubt about the origins of the Auxiliary Units Special Duties Section, as well as the Signals, the ATS subalterns and, of course, TRDs themselves. The irony is that Mackenzie (as quoted at the head of the chapter), although heading research in the right direction, may have done so inadvertently. Perhaps he was even writing about a different set-up altogether.

*

With no obvious way forward, a lifeline was thrown by Richard Hankins and VMARS. This intervention led to Operation Witney (simply a code-name dreamed up by VMARS and the Museum of the BRO). VMARS is an international society based in the UK, and set up to restore and preserve items of 'interesting' (usually vintage) electronics – covering communications, radios, radar, radio navigation devices, mine detectors and so on. About the only items the Society does not deal with are those that some readers are most likely to remember, such as 'granny's old wireless' in its polished wooden cabinet, a contraption that took several minutes to warm up, the broadcast receiver of yesteryear.

The first step came when a VMARS member was compiling a reference book covering all the known wireless sets used for clandestine purposes – so-called 'spy-sets'. This member, Louis Meulstree from the Netherlands, negotiated an exchange of VMARS expertise with the Parham Museum's acquired know-how to that date. At the time, technical knowledge of the TRD was almost nil – not least at the Museum – but it quickly became evident that a very unusual radio deserved to be rescued from the dustbin of history and, if possible, a working model built, too. Thus Project Witney was born.

*

Richard Hankins later wrote that it might be hard for readers, not aware of the history of the development of radio, to appreciate why anyone should get excited about the TRD. Surely this was just another radio? Here, then, is a look at developments in the radio field at the outbreak of WWII.

Elderly readers will remember that most homes had a 'wireless' by the fireside. This was a standard broadcast receiver that could pick up medium and long wave broadcasts – and sometimes short waves as well. *Receiving* radio broadcasts from a powerful transmitter was a relatively simple affair. By 1939, receivers were well developed, cheap to make, and simple to operate. A myriad of small wireless shops supported users well with advice, spare valves, and charging facilities for the very many sets still run on batteries. On the other hand, *transmitting* a strong radio signal required complex design and engineering.

Two-way radio is a very different matter technically. Transmitting a signal effectively is a complex affair, usually requiring a carefully constructed aerial and some skill and specific training in operating the transmitter. The receiver is similarly much more complex than the average broadcast receiver, mainly because the signals it is trying to pick up are much weaker than broadcast signals, due to the use of much lower transmitter power.

Two-way radio was much less developed in 1940 than broadcast radio. Essentially those with the equipment and skill to use it were limited to employees of certain mobile services, such as shipping and aviation, the armed forces and, to a small extent, the police. Radio amateurs were entirely self-trained in the art.

Work was carried out in obscure places in the 1930s which would lay foundations for many rapid advances after war broke out. Between 1933 and 1936 an eight-man project at Cambridge University – under W. B. Lewis, later head of the Telecommunications Research Establishment at Malvern – was created to develop a speech, two-way radio, ostensibly for the

'War Office'. Captain Ken Ward, later head of Auxunits (Signals) workshops at Hundon, was one of that team. Some information was published in *The Wireless Engineer* in 1937, as Ken recalled:

> The technique used was to have a set which couldn't easily be intercepted. It was for short-range communication, battery powered and 'Quench' operated. You couldn't hear a thing unless you rectified the carrier-wave a second time; so unless you had the second frequency built in to your receiver, you couldn't intercept it. It worked on line-of-sight. We took it on army manoeuvres in 1935 and improved it with modifications.

'Quenching' allowed the set to switch between receive and transmit very rapidly. A second set using the same technique would complete a full duplex link, just like a telephone. One interesting fact noted during the development was that an ordinary amplitude modulation receiver was unable to detect the signal that these sets transmitted. This was a fact that later was put to good use in the TRD. The Army tried to modify the set, after which it failed to work at all. Ken Ward then went one way and the radio, it seems, another. However, the reader may discern certain parallels in Mackenzie's report quoted at the head of this chapter.

*

Meanwhile, radio amateurs were quietly working away in their back rooms and garden sheds. A radio amateur was then usually someone reasonably well educated, and with disposable income to spend on his hobby. Some were in the forefront of radio development, and many proved to be an invaluable resource to the Allies during WWII. Auxiliary Units were certainly beneficiaries.

Before World War II, nearly all commercial and military radio services on the Allied side, operated at frequencies below about 20 MHz. Radio amateurs were, however, exploring higher frequencies, and had bands at 21 MHz, 28 MHz, 56 MHz and 112 MHz. As early as 1935, amateurs had discovered that 56 MHz made a very good band for contacts over distances of up to twenty miles or so, and it was also useful for keeping in touch with mobile stations. The Army also tried using these high frequencies, but failed to produce anything that could withstand the rigours of battlefield use.

The average Army radio used by the infantry before WWII was large – that is, it was vehicle-mounted (or carried by an animal such as a mule); it covered frequencies up to the region of 8 MHz; and had ranges of about five miles maximum, using a simple rod aerial eight feet high. More range could be obtained, but only by using much bigger wire aerials strung between trees or masts. This made the station non-mobile. It would transmit speech, though usually Morse was used to obtain better range. Where speech was possible, it could be picked up on any short-wave receiver tuned to the same frequency, and thus any radio links were entirely insecure.

The TRD was special, firstly because it operated at the high frequencies neglected by other services – around 45–65 MHz. As the NCOs of the design team later assembled by Auxunits (Signals) were nearly all amateur radio hams, they naturally based the TRD on their pre-war experience of the 56 MHz band. A second unique feature of the TRD was its 'secure speech' mode. No record exists of exactly how this was done, but examination of the possibilities – within constraints imposed by the number of valves employed – suggests that the TRD used a modulated sub-carrier system. This is where the speech first modulates a carrier at quite a low frequency – say around 40 kHz – and this signal is used to modulate the radio carrier wave, which might be at 60 MHz. Standard receivers are unable to make any sense of radio waves of this type and all the listener hears is 'white noise' when tuning through the signal. It would be going too far to describe this system as secure since a determined effort to recover the signal could have succeeded. It was, however, a hidden signal – and secure in the sense that the casual listener would have paid it no attention at all.

*

At the outset, VMARS had no idea where the search would lead – whether a cupboard would be found in an old shack with some of these radios hidden away since WWII, or whether they would have to work the hard way and totally recreate the TRD from scratch. The task turned out to involve more hard work than fortunate finds.

Initially, detailed research was required to ensure that VMARS had every scrap of reliable information. This involved a variety of exercises. The article from *The Wireless Engineer* took some tracking down. The publication is now an obscure journal lost in the mists of time, though apparently well regarded in its day. Eventually a copy was found in the Bristol University library and – just as importantly – access generously granted.

Two elderly witnesses were approached. The first was Bill Bartholomew ('G8CK'), a founder member of the 'Bachelors 'all Gang' at Hundon and a co-designer of the TRD. Ken Ward was the second. From these pivotal witnesses, more pieces of the puzzle were gradually assembled – not without difficulties.

The TRD was never in high-volume production. It was, however, made in hundreds and thus a full set of drawings describing it would have been produced. Unfortunately, with the TRD the drawings had all been lost. All that remained were some notes written by Arthur Gabbitas, with a rough outline of what went into the TRD and what it looked like externally, and a circuit diagram and parts' list of the unmodified predecessor sets, produced from an original contract with Brian Savage and Parsons Ltd. of Kingsbury.

Invaluable as all this was, it was inadequate to recover the design of the TRD. Consequently, the VMARS team had to *redesign* almost from scratch. Here was the hard work predicted earlier.

With regard to the secure speech system, VMARS satisfied themselves that the TRD was quite unlike any other known radio set produced either then or subsequently. Team members had no model to follow. They also suffered from the 'modern engineer' syndrome. In essence, this meant they did not think like the engineers of 1940 – they knew a lot about micro-processors and such like, but designing an unusual valve radio was very much foreign territory. Recourse to old textbooks became necessary. Moreover, there was the problem of finding vintage components of the right type. With no second-hand radio junk shops to be found, it became a matter of scouring ancient boxes and asking people to turn out their attics.

One possibly related device was the S-Phone used by SOE to communicate with agents. This was developed at Whaddon Hall in buildings adjacent to those in which the final TRDs were assembled. It was a two-way voice radio system, designed for direct talk between SOE agents on the ground and their controllers circling nearby in RAF aircraft. With short range and no need for protracted Morse code messages, there was less chance of interception by the enemy. Unfortunately, the resemblance to the TRD ended there. In particular, the TRD worked on AM and not FM and higher frequencies. Moreover the S-Phone had no secure speech facility.

*

Although the project is still unfinished, one area has been largely cleared up – the external appearance of the TRD. The dimensions were those given by Arthur Gabbitas. A replica case has been made in mild steel – the most likely material to have been used during the war, given that more exotic materials like aluminium were reserved for the aircraft industry. Opinions have differed about the positioning of the dials – on the longer side or the shorter? This was resolved by simply considering which place provided the best engineering solution and so, for the replica set destined for the museum, the longer side was chosen. Ken Ward, Bill Bartholomew, and other witnesses may well have been recalling slightly different versions. Indeed, Roy Russell, not an original participant in Project Witney, agrees that as no tuning dials were needed for Out-stations, their sets might well have had the remaining controls on the shorter side for practical engineering reasons whereas, with Control Station sets, the operator was required to use a tuning dial, which pointed to a position on the longer side.

It also transpired that different sets had different colours too. In the end, gunmetal and matt black were less favoured than the ubiquitous 'dull green' which – as any soldier knew – covered anything 'WD'. A reasonable conclusion can be drawn from the recollections of veterans about different sets and different colours. TRFs and TRMs – unlike the TRD (possibly for 'Transceiver Ron Dabbs'?), or components labelled TRWEB (after 'Transmit/ Receive William E. Bartholomew'?) – were simply versions modified with the extra knob for wavelength search, or as self-activating relay sets designed to extend transmission distance in hilly areas where line-of-sight was necessarily restricted. The numbers made – thirty-six and twenty-eight respectively – would have been about right.

With no integrated, built-in loudspeaker for voice transmission and reception, Control Station operators depended upon the faithful GPO head-and-breast set, designed for hands-on telephone switchboard operators. Out-stations were simply supplied with a standard Post Office telephone handset.

Internal circuitry was more difficult territory for VMARS. Using the circuit diagram of the earlier Savage set, the final solution was based on well-known designs of the time. A first step was to draw out a number of block diagrams that might fulfil the functions of the TRD and which conformed to the valve line-up described by Arthur Gabbitas. (A block diagram describes the function of each valve – in a shorthand way that leaves out all the complexity of a full circuitry diagram.) Ken Ward selected the most likely.

Having agreed a block diagram, the team set to work to recreate the circuit of each individual block. This involved deciding which components should be placed where, and how they inter-connected. Some of the blocks proved easy enough, since they were entirely standard functions obtained from a 1930s' textbook or radio magazine. Others fell into a 'very hard indeed' category.

At the outset, it was seriously thought that Project Witney might take as long as six months. Four years later the Museum of the British Resistance Organisation is proud to display the only replica, thanks almost entirely to VMARS and its team of experts co-ordinated by Richard Hankins.

If the development of original TRDs was a remarkable feat of ingenuity and determination under difficult circumstances, the design and roll-out of the radio network using these sets was equally noteworthy. In 1940 the business of deploying and running such networks was largely unknown. Creating a network meant finding mounting points for the aerials so that a line of sight link could be achieved, finding suitable places to mount the sets and their batteries, and carrying out the actual installation work with very limited resources. Testing the installations might well also have been difficult when no alternative communication system was available. In addition, the special requirements of the SDS meant that the aerials had to be totally concealed, as did the sets, while making sure the radio link still worked. Once installed, the network had to be manned and maintained. For the SDS, this meant setting up a regular regime of changing batteries at each end of each radio link, training operators, who were often totally non-technical, and providing a repair service for sets that failed.

It seems probable that all this came about largely as a result of Maurice Petherick's management skill. It was clearly no exaggeration for 'Bill' Beyts to have referred to him as the genius behind the Special Duties Section.

It must now be clear that the whole undertaking was entirely outside the remit of the Royal Signals. And so, we must raise our forage caps to that small group of amateur boffins, collected together early in 1941 as a result of their pre-war membership of the Radio Society of Great Britain, and then channelled into the Auxiliary Units (Signals) at Hundon. For the benefit of Britain – when the homeland was under threat – they gave their skills unstintingly.

They got no reward at all, of course. No promotion, no recognition, no cash, no patent rights. Soon after the war, the product of their genius was consigned to the bottom of a disused pit 'somewhere in England', and sealed in forever. No wonder it is still almost unfathomable to today's researchers and radio experts. Britain's secret services certainly have their own special ways of preserving the things that matter most to them.

Chapter Twenty

Causes for Concern

What is the most frequent question asked by visitors to the Museum of the British Resistance Organisation? Answer: 'Why is it still so secret?'

In view of the issues raised in preceding chapters, and the absence of any official explanation, this question and answer need to be looked at in more detail. Perhaps there is still something to hide?

If there is nothing hidden away, why have the complete Auxunits' papers not been released to the National Archives? Nearly everything else about the war can be seen there now. If it is in the public interest to permit books on nearly every aspect of SOE, to have full accounts of intelligence genius at work at Bletchley Park, and much informative detail from the archives of MI6 and MI5, why has there been no similar release of the full Auxiliary Units history? Any proposition that there is no story to tell is simply ludicrous.

Without official information, it is inevitable that any research about the Auxiliary Units will include an element of conjecture. The official decision not to expose them to the same accountability as other WWII secret services can only lead to speculation that there is still something special to hide. There *should* be no reason for the Auxiliary Units to be ignored for ever afterwards – unless someone with a very important motive has determined it is essential to do so.

Moreover, any suggestion that no records have been retained is clearly false. It is certain, for example, that Major Nigel Oxenden completed and sent to the War Office, as ordered, his personally compiled account of the history and achievement of the Auxiliary Units. It seems inconceivable that officials would ever have shredded the valuable results of this experiment in irregular warfare. Official papers which *have* found their way to Kew, including complex establishment returns, show a far more structured administration than originally supposed – certainly one whose papers were less than likely to have been casually shredded by some low-level official. One near certainty is that volumes of archive do still lurk in some Whitehall vault.

If there is nothing to hide, then unnecessary secrecy is certainly counter-productive and serves merely to fan the enduring flame of curiosity. In Suffolk, to take a comparable example, there is hardly a man or woman who doubts that the 'Mystery of Shingle Street' was a real event. Although Whitehall, after years of evasion and prevarication, now resolutely protests that there are no more papers still kept in secret, there is an indestructible myth that 3,000 (or was it 30,000?) German soldiers invaded this beach in East Anglia on the 'Cromwell' weekend of 7 September 1940, only to be incinerated by a skilfully deployed British invention that set the sea on fire, engulfing the invaders. The firmer the official protest, the wider stretches the myth, solely because such records as there were remained undisclosed indefinitely. The population of the tiny fishing village was forced – or so one of the rumours goes – to leave their homes; the RAF bombed those who refused; bodies are still secretly buried in abundance under the shingle; the local authority conspires by bulldozing all the skeletons exposed during easterly gales every winter; chemical warfare experiments were carried out; the sea was mistakenly set on fire during an exercise and it was *British* soldiers who were incinerated.

These rumours are nonsense, but this rubbish has been vigorously perpetuated on otherwise low news days, with media compliance and the exploitation of (alleged) eye witnesses, and kept in being by half a century of official obduracy and refusal to publish a handful of papers. There is no intention of creating such extreme arguments with the Auxiliary Units, but the fact remains that, with as many as 10,000 personnel involved, there must be records. Their irregular warfare experiments led to worthwhile conclusions and the development of a wonderfully ingenious radio network. Yet, apart from some miscellaneous documents at Kew and the facts leaked to David Lampe for his 1968 publication of *The Last Ditch*, the Auxiliary Units as a whole seem to have been deliberately marginalised. It should therefore be no surprise to the authorities that widespread interest persists in trying to discover why.

But, although we can only surmise what the special events were, it is certainly a worthy notion that Britain's stay-behind army of civilian men and women should not be cast aside or written off as insignificant. Their loyalty to the nation in war and their committed silence throughout the following half century of peace demands better than that.

One fact available is that the Operational Section did exist. After a succession of denials, a reluctant Ministry of Defence released a nominal roll to the (then) Public Record Office, fifty years from VJ-Day – but only after certain influential and concerned veterans such as Colonel Andrew Croft, one of Gubbins's 'originals', pressed the case. The award of the WWII Defence Medal, which sometimes followed, had previously been resisted by the Adjutant-General's office, the Army Medal Office and, perhaps even MI5 and MI6.

A whole clutch of possibilities might account for the delay in disclosure. The operational side, it is suggested, might have been needed again. The SAS and other special forces might still use some of the lessons learned by Auxiliers. However, against this is the fact that we do know that much of what the Auxiliers had absorbed in a hard, trial-and-error school was ignored by the SAS during the Cold War. More than one accredited spokesman has acknowledged that SAS troopers prepared to go underground in the event of a Soviet attack, using 'hides' vulnerable to metal detection and initially without built-in ventilation. The Auxunits' experience, a decade or more earlier, was that such bases were inevitably destined to become untenable. These facts, and their antidotes, were not only well-known to Auxiliers, but documented on their behalf by Major Oxenden in his final report to the War Office in 1944:

> Ventilation was a science of which little was known. The official teaching was that a pipe brought down to within a foot of the floor would provide an unfailing current of fresh air, but when the first 'stay in' exercise was held, most of the earlier OBs soon drove their occupants into the open, sicker and wiser men.

Although it remains a possibility, not one single Auxilier has come forward to say that an attempt was made to recruit him again *after* the stand-down in 1944. Neither, as far as is known, was any Auxilier invited post-war to join the dirty tricks exponents not unknown as field operators in the secret services.

Another possibility can be considered. Does Whitehall fear claims for compensation from men who might later think that an ungrateful establishment owed them something for the months of their lives given to patriotic, potentially dangerously exposed service? Again there is nothing to support this hypothesis and it was almost certainly the last thing the men wanted. In any case, post-war thinking was far from today's avaricious compensation culture. It is known that a number of Auxiliers were injured while training, although the circumstances are not on record.

(Sergeant Fred Matthews, in a Norfolk Patrol, lost a hand some time in 1941 or 1942. He disappeared mysteriously from his patrol afterwards. His colleagues were led to believe that he had been on a private outing, fishing with explosives – a far from unknown pastime – and that the injury was carelessly self-inflicted. He was quietly replaced in his patrol; the corporal became the sergeant and the rest moved up an appropriate notch in rank. We will return to Mathews's story shortly)

If anyone was likely to recruit former Auxiliers for Cold War dirty tricks, it was the Gladios. This pan-European organisation of cavalier stay-behinds was created in the early 1950s, mainly by the US Central Intelligence Agency, but with MI6 input. The idea, it seems, was to create secret underground armies across the western democracies – some count the personnel in tens of thousands – with access to huge stores of explosives and weaponry, and objectives not dissimilar to those of the Auxiliary Units. Sir Colin Gubbins was once reported to be involved; if so, his much-publicised differences with MI6 must have been reconciled. In any event, the Gladios were obviously too widespread and cumbersome to remain under central control, even though anti-communist officers often led the charge. Can it be doubted that former Nazis were among them? The Gladios went off the rails in a big way, especially in Belgium where the 'straight' authorities got wind of some of their less savoury activities, with resultant prosecutions and inevitably unfavourable publicity.

Again, no case has come to light of former civilian Auxiliers becoming involved. To suggest that any of their officers was enlisted would be sheer conjecture and it would be pointless to give this more of our time.

The men and women of the Auxunits' Special Duties Section are an altogether different matter. Their background and education meant they were often more broadly informed and generally politically aware. No nominal roll has ever been published but it undoubtedly rests within the archives of MI6 which, together with MI5, *could* have found a ready supply of well-trained agents already on the SDS list. Indeed, the fresh menace of the Cold War created a whole new series of opportunities for undercover employment. In turn, this called for extremes of expertise and it would be foolish to expect to learn much about this aspect of secret service techniques even now.

Internal subversion proliferated in post-war Britain, notably in trade unions, at universities, and within the civil and diplomatic services of HM government. This created a clear need for counter-measures best carried out by calling upon those who had already proved themselves. Many part-time agents were already in place in industry, commerce, or government. Personnel of the SDS were among them. In this way there was every good reason for keeping officially discreet about those men or women secretly re-selected, and, it may be argued, that if a smoke screen had to be laid down to protect the SDS, then the men of the operational patrols had to be kept similarly invisible too. The fact that recognition of operational Auxiliers' service with the award of the WWII Defence Medal was not conceded from Whitehall until five years or so after the Cold War was finished may provide some slight support for this possibility.

Technically, the Auxiliary Units as a whole came under the command of the War Office, which still depended upon maintaining its secrets by the use of the Official Secrets Acts. Every operational Auxilier, it is certain – and every agent of the SDS it may be assumed – was aware of their commitments, most having signed some sort of paper as they were enrolled. Sometimes the persuasion was more extreme. A good example was broadcast on BBC Television early in 2006. The everlasting silence demanded from personnel recruited to work at Bletchley Park during WWII was demonstrated to one man during his interview to sign the Official Secrets Act, conducted by an officer with a loaded revolver on the desk in front of him pointing directly at the signatory. This experience, and the meaning implicit, remained vividly in the forefront of the interviewee's memory.

Signatures given under the Official Secrets Acts by the men of the South Wales operational patrols may not have deterred Alan Hollingdale from organising reunion lunches for up to a hundred veterans as early as the end of the 1940s. But not one single, comparable example exists in respect of the Special Duties Section, perhaps as a consequence of even more severe threats than the one mentioned above. While security lapses such as reunions were not denied to the patrols, similar liberties were never even considered for the SDS. As far as paperwork and official releases were concerned too, the SDS embargo was almost watertight. Moreover, it was unusually difficult to break because, in most if not all cases, the cellular wartime prohibition against knowledge of other SDS participants created an impassable barrier.

In pursuit of some useful objective, however, Britain's secret services will occasionally let a calculated cat out of the bag. It is safe to assume that the public was intended to learn something about MI(R) from an early post-war stage, as an avowable diversion from even more secret interests. If Section D's closing report is to be taken seriously, the comparatively overt initiatives of MI(R) before and during the war successfully diverted attention from Section D itself, its various unavowable stratagems, and the unattributable funds at its disposal. This left serious innovation to D and financial overlordship with the Secret Intelligence Service. By implication, the SIS retained an overview from the beginning; its foresight undoubtedly filled a potentially lethal gap in Britain's war capability. The Auxiliary Units, SOE, commandos, continental escape routes – these were just some of the positive results generally channelled through MI(R).

However, by holding fast to some secrets well past their sell-by date, the secret services have shot themselves in the foot. Although the result may sometimes be difficult to distinguish from mere guesswork, a genuine release of facts from the fountainhead in good time might have forestalled all sorts of debatable propositions once and for all. A suitable maxim for today's Secret Intelligence Service to bear in mind might be 'Remember Shingle Street'!

*

With the secret services' commitment to calculated deception, it would be silly always to believe them. For example, one Section D report, dated 30 August 1940 – and now in the National Archives – on the role of the Auxiliary Units, describes the patrols as making forays through the front line, *with the army*. This was *never* a credible alternative to the technique instilled from the very start of their training. We shall never know whether the report was intended to convince or deceive the Chief of the SIS and keep the money rolling in, or to bewilder future historians. It is just conceivable that the writer was either one hundred percent mistaken or the victim of an overactive imagination.

Section D's achievements in the irregular warfare area now look less than overwhelming. However, it did maintain a degree of control over MI(R), and then supply the explosives and incendiaries to the Operational Patrols which upgraded Auxiliers from early bow-and-arrow days, and on to potentially significant achievements as a small guerrilla force.

Meanwhile, through the good offices of Joan Bright Astley, MD1 was backed with SIS money almost from the start. There was some sort of understandable competition between MD1 and the various development stations and dirty tricks' production lines established at Aston House (Station XII) and Brickendonbury (Station XVII). A good example is Stuart Macrae's contempt for the time pencil fuse, an invention of Commander Langley at Station XII.

*

If there is something still bigger to hide, we are free to look at a couple of possibilities. Under the circumstances this must necessarily be partly speculative. Perhaps neither would have been credible if the full story of the Auxiliary Units had ever been disclosed through some official or quasi-official source. If there were substance in either, however, the trapdoor of secrecy might well be firmly closed against public disclosure for ever.

Chapter Twenty-One

A Disastrous Raid on Sark

'Thus a new phase in the Commando story began. Perhaps the furious German reaction was part and parcel of a desire to curb an increasingly annoying form of warfare – one which kept the defenders guessing as to where the next blow would fall.'

Winston G. Ramsey, The War in the Channel Islands

Hitler's infamous Commando Order (*Kommandobefehl*) was promulgated on 18 October 1942. This date may be critical to any further discussion about the indefinite retention of Auxiliary Units papers within official archives, and needs to be borne in mind. This directed the German armed forces that:

> From now on, all enemies on so-called Commando missions . . . even if they are to all appearances soldiers in uniform . . . are to be slaughtered to the last man . . . even if these individuals, when found, should apparently be prepared to give themselves up, no pardon is to be granted.

By treating this as a lawful order, the enemy would seek to justify the murder of the troopers and former Auxiliers of Operation Bulbasket in France in July 1944 and many other atrocities involving properly and legally constituted Allied irregular forces fighting behind the lines.

The order had an important effect upon German military conduct for the rest of the war, although there are numerous examples – such as the experience of George Biffin from the Dorset and Wiltshire Scout Section of the Auxiliary Units after being captured at the outset of Bulbasket – of enemy front line soldiers concluding that British commandos and parachutists were simply conducting warfare in a way which they respected. Moreover, considerable prevarication and resistance was evident from the Germans near Poitiers when a firing squad was assembled to execute SAS troopers.

The question is whether Hitler's words were entirely malevolent or based upon real-life facts as he saw them? If 18 October 1942 was a significant date for his order, what motivated him to wait for no less than three years after the outbreak of war before signing it? It has already been concluded elsewhere, that his decision to do so followed one of the British commando raids that immediately preceded that date.

The Channel Islands were the only part of the United Kingdom occupied by the enemy during WWII, and they were the target of a succession of small boat raids by British soldiers, to gain experience of a task without any precedent, and to collect intelligence about enemy fortifications and troop dispositions. Critical to this was the capture of prisoners.

A look at a list of those raids – and it seems that details have long been available in public records – shows that there were three attacks on the Channel Isles, three possibilities that preceded the 18 October deadline: Operation Dryad against the Casquets Lighthouse; Cranford to the uninhabited island of Burhou; or Basalt, a raid to gather intelligence on the defences of the island of Sark – and to capture prisoners.

The next question must be 'What on earth has this got to do with the Auxiliary Units and any continuing embargo on their papers?' If full and frank records were available, the question could be answered in no time at all. As they are not, let us see if we can find any leads that fit well with the few facts available.

We can start at Parham, Suffolk, in the mid-1990s as the Museum of the British Resistance Organisation started to take shape. Knowledge about the Auxiliary Units was still very limited. Those then involved in the museum had some access to post-war correspondence which cannot now be traced. These letters apparently indicated that a small number of Auxiliers had been involved in a raid conducted by boat. The correspondence appears to have been between Norfolk Auxilier Fred Matthews and his first Intelligence Officer, Captain Nigel Oxenden. The Oxenden side of the correspondence has survived and is entirely anodyne. The Matthews letters addressed to 'Oxo' have disappeared – but the inference was left that they were the source of the 'raid' story.

Of course, Oxenden would have been the very best man in the country to mastermind a raid on the Channel Isles; he was a pre-war resident and had extensive munitions expertise dating from WWI. Moreover, he was by 1942 the Chief Training Officer at Coleshill, in succession to 'Bill' Beyts and,

being well removed from the War Office, ideally situated to co-ordinate the
various services and facilities demanded by such an irregular operation. So
had he been called upon to set up and advise on a specific raid directed at
one of the Channel Isles?

There is no definite answer to this question, but it was at or about this
time that Fred Matthews lost a hand. As we already know, he then left his
patrol colleagues in the Auxiliary Units, to appear again only after the war.
Fred Matthews was undoubtedly the leading light in a highly surprising, and
certainly unique, collection of funds from some former Norfolk Auxiliers
after Nigel Oxenden's premature death in November 1948, and the erection
of his memorial at Portelet Bay, on Jersey, as mentioned earlier. Oxenden
himself and the collection made for his memorial stone on Jersey, are still
well remembered by a few surviving Norfolk Auxiliers – and not at all by the
majority. Veteran Jim Watson remembers many incidents clearly enough but
he was not among those invited to contribute to the memorial collection.

Once he was at Coleshill, it is now clear that Oxenden had more than
one role. We have already seen how Lieutenant Roy Russell remembered
dining in the officers' mess alongside uniformed colleagues from all three
services and several different nations, all working for Special Operations
Executive. The correlation between the two secret services was not previously
realised, although with Colin Gubbins as the common denominator, it should
hardly have come as a surprise. Moreover, there is confirmation that SOE
worked directly with Nigel Oxenden at Auxunits HQ, from his daughter Joy
who, while still a young girl living with her mother and father in their small
cottage on the edge of the estate, remembers that she and her mother were
required from time to time to wait in the kitchen while her father met
members of SOE.

It is entirely reasonable to extrapolate from SOE to SSRF (the Small Scale
Raiding Force, otherwise known as No. 62 Commando), the unit of
Combined Operations specifically created to carry out pin-prick raids on
enemy-held territory as the burgeoning Commando forces outgrew such a
role themselves. Commandos were by 1942 participating in large-scale raids
such as those at St. Nazaire and Dieppe.

Is there any deduction that can be made from these granules of
sometimes circumstantial evidence? Can some context be assembled which
might compensate for the poverty of official information available about the
Auxiliary Units and account for their virtual dismissal as a subject for post-

war historical research? Does anything coincide with the irritation Hitler clearly felt in the autumn of 1942 which led to the Commando Order – an instruction to troops based on a generally incorrect and specious analysis of the principles enshrined in the conventions of war as far as irregular soldiering was concerned – at least as the British understood it?

And, in particular, do any of the commando raids on the Channel Isles provide a possible missing link? Of the three raids that preceded 18 October 1942, two were during September: Operation Dryad, where the entire crew of the Casquets Lighthouse and valuable intelligence were taken without loss to the British party; and Cranford, an unopposed scouting mission to the uninhabited isle of Burhou. The reason for Hitler's order can therefore fairly definitively be found in Operation Basalt on the night of 3 October by a uniformed force of ten or twelve (reports differ) officers and men of the SSRF led by Major Geoffrey Appleyard. Again the objective was reconnaissance and intelligence. Prisoners were the main target.

This raid had worldwide ramifications.

*

Following earlier attacks, the island's defences were already on alert but, initially, a landing was safely effected from Royal Navy *Motor Torpedo Boat No. 344*, based at Portland, and the main party of the assault group climbed from the beach to attack a small hotel occupied by enemy soldiers. A sentry was knifed and killed. Five prisoners were taken and, with the intention of getting them all back to England, their hands were bound. A considerable disturbance followed as they tried to loosen the bonds and escape while being shepherded back to the waiting RN craft, shouting loudly at the same time to rouse the rest of their detachment. Endangered by this, and about to be greatly outnumbered, Major Appleyard shouted 'Shut the prisoners up!' As some tried to make a dash for it, another British officer ordered 'If they try to get away, shoot them.' This was followed by a number of shots. The raiding party eventually escaped with just one prisoner – still in his pyjamas – leaving several bodies behind; some did have their hands still tied.

Eight of the British officers and men have been identified and named by researchers, notably in Winston G. Ramsey's *The War in the Channel Isles*. All the team survived but one – named simply as Private Smith – was wounded and had to be helped back to their boat by the rearguard.

Hitler's subsequent order led in due course to attempted German post-war justification for the murder of Allied servicemen in uniform. Prominent among these victims were the troopers of several SAS operations inserted deep into enemy-held territory after D-Day. Among these were the troopers betrayed and executed in Operation Bulbasket, who included seven former Auxiliers, at least two of them from Oxenden's Norfolk Scout Section at Wroxham.

We shall probably never know for sure, since no one in Whitehall seemingly intends to tell us, whether the SSRF party included one-off participation by two or three Norfolk Auxiliers or what, if any, was the part in the operation played by Nigel Oxenden. Is it reasonable to propose that 'Private Smith' could have been an alias for Patrol Leader Fred Matthews and that he was perhaps shot in the hand during the melée? Only by tracing his missing hand shall we ever find out. If it languishes in some Norfolk fishpond the whole proposition is dead. But, if it was left somewhere on the island of Sark on the night of 3 October 1942, much of the other evidence does fit. No doubt the associated issues are too great for us ever to be told, but if a Whitehall spokesman comes forth from his hidey-hole to tell us the truth he will be well worth a rousing three cheers.

It can be argued that the 'Matthews' theory is inconclusive, based as it largely is upon circumstantial evidence and extrapolation. However, an alternative hypothesis exists, and focuses on the pivotal character involved, Major Nigel Oxenden himself.

The SSRF group that attacked Sark included a preponderance of officers, and it is not impossible that Oxenden was one. His local knowledge would have been invaluable and it is a fact that the raiders missed no opportunity to collect intelligence from the resident population. Indeed, some of them suffered from this co-operation and were deported to Germany. There is enough smoke here to detect the definite presence of fire. And Nigel Oxenden, involved as he *may* have been in preparations for the raid, was *certainly* involved in writing the final report on the Auxiliary Units. It was previously suggested that the draft of his 'Auxiliary Units – History and Achievement', published by the Museum of the British Resistance Organisation in 1998 may have been incomplete because the full version included details of the Special Duties Section. Far more controversially, it now seems possible this was because he summarised the lessons learned from the raid on Sark. If so, Whitehall is still covering up the details of an event which led to murderous war crimes committed against properly constituted British soldiers as the result of Hitler's order. Incidentally it would also account for Oxenden's concerns about the use of noisy firearms in irregular warfare and his preference for the sound-suppressed Welrod.

In view of the significant issues that would be placed in the public domain if this is even *near* the bull's-eye, it would account not only for the cocoon of everlasting secrecy which we are still witnessing around the Auxiliary Units, but also the mysterious disappearance from Jersey of the full 20,000-word copy of his report which, after having been hidden by 'Oxo' for fifty years, vanished shortly after the discovery had been announced to the Ministry of Defence in London.

In retrospect, the British raiding party on Sark was wrong to execute bound prisoners. The victors of WWII are not inclined now to admit any blame for the resulting atrocities. If this hypothesis is anywhere near the truth, the resulting conspiracy of silence suits British interests well, even though the legal and diplomatic repercussions which would certainly once have followed disclosure have now surely passed.

Chapter Twenty-Two

Auxunits and the Rudolf Hess Mystery

'. . . the reader cannot feel he has been united with the probable.'

Rebecca West in her Introduction to Hugh Thomas's The Murder of Rudolf Hess

The background to the generally accepted pre-war policy of appeasement was discussed in early chapters. By mid-1940, with the appointment of Winston Churchill as prime minister and the defeat of the British Expeditionary Force in France, a positive, public rebuttal of any further softly-softly approach to war became the new fashion. If any doubters were still on view, pro-war propaganda soon won over all but the most dedicated pacifists, dissemblers and secret Nazi sympathisers. On the surface, at least, the day was won by the new Churchillian strategy of total victory at all costs.

However, a few people holding influential positions, or with vested interests, had their doubts and still secretly held fast to the possibility of a beneficial deal with Hitler. Supporters were recognised as the Peace Group, or the Peace Movement. They were not a co-ordinated anti-war conspiracy and their motives varied. Some genuinely believed that the interests of the British Empire would best be served by listening to the offers outlined by Hitler in speeches to the Reichstag during the summer of 1940. Had Lord Halifax, the other major contender, been appointed prime minister, the Führer might well have heard encouraging noises from the British establishment, for there was a significant minority who saw Bolshevism as an even more threatening enemy than the Nazis, and certainly one more likely to terminate their largely inherited privileges.

It seemed obvious enough to some that Hitler was merely regrouping after the fall of France, and counting upon some sort of truce with Britain, while preparing for an early opportunity to smash the Soviets. Hitler was well aware that an invasion of Britain, ill-prepared for defence as it clearly was, would be a costly and possibly protracted affair and a drain on the resources and manpower of his armed forces – thus placing in doubt their ability to attack Russia as scheduled in the spring of 1941.

The question for the Peace Group was to decide where their best interests rested. If revolutionary history was any guide, it may safely be assumed that an alliance with Soviet Russia was not necessarily the most likely way to guarantee the continuance of their influence at the top and the security of their fiefdoms. This select group of the nation's elite included Conservative members of both Houses of Parliament, aristocrats, landowners, some of the royal family, senior civil servants and diplomats. They comprised an informal but well connected ginger group, working positively, if quietly, among themselves and abroad with selected German representatives, in the direction most likely to suit their long-term interests. Unadulterated patriotism was not, in essence, a direct motive. It is not clear how deeply the Church of England was involved, if at all, and pacifists and intellectuals were not automatically included. The following prominent personages have since been named as probable supporters: the Duke of Windsor and the Duke of Kent, King George's brothers; the Duke of Buccleuch, with personal connections to the royal family, and a court appointment as Keeper of His Majesty's Household, a position removed from him (although he remained a Privy Counsellor) in 1940 because of his 'then arguably treacherous pro-German sentiments', and handed on to the Duke of Hamilton; the Duke of Bedford; the former conservative MP Henry Drummond-Wolff and the Labour peer Lord Buxton. At a political level, both Foreign Secretary Lord Halifax and his under-Secretary, R. A. B. Butler, were far from Churchillian, and Sir Samuel Hoare, British Ambassador to Madrid, is widely reported to have been in the forefront of negotiations with German emissaries.

The Peace Group, or 'The Link' as it was sometimes called, partly disintegrated after Dunkirk and the internment of known British fascists and Nazi sympathisers. However, it was later re-created under SIS control. 'C' was thus able to identify the supporters and penetrate their conspiracies. This was not all that difficult because some of his friends and family connections were well placed to play a dual role on his behalf.

Broadly, the Peace Group represented the 'old order', imperialists who respected the rapidity of Germany's economic revival and the wealth opportunities it generated while, at the same time, fearing the growth of communism. Indeed, they saw Hitler potentially as a bulwark against the proletarian revolution which would signal the loss of privileges upon which they depended. Germany – as they clearly understood – had been increasingly vulnerable to such a social upheaval ever since the end of WWI – burdened as it was with reparations laid down under the Treaty of Versailles in 1919, the wild inflation which this generated, and crippling working-class unemployment. It was this last group which had borne the brunt of casualties, both civilian and military, during the war itself. Post-war discontent contributed significantly to German instability throughout the 1920s. Mass unemployment had existed in Britain too. The working class often lived in slum housing in both town and countryside. The General Strike had been put down by troops and right-wing 'volunteer' civilian militias; and the great wealth of the British Empire was enjoyed mainly by just the privileged few of the upper classes. The end of that period of incipient revolution in Germany – replicated in Britain as it had been – was much admired by the Peace Group. By leaving the Germans free to do the dirty work in the east, the Peace Group could, at the same time, secure their own future.

Against this background, it was not surprising that Hitler and much of what he stood for, was not easily dismissed by the Peace Group. With Churchill in power and headlining a resurgence of jingoistic sabre rattling, they also feared that war would bankrupt Great Britain, leaving both the country and themselves destitute. Seen in this way, Hitler had a lot going for him. Visions of tumbrels and *tricoteuses* must have haunted those with a sense of history.

Principals in the group had the tacit support of many Conservatives, as Picknett, Prince and Prior's *Double Standards* points out:

> A study in 1938 showed that 238 Conservative MPs came from the nobility or landed gentry. Clydesdale was an MP before becoming the Duke of Hamilton and being elevated to the Lords.
>
> Britain's leading landowner, the Duke of Westminster, organised the anti-war peers into a group that would lobby the Government for Peace.

The Peace Group was by no means insignificant. With the SIS commitment to deception, the problem has since been to distinguish between those who genuinely believed that their future would be better secured through a deal with Hitler, and those who were placed within the group to report their thinking, contacts and activities to 'C' or Winston Churchill.

*

As he explained in his widely acclaimed book, *Invasion 1940*, Peter Fleming had always been uneasy about the miracle of Dunkirk:

> What seemed at the time a miracle can in retrospect be more plausibly attributed to a failure in generalship on the Germans' part. The German error was in halting on 24 May 1940, with the advance of powerful armoured forces on Dunkirk from the south, when they were only a few miles from the as yet unorganised defensive perimeter of the Allied bridgehead. The order, for whose issue there were sound administrative reasons, since the tanks were in more need of maintenance, and their crews of rest, was given by von Rundstedt, commanding Army Group 'A' and was approved by Hitler.

It was, in any event, Hitler's strategy after Dunkirk to get the British out of the way before he turned on Russia. Within his inner circle he displayed a certain admiration for the British, based no doubt, upon his experience of their fighting capacity during WWI. He also vicariously allied himself to the British because of their *Germanic* background, and waited impatiently for a positive acknowledgement of his proposals for an understanding between the two countries.

On 9 July 1940, the Nazi-controlled New British Broadcasting Company declared that 'There is at this time a real possibility, I might almost say a probability, of a negotiated peace.' Meanwhile, the Germans assembled and started to convert a makeshift fleet of highly unsuitable canal boats for the invasion of England. Enemy activity was otherwise noticeably quiescent until the Battle of Britain – the Luftwaffe's opportunity to bring the stubborn British to the negotiating table. Hermann Göring's aviators failed in that mission but did succeed in uniting most of the British public behind Winston Churchill and winding them up to a state of belated, total-war urgency and awareness. Although the ensuing Blitz was a greater threat still this, too, failed to break the British spirit or persuade them to look for a compromise settlement.

While planning an invasion of Britain, Hitler never ceased to dream of a capitulation. Invasion was a last resort. At a top-level conference on 11 July, Hitler stated that he could see no reason why the war should go on. He was to offer the British a chance to come to terms in a major speech to the Reichstag. His conviction that Britain would accept an accommodation was an intuition rather than a reasoned conclusion. Many neutral observers, including Joe Kennedy, the American ambassador to the court of St James, shared his view.

In a summary of Hitler's outlook on the British, Peter Fleming concluded:

> He often admired the British as fellow Anglo-Saxons; at other times the British inspired a venomous hatred, maybe caused by something approaching social inferiority. He alternately wanted them on his side and then at his feet.

*

During a spell of sick leave after his return from Norway in the spring of 1940, and shortly before the invasion of France, Peter Fleming wrote the imaginative novelette *A Flying Visit*. In this he presupposed the arrival by parachute in Britain of the Führer on a final peace mission. This entirely fictitious scenario very nearly came true on 10 May 1941 when, in one of the most unwisely downplayed events of the war, the *Deputy* Führer did almost that. Rudolf Hess, after what seemed at first to have been an intrepid solo flight all the way from Augsburg in Bavaria in a twin-engine Messerschmitt Bf 110, bailed out and descended by parachute in Scotland, hoping to find himself near Dungavel House, the home of the Duke of Hamilton. From the very start it was a fiasco, became a farce, and eventually developed into one of the great unsolved mysteries of WWII. In spite of boundless research, investigation and disclosures, the full story has not been revealed from either the British or German governments. Such facts as there are have sometimes been sabotaged by calculated deception.

It is not within the scope of this book to try to do better, but there is a definite, if admittedly slim connection with the Auxiliary Units Special Duties Section, which may just have involved some of the officers-in-charge – but not the civilian agents – with both Hess's visit and the Peace Group with which it was certainly associated. If there was such a connection, it could certainly account for the mysterious, everlasting secrecy which still encompasses the SDS, sweeping along with it the otherwise entirely unconnected Operational Patrols. It has apparently suited the interests of both the German and British governments – from 1941 until today – to declare that Hess had gone off his head by leaving Germany. Many of the facts are in doubt and, as usual, vary in proportion to the theories of the last source under scrutiny.

However, some things do seem certain. Rudolf Hess, an educated man, was certainly devoted to Hitler; they served prison time together in the 1920s. During their incarceration Hess helped Hitler to write his political bible – *Mein Kampf*. Until the flight in 1940, Hess and his wife lived in Munich with their only son, Wolf Adolf Karl Rudiger. 'Wolf' was Hitler's code-name during early, troubled days as the Nazi Party sought power; Adolf needs no further explanation.

Although he had recently added to his power base by establishing his own secret service as a separate entity from the Abwehr of Admiral Canaris, the closest German equivalent of 'C' in Britain, Hess had also been subordinated to Hermann Göring in the Nazi Party power battle. This tactical set-back may have persuaded him to try a single-handed attempt at concluding a peace deal with the British and – with such a master stroke – reingratiate himself with Hitler and regain his place in the pecking order. His sanity was certainly in no doubt at all until the day of his departure, for he carried a heavy and responsible workload. He was an accomplished speaker too – both for the Nazi Party itself and the German war effort as a whole.

Hess was an experienced pilot with WWI credentials, and had kept his flight training up-to-the-minute. It is recorded that he was in touch with the Haushofer family, father and son who, with impressive military and intellectual contacts, had co-ordinated some quasi-official peace feelers with the Peace Group in Britain through an intermediary. In particular, they thought they had access to the Duke of Hamilton, a serving officer in the Royal Air Force and influentially connected directly to the royal family. The Duke had also met Rudolf Hess in Germany during the Olympic Games of 1936. This contact had been intercepted by the British secret services.

Sources differ on whether 'Hess' undertook the journey with or without Hitler's knowledge or authority. However, he was photographed – and his aircraft identified – by his adjutant, during the take-off run at Augsburg. Detailed enquires tend to confirm that the Messerschmitt could never have carried enough fuel to complete the trip non-stop to Scotland, even with added wing tanks – and the take-off photograph shows no sign of them. Having over-flown the North Sea, he arrived near the British coast having miscalculated the time of dusk. 'Hess' therefore flew a delay-pattern before crossing the coast near the Duke of Northumberland's castle at Alnwick at nightfall, heading for the private airstrip of the Duke of Hamilton – Northumberland's brother-in-law – at Dungavel. A transit waypoint was the Duke of Buccleuch's seat at Bowhill. He narrowly missed Dungavel, but, in excellent visibility, continued on a strange course to the west coast of Scotland to re-orient himself before turning back inland, missing Dungavel well-and-truly on the second run. He eventually bailed out near Eaglesham, some thirty miles from his target. The significance of this is that in order to make a calculated landfall just to the north of Alnwick Castle, the pilot had to deviate from his simple westerly heading over the North Sea as he approached the coast and which, had he continued, would have taken him directly to Dungavel, where the Duke of Hamilton was waiting at his lighted airstrip. In the hangar a pair of German-built wing tanks was ready for a return flight. The Duke of Kent and secret service officers are reported to have been among the waiting reception party.

The Dukes of Northumberland, Buccleuch and Hamilton were all involved in the intrigues of the Peace Group. The Duke of Buccleuch was confined to his home under what amounted to house arrest for his unrepentant pro-German views. It seems likely that the pilot was following a pre-arranged course, both to home in accurately to Dungavel and, by flying fast and spectacularly low, deliberately to have his approach identified. These variations of course, and his low, fast flight path, contributed to yet more fuel consumption.

After his descent, the pilot was soon arrested by the Home Guard. He gave his name initially as Hauptmann Alfred Horn, was interrogated by an officer of the Royal Observer Corps, identified as Rudolf Hess and passed over to higher authority. As soon as he was identified, his secret peace mission, if that is what it was, was no longer a secret. His identity papers were minimal and his flying jacket different from that worn at Augsburg. He was in a different aircraft too. Reports differ, but indicate that there may have been a refuelling stopover in Denmark, after which the Luftwaffe protected him with an escort more than half way across the North Sea.

From the moment of his identification, 'Hess' often acted irrationally and out of character with the cool and calculating Deputy Führer. Another well-based deduction is that if Hess did land en route at a Luftwaffe base in Denmark, he was intercepted there by agents of Heinrich Himmler, chief of the Nazi Secret Police, arrested and later assassinated. Göring is also reported to have ordered that Hess's Messerschmitt be shot down. As reports of Hitler's angry reaction when he heard about the Hess flight and disappearance may or may not be true, it can be taken as fact that the public has not been given much of the full story.

In any event, it is fairly certain that the pilot who arrived, looking like Hess and primed with some foreknowledge of his peace mission, may not have been Rudolf Hess at all. Although details are not known for sure, there is some consensus that the peace terms he brought were an honourable understanding between the Axis powers and Britain; the retention of both the Royal Navy and the British Empire; and freedom to continue trading throughout the areas of most British business influence. In return, the Germans sought the cessation of hostilities in the west; freedom to seek so-called *Lebensraum* for a reunited German nation by aggressive expansion eastwards; and, finally, trade and economic dominance on mainland Europe.

All this presupposed British non-intervention during Operation Barbarossa, the invasion of Russia, which erupted just one month after the flight to Scotland but of which – apart from generous indications from German cipher traffic decoded at Bletchley Park – there was no positive foreknowledge by the Allies. The obvious question is – did 'Hess' himself know and, if so, did he tell the Peace Group or, later, British interrogators? If the answer is 'yes', Joe Stalin was more than justified in his suspicion that the British government had something to hide. His government was, in any event, desperate for any talk of peace to fail and for Britain to remain in the war to reduce the impact of any aggressive intent by the Germans against the Soviet Union. Agents of the United States are also reported to have been involved and the evidence that MI5 was at work is strong. In their case, the date of the flight is believed to have been partly determined by an MI5 agent, working in the field of the occult, bringing influence to bear on Hess through his personal astrologer. Finally, the timing of the flight may have been influenced by an announcement of an imminent speech by President Roosevelt, and the suspicion that he would proclaim the formal union of the United States with Great Britain.

Very little official information has come to light about many aspects of the Hess flight, his detention and treatment, and the events leading to his eventual death. American spokesmen have concluded that the British assassinated him at an early stage. The Russians remained suspicious of Churchill's version throughout the war, and researchers have since discovered in the National Archives a record that any remaining papers were removed to the Royal Archive in Windsor Castle. Others have gone missing without explanation.

The official position is that Hess was held in Britain – eventually by Sir Stewart Menzies' Secret Intelligence Service – and given prisoner of war status on Churchill's direct instructions, until the Nuremberg trials in 1945–6, when he was sentenced to life imprisonment. However, Hess was later medically examined in Spandau Prison by Hugh Thomas, Consultant in General Surgery to the British Military Hospital in Berlin – who also happened to be an expert on gunshot wounds. Thomas declared that, without doubt, the prisoner's chest scars were not consistent with bullet wounds that the real Hess was known to have suffered during WWI, and that, consequently, the prisoner definitely was not the Deputy Führer.

Just to confuse the story even more, careful research leading to the publication of *Double Standards* in 2001, established to the authors' satisfaction that the man who landed in 1941 was picked up by Short Sunderland flying boat W4026 on 25 August 1942 from Loch More, remotely situated in Caithness and that, together with Prince George, Duke of Kent and brother of King George VI, he set out for Sweden jointly to declare some sort of peace deal – only for both to be killed in a crash on Eagle's Rock soon after take-off, together with all but one of the crew. As there were sixteen dead men and one survivor, this exceeded by one the number on the official list of personnel aboard.

Secret services recruit 'doubles' for deception purposes and Hess – with such distinctive features – could have been among those available in either Britain or Germany. If we add up all the various conspiracy theories, we find the need not for one 'double' but a highly improbable several.

However, if we are to believe the official version of events, Rudolf Hess, the prisoner of Spandau, hanged himself in his prison cell in 1987. Hands up all those who think we know the truth, the whole truth and nothing but the truth?

And, if it all seems a long way from the Special Duties Section of the Auxiliary Units, consider this. The Duke of Northumberland was deeply involved with the peace plan. However, by luck or design, a Special Duties

Section radio Control Station manned by subalterns of the Auxunits (ATS), including Dorothy Rainey, then Dorothy Monck-Mason, was operative within the grounds of his seat at Alnwick Castle. Alnwick Castle crops up more and more. It was an important landfall for 'Hess' after a difficult trans-North Sea flight, with no track-confirming waypoints after leaving the continental coastline. It was a short diversion from due west – a compass heading relatively easy to follow – from Kalundborg, the Luftwaffe base in Denmark assumed by the authors of *Double Standards* to have been the refuelling station. A good landfall was essential to start the flight overland to Dungavel at low level and by night, without radio navigational aids except one conveniently placed broadcasting station, which he could perhaps have picked up.

This is how it was interpreted in *Double Standards*:

> It is no coincidence that both Alnwick Castle and Dungavel were the homes of high-ranking individuals who were related by marriage and were at some level involved with the peace lobby. Moreover, as Alnwick Castle is situated on the coast just a few miles off the same latitude as Dungavel and Kalundborg, could it have been transmitting a radio signal to guide Rudolf Hess's flight? Is this why such powerful radio equipment had been specially installed in the Me 110? Or, on the other hand, could somebody at Alnwick have been receiving the same signal as Hess from Kalundborg and was the specific piece of music a code for Hess's approach?

On the night of 10 June 1941, Yolande Alston, then Yolande Bromley, was on duty alone at her 'Met hut' Control Station at Thornham Magna, Lord Henniker's estate and Eastern Command HQ, near Diss in Norfolk. She recorded:

> At night I picked up this freak signal on the 'Cauliflower' network, all the way from Scotland – a range unheard of in those days. I wrote it down in plain language for the OC. It was a report that Hess had landed by parachute in Scotland.

Her normal drill with incoming messages was to take them on her bicycle to the duty intelligence officer in the main house. This, however, was not by any means a normal message. When Yolande thought about it again, she realised she had passed this one on directly by telephone, rather than leave her station unmanned. This was a special telephone line – Yolande was never to know to whom she spoke that night and the contents were received calmly by a man at the other end – but, as she was convinced it was not a simple connection to local Army HQ, it is tempting to speculate that this was a D Phone, briefly described as being far in advance of normal 'scrambling' in the Section D stand-down report. As the SDS Control Stations in the east of England were linked by secure land line directly to a point on the map in Buckinghamshire, her call was surely connected to the SIS communications HQ Station X.

Receiving the 'Hess' message at Thornham Magna was clearly freakish, since it was not apparently intended for Eastern Command. The usual range of the TRD was around twenty miles. But, in view of the especially secure design of the set, the message *could not have been inadvertently picked up from any other radio network*. In other words, the transmission specifically originated from someone within the ranks of the Special Duties Section of the Auxiliary Units.

The most likely point of origin was the Control Station in Alnwick and, as the ATS subalterns remained closeted on duty within, someone expecting the Messerschmitt 110 must have been on the look-out. The subalterns would not have accepted a message from anyone other than their Intelligence Officer, or someone with him. There is no suggestion that the Auxunits (ATS) subalterns themselves operated knowingly as part of a conspiracy, but further logical, if speculative, argument must indicate that – at a more senior level – the Special Duties Section of the Auxiliary Units was in some way associated with the Peace Group either at the centre, or very close to it.

Were the officers involved both in the transmission and reception of the message, plus whoever it was destined for, working *for* the Prime Minister, Winston Churchill, or against? If they were working *for* Churchill, the indication is that the secret services had penetrated the Peace Group and were forestalling any possible deal to bring the war to an early end. If not, then the top echelon was *assisting* the Peace Group against the established government. The merit of such intervention was debatable either way. After all, it was Winston Churchill himself who was later to declare that 'Jaw-jaw is better than war-war.'

Under the circumstances outlined in the potential peace deal, the end of Britain's struggle with Germany in 1941 would have saved hundreds of thousands of British lives plus, possibly, the Empire, and the avoidance of state bankruptcy associated with the massive British post-war indebtedness to the United States of America – which so largely allowed our friends in the Special Relationship to influence UK foreign policy for the indefinite future. The debt was finally paid off in the first decade of the twenty-first century. Together with all this, by adding strength to the Nazi assault on Russia in 1941, the Soviet establishment would almost certainly have been destroyed and forty years of Cold War avoided. In other words, Great Britain's power and influence would not have been steadily eroded after WWII. It would also, of course, have called for the abandonment of opposition to fascism and required an unacceptable compliance with Hitler's Final Solution for the Jews.

So much for supporting a peace deal. It can be taken as read that any such arrangement would necessarily have excluded Winston Churchill from further power indefinitely. Indeed, it is difficult to imagine that he could have survived at all in a post-war world of very dirty tricks.

By supporting Churchill, and the continuing fight against the Nazi regime, those opportunities had gone forever. The only recourse was a fight to the death and the pursuit, in league with the Allies, of ruthless, if slow and costly, progress toward eventual unconditional Nazi surrender. In turn, that brought about the inevitable destruction of much of Germany during the final assault, and bombing raids by night and day. Everything in West Germany then had to be rebuilt as a bulwark against the threat of expansionist communism.

After all these years, there should be space for a debate on the relatively undisputed notion that suing for peace would have been disastrous.

There is little question that the Special Duties Section of the Auxiliary Units fitted somewhere into the ongoing mystery highlighted by the 'Hess' flight and the aspirations of the Peace Group. This is probably why it was intended to disappear for all time – not unlike Prisoner No. 7 at Spandau. But even the most imaginative will find it difficult to decide just what it was that motivated 'Hess' or whomever he may have been – to join this weird conspiracy of silence until the day he died.

In a summary of the British government's reaction to the arrival of Rudolf Hess, Rebecca West, in splendidly simple sentences, concluded:

> There was obviously no reason why there should be any hurry in
> dealing with the unexpected visitor, as he could not show

dissatisfaction by going home. But the amount of foolish scurrying to and fro and brainless, impromptu chases by which the British Government reacted to this bizarre but not catastrophic surprise, arouses wonder as to how we ever won the war, even in name only.

It is difficult to believe that events were as straightforward even as that!

Is it significant that Major Maurice Petherick, the 'genius' behind the Special Duties Section of the Auxiliary Units, was replaced by his GSO1, Major Charles Randall, probably when the SDS HQ was relocated to Coleshill in 1942? Did he perhaps move upward to even greater things?

Could it be that the foolish scurrying to and fro, identified by Rebecca West, was just another deception? Was it all a cover for a very thorough witch-hunt? If so, it is unlikely that an official explanation, or corroborative papers, will ever be seen, for many heads must, figuratively at least, have dropped into the basket! Indeed, it is reported that, with the Prime Minister's backing, the threat of internment under the infamous Section 18(b) of the Defence of the Realm Act, hung over the liberty of a number of the Peace Group conspirators.

Rebecca West commented:

> There is therefore no guarantee a historian can accept that the fugitive was Hess; and there is therefore no guarantee a historian can accept that the British Government was right in handing over the fugitive as Hess after the war to the International court at Nuremberg.
>
> This, strangely enough, was what Churchill had desired from the very first . . .

And once the peace conspiracy was consigned to the depths forever, then of course, the Auxiliary Units had to follow. This was certainly bad luck for the men of the Operational Patrols who had nothing whatsoever to do with it.

Appendix One

Auxiliary Units' Weapons

These data have kindly been compiled for the author by Bathampton Auxilier Robert W. Millard, and militaria collector and former REME armourer Richard Ashley. Although issues of firearms varied from patrol to patrol the following list details weapons identified from personal experience, research and discussions with other patrol members.

Enfield US Rifle P.1917

Weight: 9 lb
Overall length: 46.5 in
Action: Mauser bolt
Cartridge: 30-06 Springfield
Sights: Adjustable aperture rear sight/blade foresight; sights from
  200–1,600 yd; battle sights at 400 yd
Muzzle velocity: 2,700 fps
Bullet weight: 11 grm
Capacity: 5-round magazine

Winchester Model 61

The Standard version of this rifle had a straight stock whilst the Expert version had a pistol-grip stock.

Weight: 6 lb 4 oz
Overall length (with silencer): 50 in
Barrel length: 20 in
Action: Slide (Pump)
Cartridge: 0.22 in Short, Long or Long Rifle
Sights: Blade foresight, Winchester Model 32 rear sight, Winchester A8
  scope

Capacity: Under-barrel tubular magazine accepting 20 Short, 16 Long or 14 Long Rifle rounds

Winchester Model 697

This rifle has a barrel-mounted telescopic sight and no iron sights to allow a lower mount that gave a lower sight line, less error and greater rigidity. Winchester had designed a new light telescopic sight for this rifle and these were designated No. 3, No. P3 and No. 5, the numbers indicating the approximate magnification of the telescope. P indicated the telescope was a post, not cross-hair, sight. The walnut woodwork comprises a stock with pistol grip and forearm. The stock is fitted with a hard rubber shotgun butt plate. There are fittings for a 1-inch sling.

Weight: 5 lb
Overall length (with silencer): 52 in
Barrel length: 25 in
Action: Bolt action
Cartridge: 0.22 in Long Rifle
Sights: Barrel-mounted Winchester No. 3, No. P3 or No. 5 scope
Capacity: 5- or 10-round box magazine

Winchester Model 74

This model uses a spring to prevent the opening of the bolt before the bullet has left the barrel. This action permits standard or high velocity rounds to be fired, although the gun performs more reliably with the high velocity round. Initially chambered for 0.22-inch Short, models after serial number 97,000 (mid-1941) were chambered to accept Short, Long and Long Rifle rounds. A number of rifles made in 1939 were chambered for Long Rifle only and were marked accordingly. The safety catch is located on the top of the receiver and operates by locking the gun's sear. The stocks are uncapped pistol grip stocks, have checkered steel butt plates and semi-beavertail fore-ends. Early stocks are $1\frac{5}{8}$ inches thick, later ones $1\frac{3}{4}$ inches thick. The early models have small loading ports in the stock; on later models this port is nearly double the size.

Weight: 6 lb 4 oz
Overall length with silencer: 52 in
Barrel length: Early models 24 in; later models 22 in

Action: Semi-automatic
Cartridge: 0.22 in Short, Long or Long Rifle
Sights: Blade foresight; Winchester No. 32 rear sight; Winchester scope
Capacity: Tubular magazine in stock, accepting 20 Short, 16 Long or 14
  Long Rifle rounds

BSA Model 12 and 12A

Principally a target rifle, it has a straight grip stock and a half-length
beavertail fore-end. The Martini action is the most suitable single-shot action
for the rapid-fire disciplines, particularly when the rifle is fitted with the
Parker Hale 'Quick Fire' loading block on the right-hand side of the action.

   The Model 12 is fitted with a target leaf sight calibrated for 25, 50, 100
and 200 yards together with a post/barleycorn foresight. The Model 12A
has an action-mounted BSA No. 8 folding peep sight and a No. 19 foresight.
This sight has a rotating post and ring element that can be interchanged by
a small lever on the right of the sight. It was optional whether the Model 12
was also fitted with a leaf-type target sight. At least one patrol had a modified
No. 12 with barrel shortened to 20 inches and threaded for a silencer, and
a scope fitted.

Weight: 8 lb 12 oz
Overall length: 44 in
Barrel length: 29 in
Action: Martini
Cartridge: 0.22 in Long Rifle
Sights: BSA No. 8 Peep sight and/or a leaf target sight calibrated for 50,
  100 and 200 yards, and a No. 19 foresight
Capacity: Single shot

Browning Automatic Rifle

The BAR M1918 is a gas-operated, magazine-fed, air-cooled weapon. It uses
a gas piston located under the barrel and a bolt with a tilting locking lug
raised to engage in the roof of the receiver. This lug is linked to the operating
piston by a swing link. The return spring is located around the piston under
the barrel and thus can be prone to overheating and loss of temper during
prolonged firing, resulting in jams and stoppages.

Weight: 19 lb

Overall length: 50 in
Barrel length: 24 in
Action: Gas-operated automatic
Cartridge: 30-06 Springfield
Sights: Similar to P.17 noted above
Capacity: 20-round box magazine
Rate of fire: 550 rd/min
Range: 600 yd

Thompson Sub-Machine Gun

Standard characteristics of the original M1921 are the Colt royal blue finish, knurled lightweight actuator, Lyman Model 55 rear sight, push-button detachable stock, checkered fire control lever and finned barrel with optional Cutts compensator. The models M1928 and M1928A1 are similar to the model M1921, but have a heavier actuator and a less powerful recoil spring to reduce the rate of fire. The Cutts compensator is fitted as standard whilst the fore-grip can be either vertical or horizontal. In July 1942 production of the M1928A1 ceased as the Thompson had been redesigned, appearing later as the M1 and M1A1.

Weight: 10 lb 12 oz
Overall length: 33.7 in
Barrel length: 10½ in
Action: Selected fire, full or semi-automatic
Cartridge: 0.45 in ACP
Sights: Lyman Model 55 adjustable or welded battle sight set at 50 yards
Capacity: 20- or 30-round stick or 50-round drum magazine
Rate of fire: 600–720 rd/min

Sten Machine Carbine

In early 1941 the Royal Small Arms Factory at Enfield produced a pilot run of a December 1940 British design to replace the Thompson. The Mark 1 Sten, which featured wooden furniture and a flash eliminator, was quickly replaced by the more easily produced Mark II. This was a very simple gun, comprising 69 parts that were mainly stamped from steel and assembled by being welded, sweated or riveted together. The Sten was the first sub-machine gun that could be fitted with a silencer and some silenced versions were

produced. Although it was not produced in large numbers, the even simpler
Mark III was probably the best version of the Sten. Manufactured by the toy-
making firm Lines Brothers, its main feature was an all-in-one body and
casing. In all, nearly 4 million Stens were manufactured during WWII.

Weight: 6 lb 8 oz
Overall length: 30 in
Barrel length: 7¾ in, 6 grooves, right-hand twist
Action: Selective fire, full or semi-automatic
Cartridge : 9 mm Parabellum
Sights: Fixed aperture, set to 100 yards
Capacity: 32-round box magazine
Rate of fire: 550 rd/min

Handguns

In August 1940 Churchill added to a memo from Colonel Gubbins, a minute
that the Operational Patrols of the Auxiliary Units were to have handguns
and this was acted upon by an initial issue of 0.32-inch Colt revolvers
obtained from the New York Police Department, still with their NYPD leather
holsters, 400 Colt 0.32-inch semi-automatic pistols and a month later by
0.38-inch Smith and Wesson revolvers.

0.32 Colt Police

Weight: 1 lb 2.5 oz
Overall length: 8.5 in
Barrel length: 4 in
Action: Double or single action
Cartridge: 0.32 in Colt Special Police (S & W Long)
Sights: Fixed V rear sight, vertical foresight
Capacity: 6-round cylinder

0.32 Colt Police Positive

Weight: 1 lb 5 oz
Overall length: 8.5 in
Barrel length: 4 in
Action: Double or single action
Cartridge: 0.32 in Colt Special Police (S & W Long)

Sights: Fixed V rear sight, vertical foresight
Capacity: 6-round cylinder

0.32 Colt Semi-Automatic

Weight: 1 lb 8 oz
Overall length: Type 1: 7 in; Types 2–5: 6¾ in
Barrel length: Type 1: 4 in; Types 2–5: 3¾ in
Action: Hammerless semi-automatic
Cartridge : 0.32 in ACP
Sights: Fixed V rear sight, vertical foresight
Capacity: 8-round magazine

Smith & Wesson 0.38/200 British Service Revolver

Weight: 1 lb 8 oz
Overall length: 10¼ in
Barrel length: 5 in
Action: Double or single-action revolver
Cartridge : 0.38 in/200 British Service
Sights: Fixed V rear sight, vertical foresight
Capacity: 6-round cylinder

Welrod Silenced Pistol

A major code-named Dolphin reportedly designed the Welrod early in WWII for dispatching sentries and use in assassinations. It is a very quiet weapon, the noise on discharge being less than that made by the gentle closing of a well-fitting door. The pistol has a grip safety mechanism and within the trigger guard is the magazine-release catch. The magazine acts as the grip and holds six rounds. The bolt action is operated by turning the knurled knob at the rear one quarter turn to the left and then pulling it back, which will eject any chambered round or empty case. When the knob is pushed forward a round is stripped from the magazine and chambered and at the same time the firing pin is cocked. The knob is then turned to the right to complete the loading process and the pistol is ready to fire. The Welrod was issued to certain Scout Sections only on a trial, rather than general basis

Weight: 2 lb
Overall length: 14.6 in

Action: Single-shot bolt-action
Calibre: 9 mm or 0.32 in ACP
Sights: Blade foresight mounted just behind the muzzle nut; rear square
  notch sight; both had radium inserts for use in poor light
Capacity: 7 rounds in grip magazine, plus one in the chamber

Ammunition Characteristics

Round	Bullet weight in grains	Muzzle velocity in fps
Springfield 30-06	180	2,700
0.22 in Short	36	1,090
0.22 in Long Rifle HV	36	1,285
0.45 in ACP	230	920
9 mm Parabellum	115	1,250
0.32 in ACP	85	560
0.32 in S & W Long	200	690
0.38 in/200 S & W	200	690

The Fairbairn/Sykes Fighting Knife

Developed in 1940 by Captains Fairbairn and Sykes, this very efficient knife
became the standard issue for the British forces and was an early issue to
Auxiliary Units as a means of dealing with enemy sentries. Its design allowed
it to be used as a stabbing or slashing weapon.

Type: Stiletto, razor sharp on both edges
Blade length: 7 in
Overall length: 13 in
1st Pattern: Checkered grip on nickel-plated brass hilt, recurved cross-
guard, polished blade with Wilkinson logo on square ricasso
2nd Pattern: Checkered grip on blackened brass hilt, blackened blade,
        2-inch straight cross-guard
3rd Pattern: Concentrically ringed grip of blackened alloy hilt, 2-inch
        straight cross-guard

Garrotte

The Monk garrotte was supplied with a cloth pouch for ease of carrying.
The high-tensile piano wire was 24 inches long, the handles 2½ inches in
length. The garrotte was used 'cross-armed' to form a loop, which was

dropped over the victim's head and then tightened. Many Auxiliers made their own.

Knuckleduster and Truncheon

Patrol members were also issued with a traditional brass knuckleduster and a weighted rubber truncheon that was 14 inches long, $1\frac{3}{8}$ inches in diameter and had a cord retaining loop.

Appendix Two

The Radio Network

These notes were kindly compiled for the author by Richard Hankins of the Vintage and Military Amateur Radio Society for the information of readers who wish to understand something of the more technical aspects of radio communication.

1. Wavelength and Frequency

Radio stations operate on a particular frequency or wavelength. 'Frequency' describes the number of radio wave cycles produced per second. Imagine yourself standing in the sea. The frequency would be the number of waves passing you every second. A frequency of 1 MHz (one megahertz) is one million cycles per second. This is in the middle of the medium wave broadcast band, and the corresponding wavelength is 300 metres.

'Wavelength' describes the distance between the peaks of two adjacent waves, and is measured in metres. Wavelength and frequency are related – the shorter the wavelength the higher the frequency.

2. Carriers and Modulation

Radio uses a 'carrier wave' to transfer information. A carrier can be thought of as similar to the pure tone produced by a tuning fork. You can hear it, but it conveys no information as such. If this tone is varied – in pitch, loudness or duration – then information can be conveyed. Morse code is made up of a series of short and long tones (of a single pitch), which conveys words one letter at a time.

If a radio carrier is varied in pitch (i.e. 'frequency') or loudness ('amplitude'), then information can be 'carried' on it. In 1940, nearly all radio systems used a means of varying the amplitude of the carrier. Speech is a signal of varying amplitude and can be imposed on the carrier wave, and thus sent by radio. This process is referred to as 'modulation', and the radio signal as a 'modulated carrier wave'.

How much of the radio 'spectrum' was in use before WWII? As radio has developed, so the frequencies in use have moved ever higher, as more spectrum is required to accommodate new services. Nowadays, mobile phone systems using frequencies of 2,000 MHz are commonplace – but in 1940 things were much more basic.

3. A TRD Block Diagram

This aids understanding of how equipment works for an engineer. While the reader will not necessarily understand what the diagram means, it should be noted that if this is not right, then trying to go further by drawing circuits is a waste of time. Drawing a block diagram is thus an essential step along the way.

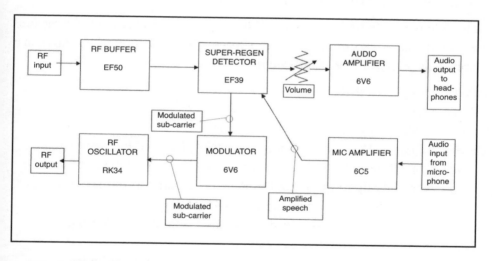

4. Block Circuitry

Each item is given in the form: NAME, function, *how easy to redesign.*
RF BUFFER Stops radiation from the super-regen detector when receiving. *Medium.*
SUPER-REGEN DETECTOR The heart of the receiver and transmitter. On receive, this stage converts the incoming radio signal to an audio signal that human beings can understand. On transmit, this stage combines the audio signal from the operator's microphone, with the supersonic 'quench' signal. The result is a modulated sub-carrier wave, with the sub-carrier frequency

being that of the quench signal, about 40kHz. *Very hard.*

AUDIO AMPLIFIER Increases the volume of the audio signal from the super-regen detector so that it is loud enough to hear the signal in a pair of headphones. *Easy.*

MIC AMPLIFIER 'Mic' refers to 'microphone'. This stage increases the volume of the audio signal from the operator's microphone, on transmit. *Easy.*

MODULATOR This stage increases the level of the modulated sub-carrier from the super-regen detector stage, sufficient to feed to the RF oscillator to modulate the radio carrier. *Medium.*

RF OSCILLATOR This stage produces the radio carrier wave, at a frequency of between 45 and 65MHz. *Medium.*

*

Description of Type TRD Wireless Set

The following details are extracts from papers then classified 'Secret and Personal', dated 28 June 1944, as the Special Duties Section of the Auxiliary Units was preparing for stand down.

Dimensions: 15½ x 9¼ x 9 in

Aerial: Dipole

Power supply: 6 volt, 85 A.H. Accumulator

Frequency range: 48–65 mcs. Transmitter is set for fixed frequency and except for minor adjustments is only changed in workshops.

Range: Normally up to 30 miles, but depends greatly on nature of terrain. Longest operational link now in use is 64 miles.

Audio: Different sets are employed for handset and loudspeaker use.

Power output: Approximately 1.5 Watts.

General: Set is designed for simple operation of R/T on very high frequencies. Panel Controls are – On/Off switch; Send/Receive switch; Receiver tuning; Volume. Minor adjustments to transmitted frequency are made by pre-set condenser.

Transmitter: Speech amplifier; modulator and push-pull oscillator.

Receiver: RF stage; super-regenerative detector; and output stage.

TRM and TRF are similar.

Bibliography

Alanbrooke, Lord, *War Diaries*, Weidenfeld & Nicolson, London, 2001

Andrew, Christopher, *Secret Service*, Heinemann, London, 1985

Angell, Stewart, *Secret Sussex Resistance*, Middleton Press, Midhurst, 1996

Anon, *SOE Syllabus*, Public Record Office, Richmond, 2001

Astley, Joan Bright, *The Inner Circle*, Little Brown, Toronto, 1971

—— and Peter Wilkinson, *Gubbins and SOE*, Pen & Sword, London, 1993

Barrington, Jonah, *Lord Haw-Haw of Zeesen*, Hutchinson, London, 1941

Beyts, Brigadier G. H. B., *The King's Salt*, Haslam, Chorley, 1996

de la Billière, Peter, *Looking for Trouble*, Harper Collins, London, 1995

Briscoe, Paul, *Foster Fatherland*, Barny Books, Grantham, 2002

Brown, Donald, *Somerset versus Hitler*, Countryside Books, Newbury, 1999

Calvert, Michael, *Fighting Mad*, Airlife, Shrewsbury, 1996

Cassidy, William, 'The Art of Silent Killing', *Soldier of Fortune*, 1979

Cave-Brown, Anthony, *Bodyguard of Lies*, Robert Hale, London, 1991

——, *The Secret Servant*, Sphere, London, 1989

Coleman, Roy, *From Creggan to Corrwg*, Alun Books, Port Talbot, 2005

Colville, John, *Fringes of Power*, Hodder and Stoughton, London, 1985

Croft, Andrew, *A Talent for Adventure*, S.P.A., Worcestershire, 1991

Cruikshank, Charles, *The German Occupation of the Channel Isles*, OUP, 1975

Cunningham, Cyril, *Beaulieu*, Pen & Sword, Barnsley, 1998

Davidson, E. & D. Manning, *The Chronology of WWII*, Cassell, London, 1999

Deacon, Richard, *A History of the British Secret Service*, Frederick Muller, London, 1969

Dodds-Parker, Douglas, *Setting Europe Ablaze*, Springwood Books, London, 1983

Dunning, James, *It Had to be Tough*, Pentland Press, Bishop Auckland, 2000

Fairbairn, W. E., *All-In Fighting*, Faber & Faber, London, 1942

Farndale, Nigel, *Haw-Haw*, Macmillan, London, 2005

Fenwick, Ian, *Enter Trubshawe*, Collins, London, 1945

Fleming, Peter, *Operation Sea Lion*, Pan Books, London, 1975

Foot, M. R. D., *SOE*, Mandarin, London, 1990

Ford, Roger, *Fire from the Forest*, Cassell, London, 2003

——, *Steel from the Sky*, Cassell, London, 2005

Forty, George, *Channel Islands at War*, Ian Allan, Shepperton, 1999

Hamilton-Hill, Donald, *SOE Assignment*, Kimber, London, 1973

Harrison, D. I., *These Men are Dangerous*, Cassell, London, 1999

Hart-Davis, Duff, *Peter Fleming*, Jonathan Cape, London, 1977

Hastings, Max, *Das Reich*, Pan Books, London, 2000

Hayward, James, *Bodies on the Beach*, CQB, Dereham, 1994

Hoare, Adrian, *Standing up to Hitler*, Reeve, Norfolk, 1997

Holt, Thaddeus, *The Deceivers*, Phoenix, 2005

Ironside, Lord, *The Ironside Diaries*, Constable, London, 1962

Jackson, Kenneth, *Invasion*, Greenhill, London, 1999

Kemp, Anthony, *The SAS at War*, Penguin, London, 1998

——, *The Secret Hunters*, O'Mara Books, London, 1986

Lampe, David, *The Last Ditch*, Cassell, London, 1968

Longmate, Norman, *If Britain Had Fallen*, Greenhill, London, 2004

Lowry, Bernard, and Mick Wilks, *Mercian Maquis*, The Logaston Press, Wooton Almeley, 2002

McCue, Paul, *Operation Bulbasket* Leo Cooper, London, 1996

Mackenzie, S. P., *The Home Guard*, OUP, Oxford, 1996

Mackenzie, W. J. M., *Secret History of SOE*, The St Ermins Press, London, 2000

Macrae, Stuart, *Winston Churchill's Toyshop*, Roundwood, Warwick, 1971

Melton, H. Keith, *The Ultimate Spy Book*, Dorling Kindersley, London, 1997

Mortimer, Gavin, *Stirling's Men*, Weidenfeld and Nicolson, London, 2004

Niven, David, *The Moon's a Balloon*, Penguin, London, 1994

Oxenden, Nigel, ed. Andy Taylor, *Auxiliary Units – History and Achievement 1940–44*, Parham Airfield Museum, 1998

Picknett, Lynn, Clive Prince and Stephen Prior, *Double Standards: The Rudolf Hess Cover-Up*, Time Warner, London, 2001

Pidgeon, Geoffrey, *The Secret Wireless War*, UPSO, Sussex, 2003

Ramsey, Winston G., *The War in the Channel Islands*, Battle of Britain Prints, London, 1981

Robins, Peter, *Gentleman and Warrior*, CQB, Harlow, 2005

Schellenberg, Walter, *Invasion 1940*, Little Brown, London, 2000

Sansom, Mark, *The Secret Army*, Lincolnshire Heritage, Sleaford, 2004

Smith, Michael, *New Cloak, Old Dagger*, Gollancz, London, 1996

Stafford, David, *Camp X*, Viking Press, New York, 1987

——, *Churchill and Secret Service*, Abacus, London, 2000

Stevenson, William, *A Man Called Intrepid*, Macmillan, London, 1976

Thomas, Hugh, *The Murder of Rudolf Hess*, Coronet, Philadelphia, 1979

Trevor-Roper, Hugh, *The Death of Hitler*, Macmillan, London, 1947

Turner, Des, *Aston House, Station 12*, Sutton Publishing, Stroud, 2006

Verity, Hugh, *We Landed by Moonlight*, Ian Allan, Shepperton, 1950

Ward, Arthur, *Resisting the Nazi Invader*, Constable, London, 1997

West, Nigel, *On Her Majesty's Secret Service*, Greenhill, London, 2006

Whittaker, Len, *Some Talk of Private Armies*, privately published

Wilks, Mick, *The Defence of Worcestershire*, Logaston Press, Wooton Almeley, 2007

Williamson, Alan, *East Riding Secret Resistance*, Middleton Press, Midhurst, 2004

Winterbotham, F. W., *The Ultra Secret*, Weidenfeld and Nicolson, London, 1974

Wright, Dennis, *Harvest of Messerschmitts: The Chronicle of a Village at War*, Frederick Warne, London, 1981

Index